INSIDE  OUT

A Guide to Writing

Maurice Scharton
Janice Neuleib

both of
Illinois State University

ALLYN AND BACON

BOSTON ♦ LONDON ♦ TORONTO ♦ SYDNEY ♦ TOKYO ♦ SINGAPORE

Executive Editor: *Joseph Opiela*
Series Editorial Assistant: *Brenda Conaway*
Editorial-Production Administrator: *Annette Joseph*
Editorial-Production Service: *Karen Mason*
Text Designer: *Karen Mason*
Composition Buyer: *Linda Cox*
Manufacturing Buyer: *Louise Richardson*
Cover Administrator: *Linda K. Dickinson*
Cover Designer: *Suzanne Harbison*

Copyright © 1993 by Allyn and Bacon
A Division of Simon & Schuster, Inc.
160 Gould Street
Needham Heights, Massachusetts 02194

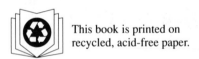

This book is printed on
recycled, acid-free paper.

Library of Congress Cataloging-in-Publication Data

Maurice Scharton.
   Inside out : a guide to writing / Maurice Scharton, Janice
Neuleib.
        p.   cm.
   Includes bibliographical references and index.
   ISBN 0-205-13769-5
   1. English language—Rhetoric.   I. Neuleib, Janice.   II. Title
PE1408.S3   1993   92–31803
808'.042—dc20   CIP

Printed in the United States of America

10 9 8 7 6 5 4 3 2 1   97 96 95 94 93 92

Contents

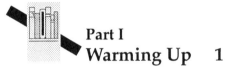

Part I
Warming Up 1

Part II
Discovering Writing Projects   53

Chapter 3 ♦ Discovering Topics   55

Chapter 4 ♦ Discovering Writing Partners   78

Part III
Drafting 93

Part IV
Revising   167

Chapter 7 ♦ Peer Suggestions for Revision   169

Chapter 8 ♦ Narrative Strategies for Revision   191

Chapter 9 ♦ Analytical Strategies for Revision   227

Chapter 10 ♦ Personal Dimensions of Revision   255

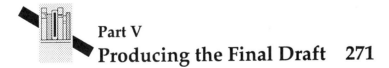

Part V
Producing the Final Draft   271

Chapter 11 ♦ Editing Your Style   273

EXPERIENCE ASSIGNMENTS

Preface

This book is about motivation to write. Why do we find ourselves writing such a book? We enjoy writing. We also enjoy working together as writers and find that our students enjoy working with other writers, too. Our purpose in writing this book is to give teachers and students multiple ways to find their own motivations for writing through writing experiences that focus and expand their interests, values, and convictions. Writers who use this book will be encouraged to move from the inside out: from inner, subjective experiences to outer objective writing projects, always maintaining the connection between the personal and social worlds. It is this connection that keeps motivational energy flowing.

A counselor friend of ours says that parents should avoid giving children rules that specify behavior that could be done better by a dead person than a living one. We found that some of the rules we had taught ourselves as writers fit into the "dead person" category: don't use linking verbs, don't write comma splices, don't start without a catchy beginning. Writing a book that emphasizes experiencing writing rather than "learning" to write or learning "about writing" seemed very bold to us at first. We wanted to help writers break away from the rules and habits that might inhibit their involvement in their own writing. We also wanted to provide experiences for writers that would enable them to find their own best focuses.

Inside Out: A Guide to Writing

- provides scores of experiential activities,
- emphasizes collaboration and community response,
- demonstrates active, ongoing research techniques, and
- puts writers in touch with motivations.

Throughout the book we look at writers writing together. We write together and with colleagues both in production of text and in constant revisions of the texts we have already produced. Many of our classes work collaboratively. Many of the classroom experiences in the book ask writers to collaborate on all aspects of writing, from discovering who they are as writers to discovering topics through every stage of revision and editing. The book demonstrates class communities and how they can work to create successful texts produced by engaged writers.

Writers read much more than they write. This book leads writers through the worlds of texts that they must negotiate in order to experience themselves as writers and guides them into those worlds as real writers. We wanted to show writers how we and our students have learned to use what we read, hear, and see to enrich what we write. Texts on texts, reading the world in many ways, contribute to every word we say and write. Finding comfortable and efficient ways to use the world of text is important to every writer. We do it by incorporating "research" into our writing at every stage, and we provide experiences for writers to use texts whenever they will enrich a paper.

Rhetoric must be at work in every stage of writing. A topic grows because a writer has something to say to a particular person or audience or wants to write in a particular magazine or journal. The first words or the first draft may or may not come easily depending on how comfortable the writer feels with his or her voice and role on a given topic. The desire to do some more research in the library or the field may arise because the writer needs more evidence to prove his or her point to the potential reader. Finally, the writer must present the work in the appropriate style, register, and format for the intended audience or forum. The experiences in this text provide many opportunities to use rhetorical techniques and activities to discover, produce, revise, and edit a paper.

Inside Out: A Guide to Writing has five major parts:

   I. Warming Up
  II. Discovering Writing Projects
 III. Drafting
 IV. Revising
  V. Producing the Final Draft

These sections follow a writer through the production of a finished text. Each part, however, also provides multiple possibilities for writing projects and offers writers many avenues for discovering both topics and directions.

The Warming-Up process proceeds through two chapters:

- Chapter 1: A Background for Writing Processes
- Chapter 2: The Satisfactions of Writing

These chapters increase writers' awareness of their writing processes and focus their attention on the intrinsic value of writing. The first
journal assignment, on earliest writing experiences, can serve as a diag-
nostic essay. By the end of Warming Up, writers will have accumulated
enough journal entries to compose an informative essay on their writing processes.

Part II, Discovering Writing Projects, also proceeds through two
chapters:

- Chapter 3: Discovering Topics
- Chapter 4: Discovering Writing Partners

Chapter 3 leads students through some experiential, intuitive ways
of finding ideas for writing: introspection, conversation, and reading.
Chapter 4 helps them to organize the human resources they need to
sustain them as they write. By the end of Part II, writers will have accumulated enough potential topics to write a proposal which describes
the remaining essays they plan to complete during the course.

Part III, once again, is divided into two chapters:

- Chapter 5: Planning a Draft
- Chapter 6: Composing a Draft

The planning chapter guides writers in defining rhetorical situations for the essays they have proposed. The composing chapter
addresses the issues of managing their composing processes to create a
comfortable and productive writing experience. This chapter integrates
three forms of invention work (clustering, matrix building, and a variation on freewriting) to help writers focus during the drafting process
itself. By the end of Part III, writers will have composed drafts of one of
the projects they have proposed and planned.

Revising, by far the longest of the five parts, comprises four chapters:

- Chapter 7: Peer Suggestions for Revision
- Chapter 8: Narrative Strategies for Revision
- Chapter 9: Analytical Strategies for Revision
- Chapter 10: Personal Dimensions of Revision

Chapter 7 provides a formal structure for peer reviews of writing
projects to keep students on task as they work in groups. Chapters 8
and 9 use rhetorical strategies to produce more sophisticated work in
revision. Chapter 10 broadens the context, fostering understanding of
the part revision plays in enabling students to assume a role in the aca-

demic community. By the time writers have completed Part IV, they will be prepared either to draft and revise the remaining projects or to proceed to Part V and produce the final drafts of their portfolios.

Part V, Producing the Final Draft, involves two chapters:

- Chapter 11: Editing Your Style
- Chapter 12: Final Details

Chapter 11 focuses on clarity, moving from logical transitions through word choice. Chapter 12 provides resources to prepare the Works Cited list and to complete the final proofreading.

At the teacher's discretion, writers may compose a test essay for the Writing for Evaluation appendix.

ACKNOWLEDGMENTS

We know a beautiful Afghan hound who always bows to say "thank you," and we wish we could bow with the same grace to all the students and colleagues who have helped us through this book.

Our first thanks go to our colleagues in the profession who do composing research and rhetorical theory. They are the godparents of this text; their names appear in our bibliography.

Our warmest thanks go to the students who wrote in our classes, whose responses suggested practical changes in the book, and who produced the essays there. Other students in graduate programs at Illinois State have contributed to the book by reading and responding to it in graduate classes, teaching parts of it in their classes, and offering revision suggestions at various stages of the writing. One graduate student in particular, Ruth Fennick, offered structural ideas through her doctoral dissertation and through ongoing discussions during the three years of an ISU NEH institute.

We gratefully acknowledge the expert advice of colleagues from other schools who reviewed the drafts of our manuscript: Robert J. Connors, University of New Hampshire; Frank Hubbard, Marquette University; David Jolliffe, University of Illinois at Chicago; Michael G. Moran, The University of Georgia; Lolly Okerstrom, Northeastern University; Chris Thaiss, George Mason University; Mary Trachsel, University of Iowa; and Irwin Weiser, Purdue University.

Finally, we thank our editor at Allyn and Bacon, Joe Opiela, who "discovered" us, got us started, and saw us through with patient encouragement and sage counsel.

Introduction

The world is full of books—many of them quite good books—that will tell you how to write. We as authors have learned from those books, and in many ways *Inside Out: A Guide to Writing* resembles them. We have tried to cover the issues that writing teachers and students would expect to find in a writing textbook, from the first moment of conceiving an idea to the last hour of proofreading a manuscript. You will be writing from the inside out, processing inner experiences into writing projects for the outer world.

Relatively few books about writing ask you to consider what it feels like to write, how writing flows from your experience of the past and present. We have always found discussions of the experience of writing to be crucial to our pleasure and productivity as writers and as teachers. In this book, we have therefore focused on the experience of writing.

When we use the term **experience**, we mean it in three ways: (1) the immediate experience of using words to convey meaning, (2) the more distant experience from which your writing habits and attitudes originate, and (3) your experience of Life with a capital L. (We confess that we regularly contemplate the meaning of life both upper- and lower-case.) We hope that as you do the work we have laid out, you'll find new lines of communication opening between your writing and your whole experience of Life with a capital L. Writing will start to feel like living instead of something you stop living to do.

In order to help you conduct an orderly search for the connections between your life and your writing, we have organized *Inside Out: A Guide to Writing* into five parts:

    I. Warming Up
   II. Discovering Writing Projects
 III. Drafting
 IV. Revising
  V. Producing the Final Draft

Our five parts represent themes which occur and recur in various writing processes. Like the themes in a piece of music, the themes of the writing process rise and fall throughout the course of the work on a piece as various melodies, rhythms, and instrumental voices emerge and then recede. Our order reflects, very generally, the order in which events often happen during writing processes.

The order of the parts and chapters facilitates study of the writing process, but we recognize that productive writing processes may vary widely from one person to the next and from one writing project to the next. Your plans, goals, and interests may lead you along paths entirely different from the one we have mapped out.

For example, you may sit down thinking that you are going to revise a piece of writing, but find yourself discovering ideas and then drafting. You may get started on a new writing project by reading over and editing a completed project. You may find that a conversation with a friend compels you to rewrite a piece of writing you thought was finished.

Since we can't be certain how you'll respond to the need to write something, we have made the five parts independent of each other. If you feel the need, you can readily skip around. You'll learn a great deal about writing if you follow your impulses and use your instincts.

We have arranged each of the chapters like a newspaper story, with the most basic information at the beginning. The further you progress in a chapter, the more advanced and complex the work becomes. You and your teacher will decide when you reach the point of diminishing returns. At that point you can skip to another chapter. You can always come back if you need to.

MOTIVATION: WHY WRITE?

Nearly every writing book asks that question somewhere, usually near the front of the text. The obvious answer in a writing course is that you write because the course requires writing. Another obvious answer in this technological world is that many jobs require writing. However, most people find those obvious answers unsatisfactory. The work we do must have intrinsic value. We need to believe that our work is worthwhile, or we don't keep doing it. What is the intrinsic value in writing? A well-written paper resembles any other finely crafted work, like a drawing, sculpture, or fine piece of furniture. Time spent on making your writing into that finely crafted work will give the same satisfaction as any other craft.

When we use terms like *connections, themes, plans, goals, interests, impulses,* and *instincts,* we intend to convey the message that why you write is important to your feeling of success as a writer. We want to increase your awareness of the ways you drive and structure your writing processes so that you can use your reasons for writing to help you write better.

Experienced writers usually work with other writers at nearly every stage of a project. Businesses assign task forces to write reports; authors work closely with editors and coauthors; scientists research and report their work in project teams. Group work in class has come late to writing instruction, but within the last ten years writing teachers and student writers have begun to value peer responses to classroom writing. You will find that most of our assignments direct you to interact with others.

KINDS OF WRITING ASSIGNMENTS IN THIS BOOK

Experiences

The first kind of writing assignment in this book comes under the heading of **Experience.** Some of these assignments are Warm-Ups, which invite you to remember events in your school, work, or personal life and to consider those experiences as a writer to increase your consciousness of how and why you write. Other assignments are designed to focus your attention on work For Your Writing Project, to invite you to work with other writers, to reflect on attitudes, and to respond to other writers' writing.

The several dozen Experience assignments ask hundreds of questions, all intended to help you get started or keep going. We don't suppose that everyone will complete every Experience or answer every question in exactly the order we have listed them. We do hope to provoke some interested, reflective response from everyone.

To give you an idea of how to respond to the Experience assignments, we've supplied many examples of student writers' responses. Some of the responses are beautifully written, some a little hesitant and clumsy. Some are from students who represent what we used to think of as the "typical" undergraduate, while others represent the growing number of older students who are attending college now. We present their work with a minimum of editing.

Your Writing Journal

Collect your responses to the Experience assignments in a **journal.** Journals in writing classes give writers a free space in which to write informal expressions of feeling and opinion, explore ideas, record perceptions, and just play with language. Most professional writers keep a journal or log of some sort to record ideas for writing or interesting information they come across while reading.

The nature of the journal can vary from writer to writer, and the content will include many different kinds of responses to this text and to other information you come across as you write. What should your journal look like? You. We will give you examples of journal entries other students write, but in the end journal entries will vary widely from one person to the next.

Journals usually are not graded since they are preliminary work and never contain final drafts of a writing project. Why would anyone assign or complete writing that will not get a grade?

One practical reason is that journals record the sort of preliminary work writers have to do before completing formal papers. You would have to think through your ideas anyway. Writing them down on paper helps you to focus on working out problems, puts the ideas in a form that makes your teacher able to help, gives you the satisfaction of seeing your ideas in language, and may even get you some credit for all that messy fumbling with language you have to do before you can produce "real" writing. A journal is a paper trail of your thinking as you plan, draft, and revise a group of papers.

Two impractical reasons are that journals are often fun and that they sometimes enable you to learn about yourself. Neither fun nor self-knowledge earns you credit hours in college, but both will make you a better writer. As you write in response to the Experience assignments, be prepared to discover, or increase your awareness of, the processes by which you write. You may find insights in the act of writing.

Likewise, be prepared to reexamine your writing with an analytical eye. You'll find patterns, and those patterns will lead you to a better sense of how writing works for you. You won't always draw the correct inference from your work, but the process of thinking about how and why you write the way you do will enable you to write more comfortably and efficiently.

As you complete the Experience assignments and make other journal entries, you'll also begin thinking of ideas for larger, more formal writing projects. Be sure to note when the ideas occur to you. By the time you have progressed through Part III, you will have begun working on more formal writing projects, and most of your energy will flow in that direction. Don't suppose that your journal work should stop at that point. You will continue to need the journal's free space to help you to talk to your teacher, your peers, and yourself about your writing processes.

Writing Projects

Of course, student writers also research, write, and revise papers for a wider audience and the customary grade. We use the term **Writing Projects** for those papers. For the most part, the topics for your papers will grow from the work you are doing in your journal and from other activities suggested in this book. In a way, you'll give yourself assignments for writing projects.

Note that the word *project* is both a noun and a verb. As a noun it means "a piece of work." As a verb, "to pro-*ject*," it means "to propose" or "to send forth into the world." Logically, if you project something, like a slide or a movie, it comes from where you are. You have ownership of it, and you send it out for other people to evaluate and use. We believe the word gives a clue to the way writing projects develop. Writing projects you value most will come from assignments you give yourself.

This book provides three sources of assistance for you to use in your search for meaningful writing projects. First, we've devoted Part II—Discovering Writing Projects—to the search for writing project ideas. By the time you've finished the section, you'll have a list of possible projects to choose from.

Second, throughout the book we describe how other writers found and developed writing projects as a result of journal assignments, conversations with other writers, reading in classes or on their own, comments from teachers, the need to say something or solve a problem, and a host of other inspirations. While you probably won't respond exactly as another writer does, you may pick up some hints and some encouragement from reading about how other people found projects that were important to them.

Third, every Experience assignment in the book has the potential to produce a writing project. When you find yourself writing more than you usually do in response to an Experience, you should ask yourself whether you have found a subject you want to deal with in more depth. When you find yourself writing that you were interested, upset, excited, sad, curious, outraged, or in any other way moved by an idea, event, or person, you will know that you have found a possible project.

Your Portfolio

Your teacher may ask you to collect your writing projects in a **portfolio,** which is a body of work designed to demonstrate the range of your interests and abilities as a writer. What should a portfolio look like? Like a journal, it should resemble you: your public self. It should contain your strongest public writing. If the formal academic essay is what you do best, then at least a couple of academic essays ought to be in your portfolio.

Your portfolio ought to show some balance as well. The writer who is most comfortable with library research should, for the sake of growth as a writer, try something less comfortable, perhaps a set of instructions, a personal essay, or even a piece of fiction. The writer who has always relied on imagination should, again for the sake of growth, get out to the library, do some interviews, or write a questionnaire to get the experience of managing factual information. The "creative" writer's portfolio should contain some practical work, such as reports and reviews, along with the more familiar personal essays and stories.

You should keep track of the projects you put into your portfolio, including drafts of the projects you complete and a letter describing the portfolio's contents. Many colleges have begun using portfolios to assess students' competence as writers. Likewise, the portfolio provides valuable evidence of your achievements as a writer for potential employers. With your teacher's assistance, you can begin preparing the documents which will help you land the job you want when you graduate.

In the early parts of this book, you will spend a good deal of time working with your journal. You should keep in mind that journal entries and writing projects are separated by the thinnest of veils. As you write your private thoughts in your journal, you will constantly glimpse the public writing which college and your profession will call on you to do.

Part I
Warming
Up

Part I helps you to build working relationships with your teacher and peers. If you are to work with each other, you have to get to know each other. You also need to get to know yourself as a writer. The series of assignments serves those purposes. By the time you have finished your work with Part I, you will be prepared to begin the process of learning and helping others to learn more about how to write successfully.

Chapter 1, A Background for Writing Processes, focuses on the attitudes, ideas, perceptions, and emotions which form the background of writing processes. An increased awareness of those background influences will help you to manage your writing more effectively. Chapter 2, The Satisfactions of Writing, focuses on the ways people find enjoyment and value in the act of writing. As you learn to appreciate the particular pleasures that help motivate you to write, you'll find that writing becomes more important to you.

Your motivations for beginning to write can vary from the need to respond to a classroom writing assignment, to the excitement of developing a multi-million dollar prospectus for a company, to the simple desire to get something off your mind. Whatever the reasons may be, we as writers all have to develop strategies for beginning to write. For some of us that may mean overcoming resistance of some kind; it may mean sorting out topics that appeal; or it may mean simply taking the time to let an idea develop before diving into the composing.

Chapter 1
A Background for Writing Processes

ATTITUDES ABOUT WRITING ABILITY

Before you begin learning more about writing, we need to review what we mean by **writing ability.** Each person's definition of writing ability probably varies a bit because each person has experienced writing and writing instruction differently. Everyone's definition of writing ability is correct, but no one's definition is complete. Each time you learn something about writing, each time you broaden your understanding of the concept of writing ability, you glimpse a wider and wider world. By the end of this section on attitudes about writing ability, you should have a heightened awareness of how personal attitudes about writing affect people's experiences of the writing process.

People often talk as if they thought that writing ability were restricted to knowledge of spelling, punctuation, and grammar. Finding an error in a piece of writing, critics cluck, "Why can't people write anymore?" But if you think for a moment, you realize that writing encompasses much more of the human personality than the part that proofreads a page of copy out of a motivation to avoid error.

Communicative Competence

Writing ability forms part of your **communicative competence**—a general ability to handle language (Hymes, 1971), not only writing but reading, speaking, and listening. Each of the parts of language ability contributes to the central task of language, which is making contact with other people.

At various times, the process of writing engages all the elements of your communicative competence—as you read a book in order to write a researched essay or as you read your own work in order to revise it; as you speak to a friend about an idea in order to clarify your thoughts before writing or as you speak your written language aloud to convey an idea

3

quickly and economically; as you listen to your own inner voices while you compose a draft or as you listen to the voices of teachers and peers who give you advice.

You were acquiring your writing ability while you were acquiring the abilities to speak, listen, and read. At each stage in your life, as you grew, your writing ability grew because you needed to communicate in order to take part in a **community**—a group of people who have something in common.

Members of a community communicate through common experiences of language, thought, and feeling. Membership in your first community, your family, began with a word—the name you were given. When you learned to speak, you began your active role in that community, and your ability to influence members of your community expanded as you learned their language.

When you entered other communities, you encountered new facts and rules about language. In school, you learned to tell a simple story, to explain a simple process, and to persuade someone to give you what you wanted. Soon you learned to write letters and stay within the lines. Spelling and punctuation came in there somewhere, as did the larger forms of writing: sentences, paragraphs, and eventually essays and research papers.

As you grew older and became more aware of your social world, you learned to use standard English, to persuade others to accept your ideas, to criticize your own and others' work, and to think through intellectual problems in a host of subjects. You learned to express not only what was in your mind, but also what was in your heart, through letters, poems, and stories.

As an adult, you possess a communicative competence which encompasses many abilities: to draw letters, to spell and punctuate, to type, to use a computer, to read, to reason, to find interesting problems to think about, to believe in what you do, to interest other people in your ideas, to take in information through your senses, to feel your emotions and to notice what other people feel, to listen to advice from others, to criticize your own work, to persist when you're discouraged, to stop when you've had enough, and to learn about yourself and other people. When you choose a friend, a lover, a college, a career, or a city to live in, you draw on your communicative competence to help you enter new communities.

ASSUMPTIONS AND THE WRITING EXPERIENCE

Each time you write, for whatever purpose or whatever reader, you bring with you a personal history that influences how you experience the writing process. From your personal history, you will have developed assumptions about writing: about the people, places, purposes, and subjects proper to writing.

You can get a sense of your assumptions about writing by trying to recall your earliest memories of writing. Your present assumptions will probably screen your memory of your early writing experiences and influence which aspects of writing seem most present and most important to you. What you remember will probably tell you a good deal about your motivations to write or, possibly, not to write. Not only will you discover something about yourself as a writer, but your teacher and your classmates will also meet you as a writer.

Perhaps you are like Scott, who showed early promise as a writer and who sees writing as a stern discipline. As you read Scott's response, note that he focuses on certain parts and certain purposes of the writing process. By becoming aware of the ways in which he limits his definition of writing ability, he can become more aware of possible new directions for growth in his ability. Scott is able to write easily and fluently because he is recovering important information about himself as a writer as he responds to the experience. When you write, don't compare your response to his. Just recall your first memory.

FROM THE JOURNAL OF S. Scott McCullough

> My earliest recollection of writing was in kindergarten. I wrote a very short book, which I entitled *Fresh Air in the House,* for my grandmother. I have long since forgotten what it was about, although I remember I illustrated it with pictures cut out of magazines, but I distinctly remember being proud of my name scrawled on its crude cover. I don't remember if I actually gave it to my grandmother, but I remember being mad at my parents for reading it and making a big deal out of it. I have searched my mother's attic, hoping it might be there, but always in vain.
>
> The first piece of writing whose subject matter I clearly recall was in seventh grade. My homeroom teacher, Mr. Short, had assigned research papers as a history lesson. Mine was to be about Harold Carter's discovery of Tutankhamen's tomb. All of the other kids did typical seventh-grade papers; a little cursory research, two pages, and hand it in on the due date. Not me. I checked out tons of books and immersed myself in Egyptology. The deadline for submission passed while I was still reading my books. Mr. Short asked me occasionally if I ever planned on turning in the paper, and I always promised to have it done soon. (I should note at this point that my teachers always made exceptions for me—I was the weird artist's son with long hair who tested beyond their scales. Their willingness to grant me extensions may have been the cruellest thing they ever did . . .)

When I finally handed in the report, six weeks late, it was over 20 pages long. I don't remember any of the words or phrasings that I used, but I do remember Mr. Short calling my parents (separately, for they were divorced by that time) to discuss my academic future. I was horrified: for some reason I loathed and craved the attention simultaneously, but it was an incredible amount of pressure for an 11 year old kid to deal with.

Oh, yes . . . I can recall the letter I included when I turned in the paper. It read:

Dear Mr. Short:

Here is my research paper on the discovery of King Tutankhamen's tomb. I regret the delay in its completion, but . . . [this part I forget]. I will not make excuses for its tardiness; excuses are loathsome to me. I hope you will judge it on its merits, not on the circumstances under which you received it.

Sincerely,
Scott M.

Scott's first writing memory is quite positive, of a piece of writing he composed for a valued person, his grandmother. However, Scott's second memory reveals some conflict: a strong drive to write well, which competes with another strong drive to meet deadlines. The members of Scott's class can expect him to be a source of positive attitudes about writing, and they should plan to help him when deadlines become oppressive.

But perhaps you are more like Martha, for whom writing has an air of mystery, of secrets kept and confidences betrayed. She recalls keeping a diary as a young girl and discovering that her mother had read her diary.

FROM THE JOURNAL OF Martha Buchanan

At seven, I was quiet as a mouse in a family of nine hungry cats who were forever waiting to pounce upon me. I spent most of my time trying to blend into the walls.

My mother gave me a diary. I was amazed that she had actually thought about me and enchanted with the idea of a secret journal. I wrote in it to fill the pages. I wanted to see pages and pages of my words. All the anger, all the rage of accepting the role of victim poured out onto the pages. I remember dispassionately writing that I hated my mother. But I was playing, playing with words, with emotions, with the implicit mysteriousness of a diary.

Long after I had safely hidden my book, long after I had gone on to a new and different game, my mother called me to the basement. I saw in her hand my diary, and in her eyes the feline satisfaction of a cat ready to pounce upon the mouse she had skillfully cornered.

Martha has learned to separate school writing from writing in which she has a personal investment. In her own words,

> [W]hen I wrote this journal piece, even after I had finished it, I couldn't understand how it connected to anything. How did this experience shape my present assumptions about writing? How did it tell me anything at all about my motivations?
>
> It wasn't until a few weeks later that I understood the connection. I reread my instructor's comment. [He had asked whether she worried that her writing would get to the wrong people and be misunderstood.] Initially, I rejected it as too simplistic, too manifestly symbolic.
>
> But the most difficult part of writing for me *is* to consider my writing in a context that would be read by more than a few readers. I am terribly afraid of being misunderstood, so much so that I reserve my best writing for myself and a few friends. I separate writing into two mutually exclusive genres—experiential and technical. Experiential writing is all writing that speaks of my life and issues that I care about. Technical writing is all that I do for evaluation.

Of course, not everyone separates school writing from more "personal" writing. Jon recalls teasing a teacher with his language ability, and he also recalls a sentimental early writing experience about writing with his mother. Jon's memories suggest that he tends to define writing ability as knowledge of the details of language. It appears that he usually writes for one of two purposes—to challenge authority or to build relationships with people who are important to him.

FROM THE JOURNAL OF Jon Neuleib

> My earliest memories of writing go back to about 1977 when I was in the second grade. The first one is an experience that is pretty clearly an anti-authoritarial one. My second grade readin' and ritin' teacher was very into answers that came in the form of a complete sentence. Because there was a problem with some of the students responding to questions with the construction "Because he wanted to," the teacher explained to the class that it was wrong to start a sentence with "Because." After a quick bit of research, I found that in many of the books that were assigned reading for the class, sentences started with "Because." I pointed this out and was subjected to at least a fifteen-minute explanation of the various uses of the word and denials that she had said that it could never be used to start a sentence.

The second experience I place in time close to the first because it dealt with a sonnet that my mother and I were writing on the subject of Minnesota. My grandfather died in 1977 so any cheerful references to his house in Minnesota would probably not have occurred after that point in time. The problem that occurred was that I could not find an appropriate word to rhyme with *skunk.* I tried to find a word that rhymed and finally came up with *kerplunck,* the noise that occurs when boaters fall out of their boats and into the water. There is nothing that seems special about this episode, but it sticks in my mind and is something I've fondly remembered even before I had to think about this prompt. I like to think that it is something I simply remember because it is warm and fuzzy.

Each of these writers brings a different set of assumptions to writing. Their responses make it clear that there is no such thing as "the writing process." Rather, there are at least as many writing processes as there are people who write, each process growing out of the writer's experiences and assumptions. When you become more aware of the background of your processes, you may find that they become both more comprehensible and more important to you.

This would be a good time for us to introduce the authors of this book as writers. We each discovered something about ourselves by writing for this experience. One of us remembered writing the little circles on the lined paper in first grade and worrying about making the handwriting perfect. She still fusses a great deal about getting her writing "right" and worries that some teacher/authority figure will look over her shoulder and disapprove of her writing. The other remembers his competitive feelings as he handed in a report on some South American country to his fifth grade teacher. To this day, whenever he writes, he sees the tidy folder handed in by the blonde girl who sat in front of him, and he wishes his writing could be better than hers.

EXPERIENCE

Once you have completed this assignment, you should be more aware of how your attitudes about writing affect your experience of the writing process.

What are your earliest memories of writing?
a. Describe the scene that comes to mind and try to recall the thoughts and feelings you associate with the scene.
   • What people are present in the scene?
   • Why are you writing?
   • How are you feeling?

- What are you thinking about?
b. Does the memory of this scene suggest any general attitudes you have about the nature and purpose of writing?
c. Discuss your responses with one or two members of your class.

AWARENESS AND COMPOSING

Right now, as you read these words, your senses, emotions, and background thoughts are helping to compose the meaning you derive from this paragraph. No one with your unique life history and combinations of abilities and disabilities has ever been where you are sitting, standing, or lying right now. Moment by unique moment, your mind makes meaning out of everything in your past and present.

Sometimes you actively and consciously compose your response to your environment, as when you listen and take notes in a class, hold a conversation with someone you want to impress, organize the schedule of your day's activities, or see a problem and create a way to solve it. Sometimes you compose more passively and unconsciously, as when you suddenly remember an appointment, have a recurring dream in which someone is chasing you, fasten your seat belt without thinking about it, or yield to an impulse to skip class.

When you respond to your world, you are composing, whether you choose to record your thoughts in a journal, say them out loud to friends, act them out in work or play, or simply keep them inside your mind. Creative people in every field learn to use the tools of their crafts to give concrete form to the compositions their minds generate every day. Painters paint, musicians compose or perform, mathematicians do equations, engineers build bridges, and, of course, writers write.

For writers, recording information on paper or a computer disk transforms inner experiences into a more permanent form. Revising takes writing still further to make it possible for others to experience your experiences in their own unique ways. But composing goes on inside of you all the time almost involuntarily.

Finding Meaning in Experience

Composing is like another complex process—dreaming. We dream every night at regular intervals and may remember nothing of our dreams. Some people even claim they never dream. But when we least expect it, an unusually vivid dream may wake us up and cause us to ask, "What do you think that meant?"

We are accustomed to simply letting experience flow through and around us, as if we were dreaming. Occasionally, when vivid waking events also invite interpretation, we wake up and ask, "What do you think that meant?" Perhaps you've just met someone whom you want to impress—say, a college teacher. You may try to interpret the teacher's words and actions in order to anticipate how the class is going to go. Or perhaps you've met another student in class, someone whom you find interesting and would like to know better. You may try to imagine how that person interpreted what you said and did in class.

We bring the same five senses, the same imagination, the same intellect, and the same feelings to every event. Why then do we experience some events as more vivid than others? We simply pay closer attention. We focus on the event and value it enough to ask what it means, what we think about it, and how it makes us feel.

Vivid events stimulate writing ability, so writers must constantly try to wake up from the dream we walk around in every day to ask, "What does it mean? How does it feel? What do I think about this experience? What does this experience remind me of?" Having awakened themselves, writers can set about rousing the sleepers around them.

One way of waking up is to write in a new environment. As you change your physical surroundings, your senses give you different information, and your mind can work on the new information. Notice how when Martha leaves her classroom to write, she becomes aware first of her general surroundings, then of her physical state, and finally of the physical sensations surrounding the act of writing itself.

FROM THE JOURNAL OF Martha Buchanan

I am outside sitting on the grass. There are a few bushes to hide me from everyone else. At least enough to pretend that I'm hidden.

I am amazed, awed by the infinite shades of nature's greens. I've spent quite a bit of time this summer studying the greens about me and trying to figure out the puzzle of how to convey the as yet unarticulated sensation that overcomes me when I pause and realize that I am immersed in a sea of greens.

I'm warm. No, I'm hot. The ground is slowly frying my ass like two eggs in a pan. The sun is magnified and intensified by my glasses; my cheeks below my eyes are slick with sweat.

There is a pleasant, unpleasant incessant tickling all over my body. Black beetles, little red ants, strange striped flying creatures are finding my intrusion either an interesting distraction or an annoyance. Sweat is gathering into beads under my hairline, below my lower lip, gathering into pools on my scalp. Drips of sweat are rolling down my neck, over my breasts, down my back. Is the itch a trickle of sweat or a bug that has found its way into my clothing armor?

Time is just about up. Soon, I'll have to close this and return to the classroom. In many ways, this writing experience feels like my personal journaling. It is not so relaxed, nor free. But it is much more relaxed and free than my previous experiences with classroom writing.

At first I missed the tools I ordinarily employ when writing for the classroom—my computer, thesaurus, dictionary. I'm breaking some of my rules for classroom writing. I don't think that I could have been quite so aware of sensation if I had had them.

Martha awoke to discover an awareness of the tools she works with. She found that by "breaking the rules" about how and when she did classroom writing, she began to question her distinction between the writing she does for school and the writing she does for herself.

Jon used this journal entry to wake up his descriptive ability. He focused on the grimy interior of a fraternity house after a party. Before he had finished his description, he had reminded himself of the famous "gonzo" journalist, Hunter S. Thompson, author of *Fear and Loathing in Las Vegas.*

FROM THE JOURNAL OF Jon Neuleib

It's morning and the fraternity is replete with all its usual smells, but the hour guarantees that there is very little noise in the house. I can hear the washer that someone has been intrepid enough to get up and start this morning. The kitchen is covered in beer cans and unwashed dishes that all combine into one scent. Quite a pleasant writing situation if I do say so myself. My mouth tastes of last night's Rhinelander and the room smells vaguely of that brand of beer. My mood is peaceful even in the midst of all this carnage. Writing a journal is not exactly a private activity, but it is something that is quite separate from the atmosphere here.

To have to describe the atmosphere is unpleasant. If I wanted to experience the atmosphere I'd stare at the wall instead of tapping it out on the keyboard. This is usually an escape time in which I encounter the inner world of thought rather than the outer one of grime.

I call it carnage because waking up early at a fraternity is similar to the end of *Platoon* when Charlie Sheen wakes up and finds himself more alive than anything else. There was a lot of violent, unpleasant activity here last night, but some kind soul came along and napalmed the whole thing. This is a secret time that exists in the same physical universe with the other things that go on here, but this one is not seen by most people and that makes it special. The only thing that really changes between this time and that time is that the sun comes up in the morning and you can

see everything as shitty as it really is. At night there is a nice illusion that
happens because you can't tell what is dirt and what is shadow. I'll miss
it.

Great Hunter S. Thompson! *Beer and Loathing in the Frat House.*

You can tell that both these writers enjoyed the writing that occurred
when they woke up. While Martha interpreted her waking dream as a
message about her divided attitudes about writing, Jon found that his
grimy surroundings caused him to write quite naturally in Hunter S.
Thompson's style.

Some writers find that waking up gives them some not-so-pleasant
information. If you encounter anxiety when you write in response to the
Experience below, you should try to understand where the anxiety is coming from. There's a good chance that the anxiety was there in the background all along, inhibiting your productivity. If you wake up and deal
with it, you'll probably be a more comfortable writer, which should lead in
the long run to improvements in the quality and quantity of your work.

EXPERIENCE

1. Pretend that you are just awakening from a dream.

   Find a comfortable environment different from your usual
   writing environment. Take a moment to focus on what is going on
   around you and inside you as you write. Begin writing and then
   try to write about the experience of writing itself.
   - What do your senses of sight, smell, hearing, taste, and touch
     tell you?
   - What kind of mood are you in right now?
   - What thoughts have been running through your mind today?
   - Does this experience remind you of any other experience?
   - Write down as much of this sort of information as seems interesting.
2. Interpret your experience as if it were a dream. Reread what you
   have just written. Focus on the feelings and sensations which
   accompany the act of writing.
   - What does this experience mean?
   - What does it tell you about your writing?
   - How does the state of mind you just described compare with
     your usual state of mind when you write?

COMPOSING STYLE AND PSYCHOLOGICAL TYPE

As a writer, you probably have a composing style different in some
ways from every other writer you know. Your composing style is learned

behavior. You picked up most of your methods in school, and most schools have some pretty definite rules. Ideally, your composing style should fit you comfortably and should help you work effectively, but sometimes you can pick up methods that don't work well for you. For example, like one of this book's authors, you may have found the outline to be an essential preparation for writing. But perhaps your composing style resembles that of the other author of this book, who, while he was in school, secretly wrote his papers first and his outlines afterward, as part of the revision process. When you have finished this section, you should begin to see that productive composing styles can differ from person to person, and, with a new consciousness of your own style, you should be prepared to learn some techniques from others.

Some writing research (Jensen and Ditiberio, 1984) suggests that we can understand people's composing styles by looking at something called **personality type.** Many theorists of human psychology have suggested that people differ systematically, and that those differences give rise to personality types. Discovering personality type may help a writer to make productive decisions about work habits.

The descriptions that follow are derived from a system of personality types proposed by the Swiss psychologist Carl Jung (1921) and elaborated by Katherine Briggs and Isabel Briggs Myers, a mother-daughter research team. The theory (Myers, 1980) suggests that four pairs of personality traits may help you to understand people's behavior. The pairs of traits are extravert/introvert, sensing/intuition, thinking/feeling, and judgment/perception. Most people have some preferences for one or the other trait in the pair.

- Extraverts prefer to focus attention on the outer world of people and things, while Introverts prefer to focus attention on the inner world of ideas and symbols.
- Sensors prefer to use their five senses to perceive the concrete, practical dimension of information while Intuitives prefer to use a sixth sense to perceive the imaginative, theoretical dimension of information.
- Thinking types prefer to make decisions using impersonal processes of logic and analysis. Feeling types prefer to make decisions using personal processes of valuing and relationship.
- Judgers prefer to organize their lives around schedules that help them to finish projects. Perceiving types prefer to live unstructured lives that help them to discover new interests.

According to the theory, people exhibit a preference for one element in each of these pairs of personality traits in a way that resembles handedness. You can illustrate the idea for yourself if you stop right now and sign your name with your less-preferred hand. Notice that as you sign your name (with your left hand if you are right-handed or with your right hand if you are left-handed), you feel awkward, out of control, unnatural, disadvantaged, weak—you can add other terms that describe your reaction. According to theory, you were born with a preference for one hand or the other. Over the course of a lifetime, exercising your preference caused you to learn to control one hand more than the other. If you have learned to type or play a musical instrument, you may have developed your less-preferred hand. Whether you developed your "weaker" hand depended on circumstances—your parents, your school, your friends, and other factors.

Personality type works in the same way: a preference (possibly inborn) for behaving a certain way (reinforced over a lifetime) leads to comfort and often to skill in the preferred behavior. The preferences are subject to change over the years as you change environments: new people, jobs, and interests change your taste. Since these preferences are broad and general, they influence many patterns of behavior, your writing being an important one.

According to theory, each person has a "true type," which is inborn and which it is the person's lifework to discover and develop. Although some scientific research has suggested a biological basis for extraversion and introversion (Eysenck, 1975), we can't safely generalize that true type exists, let alone that we can measure it. Type theory seems valid to the authors because it often explains writers' behavior in a reasonable, helpful way. As you continue reading, you'll encounter paragraph descriptions that synthesize some qualities of type in a way that may help you to think about your writing processes. But we make no claims to validly assess your preferences. Of the various psychological instruments that assess the preferences we have described, the Myers-Briggs Type Indicator has the best research background. If you become interested in personality type, you may find that your school's counseling center will be willing to give you the Indicator and discuss the results with you.

For present purposes, we'll introduce each of the personality traits with descriptive paragraphs, asking you to choose which paragraph describes you best. We'll first ask you to identify the trait in the context of your life in general. Then we'll introduce you to the trait in the context of writing and again ask you to choose which paragraph describes you best. As you read the paragraphs, you should try to choose the paragraph which describes your preferences—the behavior patterns which make you comfortable. Many environmental factors—your culture, your gender, your parents and friends, your job—can influence you to decide that a way of behaving is "right" or "wrong" rather than comfortable or uncomfortable. If you can, try to choose with a "shoes-off" mentality, thinking about what *you* would like, not about what teachers, friends, parents, or anyone else has taught you is appropriate.

As you consider each of the preferences in turn, you'll form groups with people who have the same preferences as you, and discuss your writing style. You may discover that your group members use the same methods and encounter the same advantages and disadvantages you do. If so, you'll have the comfort of knowing you're not the only one in the world. You may also discover that someone in your group has a trick or two you may want to pick up. You should be sure to contribute your insights to the group and to take notes on your group discussion as you listen. We'll ask you to do some writing about the experience.

Extraverted and Introverted Planning Styles

To begin, consider which of the following descriptions sounds more like you.

Extravert Description 1

Extraverts like to stay connected with the outside world most of the time. They enjoy dealing with people and things. Extraverts would usually rather deliver a message orally than in writing. They feel charged with energy when they get to interact with a lot of different people in a short space of time.

Introvert Description 1

Introverts like to stay connected with the inner world most of the time. They enjoy dealing with ideas and symbols. Introverts would usually rather write a message to someone than deliver it in person. They feel charged with energy when they can interact with one or two people in depth.

The extravert/introvert difference has to do with personal energy, with what makes you feel charged up and what makes you feel run down. Extraverts tend to find the external world of people and things more energizing, whereas introverts find the inner world of ideas and symbols more energizing.

Did one of the descriptions clearly fit you? Or did you find that both descriptions fit you to some degree?

To help you clarify the difference, let's think about the following situation. Suppose that the weekend has begun. You've had a tough week and you're exhausted. Which of the following descriptions comes closer to what you would like to do to recharge your batteries over the weekend? (We'll assume that one thing you would do would be to sleep until you felt rested.)

Extravert Description 2

Extraverts would like to get out of the house and get involved in some sort of activity with friends. They would want lots of different activities. They would go boating or swimming, do a group project of some kind, play on a team, or organize a picnic or party. Later on, they might feel like spending some quiet time alone. In the evening, extraverts might want to go to a party and meet some new people.

Introvert Description 2

Introverts would like to have some time by themselves to rest up. They might read a book, sew, take a walk, work on a hobby or do some small project. It would be good to go to lunch with a close friend and spend a couple of hours talking seriously. In the evening they might go to a play or movie. They might go dancing or to a party if there were going to be people they knew there.

Now look at the paragraphs describing extraverts and introverts. Try to decide which fits you better. Think about what would make you most comfortable: not what your parents would like you to be, not what you think your teacher would like, not what your best friend or elder sibling is like, but what you would really prefer.

Let's try one more pair of descriptions, this time having to do with how you write.

Extravert Description 3

Extraverts like to generate ideas by talking about the topic, interviewing people, or actively experiencing the topic. They prefer to start writing without much preplanning. Extraverts develop lots of ideas while they write, sometimes starting out in confusion and working toward a clear understanding of the topic. They often stop while writing to plan what to do next. Extraverts don't mind revising, but they sometimes create drafts requiring so much revision that they lose interest in them before they finish.

Introvert Description 3

Introverts like to plan carefully before they write to avoid a lot of rewriting afterward. They would rather do research with books than with people. Introverts like to deal with advice by going off and thinking about it before revising. Since they work ideas through before they write them down, introverts don't change much between first and final drafts. They outline so carefully that they rarely come up with new ideas while writing.

One of this book's authors prefers an extraverted composing style—easy on the planning and heavy on the revision. The other author prefers an introverted composing style—heavy on the planning and skip-the-revision-please. The combination of styles can help create a nicely balanced work relationship or can create friction. In our case it seems that the differences mainly complement one another. Since writing places a heavy burden on both planning and revising, a writer needs to have some competence with both processes, but a writer also needs coauthors, editors, and friends to render aid when it is needed.

EXPERIENCE

1. In class, form a group based on the choices of paragraphs you've made. We'll determine the group memberships as follows.
   - Group 1 chose all three extravert paragraphs.
   - Group 2 chose all three introvert paragraphs.
   - Group 3 chose two extravert paragraphs and one introvert paragraph.
   - Group 4 chose two introvert paragraphs and one extravert paragraph.
2. Once you've joined your group, list some of the steps you take in writing a research paper.
   a. As you compile the list, check items shared by most of the members of your group. Which parts of writing the research paper are easiest? Which cause the most problems?
   b. Note ways in which your personal preferences resemble those of your group and of your teacher.
   c. If you are in an Extravert group but did not choose Extravert Description 3 or if you are in an Introvert group but did not choose Introvert Description 3, what differences do you note between the way you draft and the ways other members of your group draft? What could they learn from you? What might you learn from them?
3. Use what you have learned from this experience to write a paragraph describing your preferences as a writer. Note both strengths and weaknesses that proceed from your preferences.

Sensing and Intuitive Views on Assignments

The second pair of differences in Jungian personality type is between sensing and intuition. This pair of traits helps define how you like to take in information. Sensing types like to use their five senses to focus on what they are learning, whereas intuitive types like to use their imaginations more.

Sensing Description 1

Sensing types prefer to be realistic. They focus on what is actually happening around them. In class they like teachers to give lots of examples and illustrations of each idea presented. They are interested in details and patient with handling them.

Intuitive Description 1

Intuitive types prefer to be imaginative. They tend to read between the lines and look for possibilities inherent in their situations. Once they "get" an idea in class, they like teachers to move quickly and skip the irrelevant details.

Does one of these paragraphs sound more like you than the other?

Try this little perception exercise to see if you can extend your understanding of sensing and intuition. Take out a sheet of paper and spend a few minutes taking a tour of your surroundings. Wherever you are, simply observe and take in the information and then jot it down on the sheet of paper. Don't read further until you have taken your tour.

Sensing Description 2

Sensing types probably got up out of their chairs and literally toured the surroundings, finding information about the size, shape, number, color, weight, smell, and feel of the surroundings. They may have come up with a good deal of practical knowledge about the place. The information was probably arranged in a list as they happened upon it in the tour.

Intuitive Description 2

Intuitive types may have interpreted this direction as an invitation to take an imaginary walk. Without stirring from their spots, they may have picked up some bits of sensory data and then thought of an association: a color might bring to mind a feeling, a shape might suggest something shaped similarly, objects might suggest the people who used them, and so forth. Some of the connections might be far-fetched.

As a last clarification of this difference, consider the following descriptions of how sensing and intuition may affect the writing process.

Sensing Description 3

Sensing types like detailed and specific directions. They enjoy writing about things they have experienced directly. They tend to work in a step-by-step process that begins with facts and works gradually toward ideas. They are good with concrete examples and careful about details such as handwriting, spelling, and mechanics. They sometimes remain stuck in the details and never get round to the big ideas. Readers sometimes react to their writing with a so-what attitude.

Intuitive Description 3

Intuitive types like a few directions which give them lots of latitude. They need to be able to take a unique and imaginative approach to a topic. Their ideas come quickly, and they sometimes aren't sure where the ideas come from. They tend to "fake it" or make it up as they go along, rather than follow an established writing procedure. They are adept at inventing organizational patterns. They sometimes confuse readers because they skip from one big idea to another. They sometimes confuse themselves with their complex organizational patterns.

Both authors of this book use a strongly intuitive composing style. Since we value originality very highly, we have to work twice as hard as sensing types to cover all the details, and we have to constantly remind ourselves to go into detail and use illustrations and examples. We rely on our sensing students to remind us to supply enough details when we give an assignment to enable them to work comfortably and effectively.

Sensing and intuitive writers can work together quite productively, the intuitive types spinning out original ideas and organizational plans and the sensing types asking and answering the hard questions about practical details of getting a writing project finished.

Now that you've had a chance to make three choices, try the following experience.

EXPERIENCE

1. In class, divide into four groups as they are indicated below.
   - Group 1 chose all three sensing paragraphs.
   - Group 2 chose all three intuitive paragraphs.
   - Group 3 chose two sensing paragraphs and one intuitive paragraph.
   - Group 4 chose two intuitive paragraphs and one sensing paragraph.
2. Now meet in your groups to list and discuss the writing assignments which have helped you write most successfully.
   a. Describe the assignment.
   b. What particular features of the writing assignment helped you the most? Put a check mark next to any features which occur to more than one writer.

3. Discuss your lists with the other groups.
    a. Which group do you resemble most closely?
    b. Note ways in which your planning methods resemble those of your group and of your teacher.
    c. If you are in a Sensing group but did not choose Sensing Description 3, or if you are in an Intuitive group but did not choose Intuitive Description 3, what differences do you note between the way you draft and the ways other members of your group draft? What could they learn from you? What might you learn from them?
4. Use what you have learned from this experience to write a paragraph describing your preferences as a writer. Note both strengths and weaknesses that proceed from your preferences.

Thinking and Feeling Relationships to the Reader

Two ways of making decisions are thinking and feeling. Feeling types like to use human values to make up their minds on any issue, and thinking types like to use logic.

Thinking Description 1

Thinking types aim for impersonality in decision making. Thinkers like to be sure they are being fair, consistent, and reasonable. To thinkers it is important that all the information be organized logically so that the conclusions drawn relate to the information given. Human factors will be part of the information but will not be the predominant factor.

Feeling Description 1

Feeling types make decisions by considering the human factors—values, emotions, personalities, and so forth. People with the feeling preference tend to focus on whether something is good or bad, beautiful or ugly, pleasing or displeasing. If a feeling type has to make a decision, he or she will use logic as part of the process, but will trust subjective judgment and personal values more than logic and therefore subordinate logic to feelings.

The scoring system for the Myers-Briggs Type Indicator weights the feeling score of males and the thinking score of females to compensate for cultural pressure. Although any of the preferences may vary according to pressures of various kinds, statisticians have been able to observe gender-role pressure on this particular dimension which is strong enough to warrant adjusting scores. Males may feel social pressure to choose the thinking description, and females may feel similar pressure to choose the feeling description. Try to focus on how you really prefer to operate rather than how you think your social sphere expects you to operate.

To help refine your understanding of the difference between thinking and feeling, define the word *love*.

Thinking Description 2

Thinking types will tend to react to this request with a groan. "Please don't make me do this!" Thinkers may believe you can't define love, or they may prefer highly abstract definitions ("Love is a condition in which personal needs are subordinated to those of the object of affection"), cynical definitions ("Love is a glandular disorder") or even sexual definitions ("Love means never having to say you're horny").

Feeling Description 2

Feeling types may value tenderness, accommodation, affect, and compassion. Feeling types focus on human values and relatedness. Feeling types have a refined understanding of this feeling because it is the core of so much of their experience. Their definitions reveal the various forms that caring can take as it is played out in relationships between friends, lovers, parents and children, and people and God.

For the third set of choices, we again turn to some differences between the ways thinking and feeling types like to write. We'll focus particularly on how the two types differ in the ways they prefer to manage their relationships with their readers.

Thinking Description 3

Thinking types appeal to readers through logic and organization. Thinking types may assume readers are interested in analysis and in ideas for their own sakes. Thinking types may tend to be abrasive because they regard their ideas as objectively true. Thinking types may become confused about how to approach the reader if they don't see the purpose of an assignment, when they think the reader is unfair, or when they cannot find a comfortable organizational structure.

Feeling Description 3

Feeling types appeal to readers through deep personal conviction. They are more interested in appreciating an experience than in analyzing it. Feeling types may tend to be evasive if they are afraid that their ideas will offend someone. Feeling types may find difficulty approaching the reader through rigid organizational plans, when they lack personal involvement in what they are doing, or when they cannot find just the right word or phrase.

Both of the authors of this book are thinking types. As teachers and writers, we tend to focus on logic and analysis, believing that when we have given a reader good reasons, we have done enough. Feeling-type students and colleagues have taught us the importance of taking personality into account, of occasionally telling stories to make a point instead of relying exclusively on debate tactics, and of choosing a writing project carefully to be sure we believe in what we are doing.

For our part, we have helped other writers to stand at an objective distance from their work and the problems they are having, to analyze a writing problem, and to develop logical solutions to problems.

EXPERIENCE

1. In class, join a group based on the following criteria.
   - Group 1 chose all three thinking paragraphs.
   - Group 2 chose all three feeling paragraphs.
   - Group 3 chose two thinking paragraphs and one feeling paragraph.
   - Group 4 chose two feeling paragraphs and one thinking paragraph.
2. In group, discuss how you try to appeal to your reader.

   What do you do to try to make your writing interesting to your reader? What part of writing is least interesting to you personally?
   a. Make a list that includes the suggestions of everyone in your group. Put a check mark next to the suggestions which are shared by most members of your group.
   b. Note ways in which your personal preferences resemble those of your group.
   c. If you are in a Thinking group but did not choose Thinking Description 3, or if you are in an Feeling group but did not choose Feeling Description 3, what differences do you note between the way you appeal to the reader and the ways other members of your group appeal to the reader? What could they learn from you? What might you learn from them?
3. Use what you have learned from this experience to write a paragraph describing your preferences as a writer. Note both strengths and weaknesses that proceed from your preferences.

Judging and Perceiving Styles of Managing Writing Processes

Judging and perceiving are two lifestyles, two ways of dealing with the world around you. Consider the following descriptions of the two types.

Judging Description 1

Judging types like to order their lives. They make decisions quickly. They have no difficulty deciding when they have heard enough. Judging types will agree or disagree with an idea soon after hearing it. Once their minds are made up, they don't like to reopen them.

Perceiving Description 1

Perceiving types would rather just live their lives than order them. They are always waiting for new information to come in before making a decision. They will suspend disagreement or agreement in order to avoid making irrevocable errors. They have no difficulty reconsidering a decision.

As you can probably guess, these two types of people get on each other's nerves if they go out to eat together. The judging types make up their minds quickly about what to order. The perceiving types always want someone else to order first.

You can see the difference in behavioral terms if you consider the following situation. Suppose that you were about to go on a trip. Make a list of the preparations you would feel necessary before you go.

Judging Description 2

Judging types are list-makers by nature. Their travel is preceded by an immense amount of arrangement: cancelling deliveries, arranging tickets, getting pet-sitters, packing for all kinds of weather, getting replacements at work, and so forth. If your travel list is a long one, you are probably a judging type.

Perceiving Description 2

Perceiving types are problem-solvers by nature. They would rather just pick up and go. Whatever happens, happens, and they'll deal with it then. If your list was short or nonexistent, you are probably a perceiving type.

Finally, consider the ways these two types manage a composing session.

Judging Description 3

Judging types often focus on goal setting. They tend to write in as orderly a manner as they travel. They are emphatic and sometimes opinionated (at least in their tone). They write short first drafts and usually finish before the deadline. Judging types don't mind committing themselves to a regular writing schedule, but they find that it is difficult to alter their schedule once it is set.

Perceiving Description 3

Perceiving types often focus on research and analysis. They are ambitious in their choice of topics and in their approach. They are thorough and always open to new information. They write long first drafts and often depend on their ability to build up speed at the last moment to make deadlines. Regular writing schedules often depress perceiving types, but they sometimes wait too long for inspiration to strike them.

The authors of this book differ on this preference. The first author is a perceiving type and the second author is a judging type. As a student, the perceiving-type author always took a devil-may-care attitude toward deadlines. He usually asked for and received extensions from his teachers. One day during his senior year of college, he was in the process of asking for his usual extension, and his teacher was mercifully giving him an extra week when he suddenly grew annoyed with himself. He respected the teacher and knew that that the teacher personally never missed a deadline. He spoke snappishly to himself: "Are you going to be a weasel your whole life?" He turned on his heel, drove back to his apartment, sat down at his typewriter, and turned out the writing project by the deadline. He has missed deadlines since that time, but missing deadlines has never again felt like the normal way to behave.

The second author zipped through college making every deadline and accumulating scholastic honors. After becoming a college professor, she continued to set early deadlines, complete her writing, and secure places of publication for it. But a few years ago, she began work on an article which was personally important to her. Since she wanted to place the article with a particular magazine, she gave herself plenty of time to meet the expectations of that magazine's editor. Still, the editor asked for revisions, and more revisions, and still more. She missed many personal deadlines but eventually placed the article in the magazine. Since that time, she has become more flexible about restructuring deadlines to allow sufficient time to produce the level of quality she now expects of herself.

In both those cases, encounters with opposite types taught a writer an important lesson. The perceiving type learned that flexibility carried too far can become sloppiness, and the judging type learned that orderliness carried too far can become a willingness to sacrifice quality. Each type needs the other for balance to keep strengths from growing into weaknesses.

EXPERIENCE

1. In class, divide into four groups according to the following criteria.
   - Group 1 chose all three judging paragraphs.
   - Group 2 chose all three perceiving paragraphs.
   - Group 3 chose two judging and one perceiving paragraph.
   - Group 4 chose two perceiving and one judging paragraph.
2. List the actions you would take to complete a writing project that is due in four weeks.
   a. Put a check mark next to actions most people in your group agree on.
   b. Note ways in which your personal behavior resembles that of your group.
   c. If you are in a Judging group but did not choose Judging Description 3, or if you are in a Perceiving group but did not choose Perceiving Description 3, what differences do you note between your methods of managing the writing process and the ways other members of your group manage the process? What could they learn from you? What might you learn from them?
3. Use what you have learned from this experience to write a paragraph describing your preferences as a writer. Note both strengths and weaknesses that proceed from your preferences.

Putting the Preferences Together

If you work out all the combinations of the eight preferences, you will see that they produce sixteen possible personality types. Of course no one can capture an entire personality in a simple set of categories like this one, but type theory can help people to understand themselves more deeply and to recognize, honor, and make use of the ways other people differ from them. As an example, consider the preferences of this book's authors. On the Myers-Briggs Type Indicator and the paragraphs we have provided, Janice Neuleib comes out an Introverted, iNtuitive, Thinking, Judging type (INTJ). As a writer, she has an introvert's preference for planning before writing and an introvert's fondness for concentrating deeply on the task at hand. She has an intuitive's fascination with theory and originality in writing, a thinker's tendency to enjoy scientific methods of reasoning, and a judging type's tendency to turn out work in large quantities and always on the deadline. The other author shares two of her preferences, for intuition and thinking, but he prefers extraversion and perceiving, which give him the personality type labeled ENTP. His extraverted composing style is discovery oriented: he often writes to see what he thinks, in a written version of thinking out loud. He enjoys skipping from one part to another of a writing project in a flexible perceiving-type way.

Each of the composing styles carries with it a tendency to do some work more and some work less willingly. Various aspects of writing projects may require you to engage in every one of the behavior patterns associated with the sixteen types, and you cannot possibly prefer all of them. Fortunately you have people of various preferences around you from whom you can secure help and advice. The authors have found that the preferences we share enable us to communicate with each other effectively and to assist each other in working through problems with the writing process. However, those common qualities become a bit of a disadvantage when we need to critique each other's work. We find that the advice of people who do not share our preferences helps us a great deal. We especially need sensing types to help us to see where we fall short in presenting details and finding applications in our theoretical intuitive way. We need feeling types to help us see where we unwittingly ignore the human element in our brusque thinking way.

We will therefore suggest that you cultivate two kinds of relationships with the people in your class. For advice and assistance in carrying out your writing processes, we suggest that you form a working group with several people who share two or more of your preferences. You'll find that those people experience their writing processes in ways that resemble your own experience. From the basis of those common experiences, you'll be able to converse and advise one another readily. For advice and assistance in locating problems that require revision in a writing project, we suggest that you form a reading group with several people who share only one or even none of your preferences. Since you will differ in the ways you write and read, you'll be able to exchange insights you might not gain from people who are more like you.

The terms *introversion, intuition, feeling,* and *perceiving* denote a quality of mental experience which we can describe as "subjectivity." We would choose *extraversion, sensing, thinking,* and *judging* as terms which describe "objectivity." Writing involves giving subjective knowledge an objective form. In this book, we have arranged our chapters to move from a relatively subjective to a relatively objective view of the writing processes. So far you have concentrated on comparatively subjective work which may seem personal and oriented toward your inner life. As you move through the book, you'll find that the work becomes progressively more objective, more textual, and more oriented toward the outer world. As we go along, you may notice that we explain the same idea from a couple of different perspectives. For example, when we present a theoretical explanation, which we know intuitives will like, we usually balance it with a practical example or analogy, which we hope sensing types will like. We offer different ways of approaching the subject matter in the hope of making our information accessible to as many types as possible.

Depending on your preferences, you will find some parts of this book more comfortable than others. If you happen to be an INFP, you've probably been finding the work quite comfortable thus far. If you happen to be an ESTJ, you're probably wishing we'd get down to business. Later on, as we focus on revising for an audience and preparing the final draft, the INFP will wonder what became of writing about core issues in the journal. The ESTJ will be glad that we've finally come to our senses and concentrated on the portfolio.

You may even notice that our writing style changes. It may seem to you that the early part of the book is more personal and the later part is more intellectual. We think you'll be a better writer if you can learn to see past that dichotomy. Writing is personal and intellectual, subjective and objective, intuitive and sensing, perceiving and judging, feeling and thinking, extraverted and introverted. For the sake of teaching and learning, we've used the concepts of "journal" and "portfolio" to divide the subjective from the objective parts of the writing experience, but we really believe that writing necessitates a constant interplay between the states of mind those concepts represent.

Finally, we want to note that type is an explanation, not an excuse. We jokingly say things like, "Intuitives shouldn't have to proofread," or "Introverts get to be their own peer group," but we know that preference does not release anyone from responsibility. The exercise of writing ability requires your whole personality, every bit of energy and experience you can bring to bear.

EXPERIENCE

1. Assemble the four paragraphs you've written in response to the four experiences of psychological type to create a description of yourself as a writer.
   a. Trade descriptions with a peer who shares two or more of your preferences. Take notes on your peer's description where that description gives you further insight into your own preferences. Revise your own description as it seems appropriate.

    b. Trade descriptions with a peer who shares none or only one of your preferences. Note the preferences that would be especially problematic for you.

2. Form a working group with two or more people who share two or more of your preferences. When you need to discuss your writing processes, turn to these people for advice and assistance in understanding and solving problems.

3. Form a reading group with two or more people who share none or only one of your preferences. Show drafts of your writing projects to these people, and ask them for suggestions for revision.

Chapter 2
The Satisfactions
of Writing

MAKING THE TIME TO WRITE

When you were small, like all children you enjoyed expressing yourself with pencils, crayons, computers, or clay. Somewhere along the way, for many of us, writing became toil rather than expression. You can relearn that earlier joy of writing and expression by writing about valuable parts of your experience. You confer importance on an experience when you decide to write about it, and you confer importance on writing when you use it to record important experiences.

Think of a photograph you're familiar with. Can you visualize the scenery in it? The people or animals? Were you part of the picture? Did you take it? Can you remember what was happening that day?

Notice how just the fact that someone took a picture lends a kind of importance to the most common people and events. Suppose you went your whole life without taking any pictures of the people, places, or events that were important to you. You'd never have the chance to freeze a moment of experience, hold it in your hand, and look at it. Nor could you look at the experience later and summon exactly what was going on at that time. Nor could other people who were not present share the experience as it looked through your eyes.

Pretend to take a picture right now by making a frame with your hands. Notice that you choose a center, a focus to view through your frame. And notice that you see the focal object more clearly; you experience it more fully.

Like photography, writing enables you to experience the present more fully. The slow pace and large vocabulary you use when you write enable you to make subtle distinctions of thought and feeling, to ask and answer complex questions about what you are learning, and to choose inventive ways of expressing yourself so that you and your readers can glimpse various sides of your character, as well as accomplishing practical purposes like getting your schoolwork done.

As you look through the lens of writing, you frame experience and give it logic and beauty. Writing even gives you the artist's power to envision something that hasn't happened yet, experience it imaginatively, and preserve your imaginative experience for others. If you only speak, you're limited to the words you happen to be able to find at the moment. In effect, you're captured by the time and space you live in.

Like a photograph, a piece of writing freezes a moment of time. The written language has concrete form and color that oral language lacks— different papers and inks, different typefaces and sizes. But, better than photography, writing gives you the power to go beneath the surface to capture the parts of experience that happen inside of you. If you never write, you never have the chance to re-experience, reconsider, or share your inner life. And when you are gone, there is no trace of the part of you that you think of as "I."

Spending Time Writing

Since you're reading this book, we can assume that you're about to spend some time working on your writing. Have you ever said or thought something like this?

"I don't have time to sit down and write. I've got school, a job I have to keep to pay the bills, and my friends and family to think about. I won't even talk about finding personal time to relax and do what I want."

"There just aren't enough hours in the day to do everything. You have to be so disciplined to write. Maybe if I slept half an hour less each night . . . ."

Writing can solve some of your problems and add quality to your life. Like everyone else, the authors of this book sometimes put off writing, but we know that when we do, we lose rather than gain time. We write to solve personal and practical problems, to express ourselves, and to communicate with others, but most importantly, we write because the experience of writing itself fills an important need in our lives. Far from taking time away from our friends, our families, our studies, or our leisure, writing deepens our experience of those parts and all the other parts of our lives. For us, saying, "I don't have time to write," is like saying, "I don't have time to live."

Consider what it means to say, "I don't have time." When someone says, "I don't have time for X" or "I can't spend time to do Y," it often isn't that the person literally couldn't find the time for X or Y but that he or she doesn't *value* X or Y as much as some other thing he or she might be doing. People spend time and money on what they value, but they also find that they begin to value what they spend time and money on. To people who don't spend time writing, writing never becomes valuable. This book's authors find that when we write every day, we want to do more and more writing, but when we get away from writing, for instance during the end of a semester when we have many papers to respond to, we tend to find ourselves thinking of it as a chore.

We know many busy people who began by making time to write, but who now find that writing makes time for them. Donna, a woman with a family, has returned to college. If anyone could be said not to have time to write, it would have to be someone like Donna. Her journal entry illustrates how value can return from value invested in writing.

FROM THE JOURNAL OF Donna Svob

Today, Wednesday, I don't have a class until 1:00. I planned to leave early, though, and spend some time in the computer lab in the library working on the materials for this course. My husband and daughter left for work and school at about 7:30. My plan was to shower and leave home around 8:30. As soon as everyone left, my 10 month old black Lab threw a temper tantrum, tore up some papers and chewed through an electrical cord (the one my husband had just put a new end on two nights ago). I put her in her crate and went to shower—greatly agitated. In this state I began to think of a commitment my husband informed me of last night, one that I didn't expect.

He had forgotten to let me know that I am to teach a canoeing class September 7 and 8. Since I didn't even know this was in the works, I am totally unprepared. I also have never taught a purely lecture section—I'm used to teaching at the river, with equipment in hand. For this course, I am expected to teach three hours of classroom; the second day will be hands on at some lake or river.

Well, I was fuming anyway about the dog, so I just added this to my subjects to fume about. While in the shower, though, my thoughts took a turn and my attitude moderated. I began to think about how I was going to handle three hours of lecture. What a frightening thought for someone who has never given a formal lecture before. I decided that I needed to put together some sort of "script" for the session and I began to put words together in my mind, imagining myself standing in front of the group. All of a sudden I had so much to say I had to write it down!

After my shower I went directly to my pencil and paper. My hair dried out of shape; the dog whined because she wanted out of her crate. But I had to write!

I was aware of being annoyed at the pencil. I'm used to writing at a keyboard, but my PC wasn't up and I didn't plan on being around very long so I decided to write "manually." My pencil couldn't keep up with the thoughts and the muscles ached from trying to write so fast. My words were written in a sort of shorthand—I couldn't take the time to add the last "e's," cross the "t's" or dot the "i's."

I was unaware of what was happening around me. I don't know if the dog stopped whining. I was totally focused. I wasn't even annoyed anymore about having to do the project. It might be fun and, since someday I hope to teach high school English, it would definitely be a learning experience.

I was excited emotionally. I felt an energy that has carried over to this moment, approximately three hours later. It will probably carry me through the day.

I wrote until I *knew* that it was enough. I had reached the point where thought was no longer flowing, and I was going to have to think about what should come next. I decided that it was time to stop.

From her experience in this journal entry, Donna learned that writing felt like a natural outlet for the energy she had built up. Once she had used writing to focus her awareness, she found that the sense of focus carried over into the rest of her day. As she continued to find time to write, she learned to expect writing to help her get through her days.

Maybe you've developed a belief that good writers are geniuses. Or famous writers are rich and have their mornings free. Or successful writers have to have their own computer and printer. Or passionate writers have to have lived an unhappy life. Or brilliant writers have to have studied philosophy with the great thinkers. Or productive writers have jobs that make them write all the time. Or happy writers have permission from their spouses to write instead of making dinner or taking out the garbage.

Each of those beliefs may have a kernel of truth in it, but the larger truth is simpler: writers are people who value writing enough to spend time doing it.

Any success or satisfaction you may enjoy from writing will follow from that truth. If you "don't have time to write," we hope to help you relearn what you always knew, that the experience of writing, like the experience of living, is worthwhile for its own sake.

EXPERIENCE

Slow down and spend some time writing.

Choose a time of the day when you would ordinarily have a hundred things to do and feel rushed and stressed—perhaps early in the morning as you are trying to get ready for school, or perhaps between classes. Stop for a few moments and write about what's on your mind.

WANTING TO WRITE

What does it feel like to want to write?

Do you have to be told by a teacher or textbook to write? Do you want to get an A, impress your friends, or just pass a course? Do you want to win the heart of your true love? Do you want to be remembered forever like Shakespeare? Do you want to set down profound thoughts to be admired by the intellectuals of the world?

There are many feelings you can interpret as a desire to write. You have to learn how to interpret the feelings because they aren't always as obvious as a burning ambition to win the Nobel Prize for literature.

It may be simply that a certain thought keeps running round in your head. Writing about what was on your mind when you woke up this morning is a good way to get it off your mind so that you can think about something else. You may want to write because you have just read a book or article that made you mad or curious. You may have just heard a lecture that excites you or fascinates you.

You may be traveling, experiencing so many new sights, sounds, and smells that you need to write in your diary at the end of the day to calm yourself down. Writing about your reactions is like chewing your food. It puts the experience in a form that you can use.

You may experience the desire to write as a sort of physical itch for the sensation of fingers on a keyboard or a pencil on paper, or you may want to see elegant lines flowing from a calligraphy pen. As your fingers hit the keys, you may experience a satisfaction like hitting a nail and watching it disappear into a board.

You may feel a dreamy desire to go off by yourself and think your thoughts, begin writing in your journal, and find yourself asleep in a few moments. You may wake up in the morning or in the middle of the night feeling jittery with your mind racing. Writing when you have insomnia won't necessarily help you get to sleep—it might wake you up even more. But at least you will be doing something other than thinking about the monsters in your closet.

You may have met someone so interesting last night and had such a wonderful time that you feel the need to sort your thoughts or feelings out in order to make them clear to you before you decide whether you've really found the love of your life.

You may be bored with the class going on around you and suddenly discover that it's far more interesting when you begin to write responses to what is being said. You may be experiencing emotional pain or pleasure— joy or sorrow or anger or fear—and use writing to try to capture the feeling because it has meaning for you.

You may feel distant from someone you want to be closer to, or close to someone you want to distance yourself from, so that it seems necessary to write a letter. You may be about to go to the dentist, a job interview, a speech you have to give, or a test you have to take, so that you need to tap off some of your anxiety in order to be able to concentrate on dealing with the situation.

As a student, you probably do most of your writing at the behest of your teachers, so it may seem that you write mostly for evaluation. As you gain more experience with writing, you will begin to develop a greater sense of your own reasons for writing, and you'll realize that you rarely write just for school or just for a grade. To illustrate this point, we'll show you the writing of a couple of more experienced student writers.

Pat, the writer whose work you are about to read, is an older student who is undergoing some changes in his attitudes about writing. As he warms up to the idea of writing, he is learning to find his own desire to write in assignments for school.

FROM THE JOURNAL OF Patrick Mulvihill

The very last thing I wrote was for the previous exercise, "Awareness and Composing." I began it because it was an assignment. It didn't feel like an assignment—I somehow felt purged of a loneliness I didn't know I felt until I started to write. Very early on, it seemed like an entry into my personal journal (not the one for this class), more than it did an assignment.

Before that, the last thing I wrote was an essay on the Buddha's argument for non-self for a philosophy class. I kind of enjoyed that assignment. The structure of the essay was already apparent—it simply followed the structure of the Buddha's argument. I thought about it off and on for a few days before I started to write it. I felt as though I knew the material and would be able to write the essay in a short time. Altogether, it took only about seven hours to write four pages, seven hours of sitting at the computer. I kept floating back and forth between the essay and a letter to a friend so I can't say how much time the essay actually took.

The experience was somewhat typical of my reason for writing. The bulk of my work has been for assignments but that is changing. I find myself writing more and more for myself. This class has a lot to do with that—I must be easily inspired—a basic Art Appreciation class inspired me to buy some oils and canvases. I'm no visual artist but I've very much enjoyed blending paints and making a mess. Like spontaneous writing, spontaneous painting gets me in touch with my emotions. The difference is, with writing I'm using my mind, and with painting I use my feelings.

To get back to the essay: I felt pretty free while I was writing it, totally involved in it, as though my life were ordered and meaningful. I was doing what I felt like I should be doing.

You may never have to write an argument on "the Buddha's argument for non-self," but you probably have your own difficult, abstract, and obscure topics. When you find your own reasons for writing, you will find, like Pat, that you feel you are doing what you should be doing.

Another older student, Donna, has returned to school and is finding that the writing she used to do strictly for the professor now seems to have more intrinsic interest. Donna writes carefully and conservatively, but you can discern the pleasure her changed attitudes have brought to her work.

FROM THE JOURNAL OF Donna Svob

The last major writing project I had to do was associated with one of the courses I took over this past summer. It was a literature course—"American Literature to 1865." It had been a good many years since I had done any critical literary analysis, and even that had been early in my studies so it was somewhat immature.

My initial reaction to writing about the writings of others was terror. These writers were the "greats"—how could my interpretations possibly be of any note? But I soon got into it, got over my fear, and loved every (almost) minute of it.

The writing was prescribed; my professor expected certain questions to be explored. The nature of the exploration, though, was personal. We were not expected to all have the same opinion of the meaning—we were just expected to have an educated opinion. I thoroughly enjoyed it!

I found the format most conducive to writing. I was given a structure to work within—for "Young Goodman Brown" we were to discuss the meaning of Brown's encounters with the characters from his life during his journey to the woods. There were so many directions from which to attack this question! I found that the words flowed—sometimes with agony and sometimes with a feeling that my fingers could not type fast enough to keep up with my thinking! It was exhilarating!

To each of these assignments I was able to bring to my writing any academic knowledge that I possessed, my personal experiences, and often, my personal belief system.

Both these writers have begun to experience considerable personal satisfaction in their writing. As they reflect on that satisfaction, they become more alert to its influences on their writing, and they become accustomed to writing because they want to. The satisfaction was always there, waiting for them to notice it. Like them, you have your own reasons for writing.

Once you find them, you'll experience satisfaction in the process of writing, you'll write more and more willingly, and, eventually, you'll write more skillfully.

EXPERIENCE

Recall something you've written, perhaps the most recent piece of writing you've completed. Reflect on your reasons for writing.
- What caused you to begin to write?
- Was that experience typical of your reasons for writing?
- Can you describe what it felt like to write?

"RULES" FOR WRITING

You probably learned at some point that there were rules for how to write papers.

Maybe someone told you to outline before you started. Maybe you learned to brainstorm, to vary sentence and paragraph length, to be careful about your punctuation and spelling, to think of a snappy opening, or to write your thesis statement at the end of the first paragraph. Perhaps you were rewarded for being funny, for using long sentences and big words to sound formal, or for ending in some grand and inspiring manner.

Any such bits of writing advice can become internal rules that you feel compelled to follow each time you write.

You can also give yourself rules. Do you absolutely have to clean your room before you write? Do you feel you have to write with a pencil, compose at the typewriter, write between eight and ten in the morning, or get somebody's opinion about your writing right away? Do you feel that you have to go back and correct spelling errors even though you're just working with a rough draft? Do you always wait till the last minute and then write a whole paper in one sitting? Do you always try to do something strikingly original?

You probably have good reasons for the rules you have. You learned them from someone you trusted, or you developed them as a consequence of experience. Wherever your rules came from, you believe that that they help you to write. If you didn't, you wouldn't follow them. If a rule makes you more comfortable with writing, it needs no other justification.

Rules That Get in the Way

Personal preferences for writing, such as "Always begin with an outline," are intended to help a writer to work efficiently. If outlining is one of your rules, you probably have found that it helps you to be more satisfied with your writing.

But preferences get in the way when they become inflexible rules. Believing that you must begin with an outline, you may experience frustration if you're really ready to write and don't need the outline, or if the outline keeps you from writing about what interests you.

Of course the same goes for any rule. If your rule is that you have to write with a pencil on a yellow legal pad, you're stuck unless you have a pencil and a legal pad. If you have to write in your room in the morning, you can't write until it's morning and you're in your room. All these rules can keep you from starting, or finishing, a project.

Staying Flexible

Research (Rose, 1980) suggests that writing requires flexibility at least as much as it requires discipline and rules. You should distrust any rule that keeps you from writing, especially if the rule sets up restrictive conditions for the act of writing. "I can't write without an outline, and I have to get to the library to do the research before I can write my outline." "I have to write in my room but I can't write when my roommate is there, and she's never gone." "I have to be in the right mood."

If you aren't writing or aren't getting satisfaction from your writing because your outline won't work, try writing without your outline. You will find that the world doesn't end. Ask your roommate for an hour alone if you need one, or leave. Tell yourself that you're going to write no matter what your mood is.

If breaking your rule allows you to continue to write, and if you feel good about what you are doing, then the rule was probably the major problem. Breaking the rule this time was right.

Inflexibility

If, on the other hand, you feel you absolutely can't write until conditions are perfect, you should ask yourself, "Why am I setting up conditions guaranteed to make it harder for me to write?" If your rule won't let you write, and you won't let go of your rule, *you have to suspect that you don't really want to write.*

When the authors of this book can't get started on a project, we often find that we are getting some benefits from setting up inflexible conditions. We have rules about straightening the office or the study before we write; if we find ourselves washing the windows and making two or three trips to the library as well, we try to figure out why we are avoiding the project.

We don't mean to suggest that people never have good, writing-related reasons for hesitating. Often the feeling that you should stop and think before you go on can keep you out of trouble.

We like to compare getting stalled on a writing project with getting stranded while traveling. The plane arrived late, and we missed our connection. The weather turned ugly, and the police closed the road. The route that looked so clear and simple suddenly grew dark and complicated, and the signs said slow down or stop. We have a strange reaction to that situation. We've bought our tickets, and we've found a dog-sitter. So we're going whether it's smart to continue or not. The same sometimes happens to us when we are writing. The more stuck we feel, the more we want to forge ahead. Sometimes we have discovered that we need to pay attention to the stuck feeling.

We sometimes feel physical symptoms—tension or a knot in the stomach. We have learned that when this happens to us, some part of our minds is trying to get our attention.

We continue to write, but the pace slows down and we're less certain of what should come next. We stop then and try to figure out what the message means. Often it's that we have begun over-explaining some small point, or we need to stop and do some research in the library.

A more serious signal is a feeling of boredom. We hate being bored, so we know that if we are bored with a writing project, we had better find out why before we drop the whole thing. Sometimes the solution is as simple as skipping to another part of the paper, but sometimes boredom may mean that the topic or the approach really isn't the right one for us.

At other times we feel full of too much energy to sit still and write. We switch gears for a while. If we distract our conscious attention by writing a letter to a friend or going for a run, we often find out that we suddenly see the writing problem more clearly.

The point is to try to stay open to internal signals about writing. You don't want to become so anxious about writing that you aren't producing anything, but neither do you want to lose touch with your best instincts as a writer. If you can bring the reason for hesitation to conscious awareness, you can ask advice from your teacher or from someone in your class who shares your personality type and composing style.

EXPERIENCE

1. List the rules you have for writing.

    You may have rules about how to begin to write, how to produce a rough draft, how to revise, or how to proofread. You may have rules about where and when to write, how you should be dressed, how to type, how to do library research, how long you work at a sitting, who gets to read your papers, or what subjects you can and can't write about. Put down anything and everything that occurs to you, no matter how trivial or silly it may seem. If you need to have a bowl of jellybeans and wear a baseball cap backwards while you write, say so.

2. Look through your list of rules to find the four most important ones.
   - Where did you get those rules?
   - Explain why your rules are important.
   - Do they speed up your writing or slow it down?
   - Do they make writing more pleasant or less pleasant?
3. Can you remember a time when you were unable to write something you wanted or needed to write? Describe the circumstances.
   - How did you feel?
   - What do you think made it difficult to write?
   - Were you finally able to do your writing?
   - If you never got unstuck, what were the consequences?
   - What did you learn from the experience?
4. Think of a time when it looked as if you were going to get stuck, physically or psychologically, in some situation (not necessarily involving writing).
   - How did you react to the prospect of getting stuck?
   - Did you stop or did you forge ahead?
   - How did it turn out?
5. Write a rule for getting unstuck.
   - Reread your responses to 3. and 4.
   - Describe factors or strategies which helped you to get unstuck in the two situations.
   - Use factors or strategies you discover to write a new rule such as "I have to feel I have someone else's support and approval to go ahead" or "I should remember that writing is like driving on the interstate with the radio turned up: If I hit heavy traffic, I should slow down and turn off the distractions that prevent me from concentrating."

GOOD WRITING

To gain people's attention, the authors sometimes compare writing to play: if it isn't fun, you aren't doing it right. As part of our campaign to get you committed to writing, we'd like to focus your attention on the little satisfactions of writing.

What does good writing feel like? Let's distinguish **good writing** from **writing well.** You write well when what you write is useful to someone else, a reader. You usually have to revise to make your writing satisfying for readers. Other people get to decide whether you have written well because they know whether your written product suits their purposes. You should always consider readers' opinions about your writing, and, if you can, you should try to use readers' opinions to help you to get more out of your writing.

Writing and Play

But let's leave readers out of this for the moment and explore how writers experience writing itself. In this context, **good writing** is writing that feels good to the writer. Writing that you enjoy won't always please readers. Indeed, sometimes people will look at something you enjoyed writing and make comments which persuade you that you haven't communicated your meaning very well. It's important that you know that writing for yourself may differ from writing for others. Like good play, though, sometimes what amuses you may please others, too, as does good football or fine cross-country horse racing. Writing for pleasure, then, has two possible outcomes. You may get enjoyment and satisfaction that others never share, or you may find that what you have enjoyed writing is just what your classmates or a wider audience also enjoy. From your standpoint as a writer, writing is good when you get satisfaction from your work.

Scott's "game" is motorcycling. When he began writing about riding his motorcycle he discovered, as people often do, that his interest carried him along. He wrote a long entry which could easily develop into an entertaining essay.

FROM THE JOURNAL OF S. Scott McCullough

The game (actually, it's more of a recreational activity) that instantly came to mind is motorcycling. Even as a very young child, I was fascinated by motorcycles and craved the experience of riding one. That craving became acute at the age of eight, when my father took me to see *Easy Rider*. At about the same time, I began to notice the people riding motorcycles as much as the bikes themselves. Suddenly, I realized that motorcycling was not merely a physical activity, but that it was also highly social, bringing together people with highly divergent interests and backgrounds who shared the love of riding. Bikers always seemed to enjoy life more fully and expansively than any people I had ever met before. I knew that someday I wanted to be one of them, forever travelling to wonderful and mysterious destinations.

Many people are cowed into believing that such a joyous life is somehow evil, or illegal, or a waste of time. What a sad and beleaguered attitude! I believe that life is to be lived as fully and completely as possible without harming others. Those who fear death the most often seem to live the least, while those who love life the most are often most willing to risk it. Bikers are perceived to be so threatening largely because they challenge risks instead of fleeing them, and because they often refuse to succumb to social pressures to conform. Most people spit out "biker" like a shameful label, reserved only for the lowest and most pitiful dregs of society. I have known many bikers, have lived among them, loved them, have ridden and partied and laughed and cried with them, and declare with pride (rather than admit with shame) that *I am one of them!* I could use the innocuous title of "motorcyclist" instead, but it seems to imply a sense of reservation and equivocation that I do not mean to convey.

Actually the term *passion* seems more appropriate than *interest* to describe Scott's enthusiasm about motorbikes. If you have a passionate interest to write about, by all means write about it. You may find, as Scott did, that writing about something you love feels like opening a door into a spacious new room, an area of your experience in which you can stretch out comfortably as a writer.

Think of something you like to do, something you think of as play. Be loose in your definition of *play*. Some people enjoy working and have to remind themselves and others that they are playing. Play can be drawing, dancing, playing an instrument, riding a horse, solving a complex chess problem, making pizza, walking to school in the morning, going to rock concerts, or staying up late to talk with friends.

Notice that when you're playing, you get pleasure of different kinds all the way from the beginning to the end of your game. You're glad you thought of the game, you don't mind building your day around what you want to do, it's fun to get the materials together, you're eager to get started, you lose track of time as you're playing, and no one has to urge you to continue or tell you to stop when you've had enough. You usually think pleasurably back over the game, but even if you didn't play very well, you're already planning when you can play again.

That's what good writing feels like. You've probably experienced good writing before. If you think back over your history as a writer, defining writing loosely to include work you have done both in and out of school, you'll probably recall some piece of writing that you enjoyed more than usual. If you think about that piece of writing, you'll notice that the trick is to treat writing like a game. You have to think of writing as something you do for yourself, not for someone else. You have to start when you want to and stop when you're tired. You have to write about what interests you. You have to be willing to take some chances and accept failures as well as successes.

EXPERIENCE

1. Tell the story of how you got involved in one of your favorite games.
   - Did you discover it yourself, or did someone push you to get involved?
   - What was it like to learn the game?

- How long did it take you to get good at it?
- What parts of the game give you the most satisfaction?
- Have you developed relationships with friends who are involved in your game?
- What are the most important benefits you get from your game?

2. Tell the story of how you got involved in your favorite writing project.
   - Did you discover it yourself, or did someone push you to get involved?
   - What was it like to work on the project?
   - How long did it take you to finish it?
   - What parts of the project gave you the most satisfaction?
   - Did you develop relationships with anyone as a result of working on your project?
   - What were the most important benefits you got from your project?
   - Can you see any game-like qualities in your writing process?

GOOD WRITING AND FLOW

Flow is an experience you have when you encounter a problem that perfectly matches your skills (Csikszentmihalyi, 1990). When you play a game with just the right opponent—someone whose skills challenge your skills without overwhelming them—you may play a match in which you lose the sense of where you are, who is watching you, or how long you've been playing. That sense of total absorption in an activity is flow.

Flow in writing may feel like fascinated reading. Think of the last time you were really drawn into something you read. Perhaps it was a "trashy" novel. It could have been your favorite magazine. It might have been a book about a person you admire or about one of your special interests. It might even have been what people consider "great literature."

Remember how you were drawn into another world when you read. You became absorbed in your activity, forgot where you were and how long you'd been there, and didn't notice fatigue or hunger. Like Alice in Wonderland, you had fallen down a rabbit hole into another world with a series of fascinating problems you had to solve before you could return to reality.

For some people, good writing is like that. You feel focused, as if you are writing from some stable point within you or toward some clear goal outside of you. You feel that you have found a channel for your thoughts and feelings, as if you had tuned a radio past several stations that weren't coming in well and found a local station with a clear, strong signal.

Good writing may be akin to tidying your desk. When you are tidying a familiar space, you can see exactly where everything goes, you can usually see the most efficient way of putting everything in that space, and you know exactly when you are finished. You can even stop in the middle and come back to the activity because you know where things go. Familiar subjects are especially likely to give you this experience of good writing.

Good writing may be just like good talking. You may visualize a person you know well to whom you want to say something. You may simply begin talking on paper, imagining the person's reactions and working those into what you are writing, hearing the person's voice answering your own, imagining the gestures you would use, feeling your own breath as you talk, and tasting your mouth. Good talk usually happens between two people who know each other well and who are comfortable with their surroundings. This experience of writing often occurs when you write to a close friend or an intimate enemy. You know how the person thinks, so you are able to communicate easily, swiftly, candidly, and passionately.

Good writing may be a plunge into the mysterious, like a dream. In this state, writers begin writing with only a vague inkling that they understand the answer to a question, and they write until the answer is complete, often using a personal code language that would be difficult for another to understand. They surrender to the experience and become lost in their own thoughts and feelings, losing track of time and forgetting to eat or sleep.

This sort of writing is likely to occur when you're solving a problem about a favorite subject. You grow absorbed in the subject matter and write more and more quickly as your curiosity becomes aroused, like someone searching through a drawer for a particular pair of socks. You know they're in there. Pretty soon socks are flying in all directions, and when you find them you often discover that you've made a mess. When you write to discover something personally important, you should expect the writing to interest other people about as much as the inside of your sock drawer. Usually this sort of writing requires considerable revision before another reader can appreciate what you've discovered.

Some people may experience good writing in a physical way, as a kind of heart flutter, as a sense that the hairs are standing up on the back of the neck, or as some other form of excitement that tells them they are on the right track. Experienced writers know that when they feel that excitement they should write steadily, for their minds and bodies are in synch, and that when the feeling goes away, they should stop writing and think or reread for a while to try to get the feeling back again.

Good writing may be a kind of euphoria in which the words and ideas sort themselves out effortlessly into sentences and paragraphs, like blood flowing through the veins. This smooth rhythm of thought develops a sort of momentum that carries the writer from paragraph to paragraph and page to page. The writer may choose to continue writing even though he or she begins to depart from the point. Rather than allowing the productive rhythm to falter, an experienced writer may simply continue working with the flow of language, knowing that revision can remove the parts that are of uneven quality. If you find this kind of rhythm, you may discover that you've written much more than usual with little sense of effort.

Most people have an experience like flow during parts of the writing process. Some of us lose track of time and place when we are dreaming about getting started or organizing ourselves and our materials. Others fall out of everyday reality when they draft or revise a paper. Some people will pause for hours to polish a manuscript to a high sheen. A few writers love it all.

FROM THE JOURNAL OF Martha Buchanan

My fingers can't move fast enough. I hear nothing. I see nothing. The entire universe becomes triangular. At the crest is my mind. The base is composed of my fingers and the word processor. All the trappings of my life fall away. I am no longer concerned with mere mortal needs. I am transformed. I am absorbed, consumed. I am a goddess.

I wrote a piece four years ago that I love. I've worked on it on and off and am beginning to suspect that it will never really be at a point that will feel finished. It began as a research paper for my introductory English class. I read more and more and became addicted to my topic. I was taking only one class that semester. I spent all my spare time for several weeks before I began writing reading and researching, jotting down phrases and possibilities.

When I had to stop researching and begin writing, I was obsessed. I wrote from the time I had my first cup of coffee to the time I knew I had to give it up and go to sleep. I was excited. I believed I saw clearly where others had seen only dimly. When I was finished with my first draft it was four times the maximum page numbers.

I look back at that experience as one of my most satisfying because it was analytical, yet based upon my uniqueness as an individual. I never knew exactly what the professor thought of the piece. I didn't want to know. I handed it in as my final paper and didn't pick it up after the break. It was the first piece of writing that I did that gave me intense satisfaction. It was the experience that addicted me to writing.

Flow, as I experienced it, was most like your last description. It was euphoric and effortless. Until that point, I had no idea that writing could be an experience that pleasurable.

This first experience felt very much like the first time I experienced good sex. It was a bit shocking. (You mean that wasn't really all there is?)

It was a bit frightening. (What is happening here; is it safe?) It left me wanting more.

It certainly doesn't complicate life as much as sex does. This experience makes me realize that I can write to feel good. It is a high, euphoric feeling to experience flow, to know that it's there, that it's right, that it's working.

I have thought of personal writing as satisfying, a way of calming down, of centering, of knowing what is in me, what is me. But I've never thought of "writing" as a tool for living more joyfully, or of joyfulness as a tool for writing.

Unfortunately, flow is a state that I usually have to work hard for. It's forcing the words into sentences and the sentences into paragraphs until something magical transforms us, merges us into one being.

Writing *is* work. But it's also a safe and productive way to experience euphoria. When you become engaged with the process of writing, rather than fixated on achieving the product, you understand why people write through hardship and discouragement. Like a dancer who becomes obsessed with a rhythm, the person who experiences flow while writing will go over the same passage again and again. Tireless repetition of the activity will eventually improve the person's skill, and the person will continue to complicate the activity to make it more interesting. In time, the person acquires the ability to perform highly complex activities with effortless grace. Writers who have learned to create flow for themselves keep returning again and again to a piece of writing to renew their sense of absorption in the process. They expend exorbitant quantities of time and effort on their work, and it shows. As writing session follows writing session, they accumulate experience and insight, and they write more efficiently, more comfortably, and more skillfully.

EXPERIENCE

What parts of the experience of writing are most absorbing to you?

Turn to the Table of Contents of this book to remind yourself of the many elements of the experience of writing. Choose those that you find the most interesting and explain why you like them.

MAKING WRITING FIRST

Look back at your responses to all the experiences so far. The point of those experiences was to help you wake up to your own interests and mental processes so that you could find satisfaction in writing.

We would like you to take another step into the inner world of writing. This one has to do with the hours of the day when you feel most alert, most wide-awake, most aware—when you have the best energy of your day. Most people use their best hours for the work or play they consider most important. That may be attending class, reading books, talking to people at work, exercising, seeing family, or any of a number of other things.

Writing during Your Best Hours

A halo effect lingers over what you do during your most energetic hours. You associate the energetic feeling with the favored activity, and you get more and more connected to the activity because you feel energetic while doing it.

Your wide-awake times come to be reserved for that activity. You set up your day so that you can do what you want during your wide-awake time. You're annoyed when something interferes. You probably notice that on weekends and vacations the wide-awake feeling occurs at approximately the same time of the day, and it enhances whatever recreation you're enjoying.

Writing is a very complex form of human behavior. It taxes your intellectual, emotional, and even physical resources. So you need to have the maximum amount of energy available. If you'd like to experience flow in writing, choosing the best energy of your day may help you.

People sometimes experience unexpected emotions in this sort of writing. Emotional content is an important part of the writing experience, so you should try to analyze your responses. One way to look at emotions is think of them as variations on four basic themes—joy, sorrow, anger, and fear. Each of the themes has positive and negative versions. You can feel a joy that is pure delight when you win a race, or a joy that is painful when you remember someone you loved and left behind. Sorrow can feel sweet as you leave behind one part of your life and look forward to another, or sorrow can be merely despair when you have failed at something you really wanted to do. Anger may feel right because you are fighting an injustice or it may wound you over and over as you remember an injury someone has done you. Fear may be simply caution about how you handle a fragile vase or panic that immobilizes you in a terrifying dream.

In the journal entry which follows, Pat uses his best time of the day and finds himself writing about his interest in music and its connection with the important people in his life. He produces a long journal entry, a signal he has found a subject he should probably pursue in a writing project. As you read Pat's entry, consider how you would advise him to proceed. What parts of this entry interest you most? Can you imagine a writing project on this subject?

FROM THE JOURNAL OF Pat Mulvihill

It's nine A.M. on a Friday morning. I'm not always wide awake at this time but today I feel fairly energetic. This will be a good time to try this experience.

I walk into the computer room at my sister's place and see my guitar, my '59 Gibson, on its stand and I know that's what I'm going to start to write about.

Ever since I can remember I've wanted to play a guitar. Like so many other 12 year old boys, I wanted to be a rock star. My father wouldn't let me have a guitar—I had the money to buy one myself—I'd been caddying since I was ten and had money in a bank. One day, I got up the courage to defy him, went to the bank to withdraw some money, but they called my father at work. I didn't realize they would do that. I got yelled at but I guess he realized I wanted a guitar awfully bad to take a chance like that. He finally relented, on the condition I take lessons. I had to pay for the lessons myself. I only took them for about six months. By that time I realized I didn't have much talent but I also learned that to play rock and roll or folk music, I didn't need much talent. I also realized if I wrote my own songs no one could compare me to anyone. So that's what I did.

I met other kids who played guitar and my life changed. The common interest brought me into circles I would not have otherwise travelled. I played in what they use to call a "garage band." We were terrible but we had a lot of fun, thinking we would all be rich and famous one day and girls would chase us down the street. Most of those people quit playing when they realized the fame and fortune thing wasn't going to happen for them. For me though, the guitar became a voice. When I get emotional, whether it's from joy or sadness, I like to pick up my guitar and just bang on it. When you were talking about the sensory feeling you get with the computer keyboard in class one day, I thought about the guitar—sometimes I just have to feel it. I'm starting to feel that way about the computer keyboard—I think I'm entering into a new period of life, full of frustration and fulfillment—I find myself playing the guitar less and less and typing more and growing younger all the time.

I remember having an awful lot of trouble making a G Major chord. It's an easy enough chord to make but my fingers just couldn't do it. I tried and tried and finally it happened. I was really proud and really happy. I can't imagine life without a guitar now.

I have a couple circles of friends and music is at the center of both of them. The first circle has been together since grammar and junior high school—I think that's really special. When we get together, we sing

some of the songs we were raised on and just generally make fools of
ourselves in front of the kids—but those kids—they're like cousins.
Playing those old, old songs with those lifelong friends is better than
performing for a bunch of strangers. For me those old friends are family
and music is the blood that makes them so.

The second circle of friends I have is newer. Music was at the center
of this circle right from the start. Probably the main difference between
circles is this: the first group of friends only gets together a couple times
a year and we are all financially and socially different—from a drifter to
a high school principal. We are siblings without the blood and very few
judgments are made from one about another. We accept each other
totally and never never let things we do get in the way of our feelings for
each other. Success and failure are both the same in this group. We are
family. The second group of friends I have formed out of common
interests and when a person changes his or her interests, gets married or
something, the group changes. We care about each other but not like
family. Music is the glue that holds us together.

Music . . .

My father and I had some of our best arguments around the guitar.
When I was a teenager we disagreed about everything and it always
came back to the kind of music I listened to. He hated Bob Dylan,
blamed him for my rebellion. We didn't talk for several years after I
turned 18 and left home. When I was in a re-hab program, I would play
my guitar and sing for the other patients sometimes. Once when my dad
came to visit me, I was in the middle of a song—I was embarrassed—he
hadn't heard me sing or play since I was in high school. He looked kind
of proud while he was listening. I was singing a song I'd written and he
laughed at all the right places and our relationship changed after that.

He died of cancer a few years later. He was lucky in that he got to
die at home, in his own bed. There was no Hospice in the area at that
time but because my mother had been a nurse and because she'd
worked for the state and accumulated a lot of sick time, she was able to
take care of him. His dying brought us all closer together—my brother,
sister, mother and me. I would stop over to my folks' every day after
work and bring my guitar with me. I would play some songs for him—he
loved to hear Steve Goodman's "City of New Orleans"—he was a
railroad man and had ridden on that train several times. It wasn't the
guitar that had driven us out of each other's life all those years before—it
was stubborn pride on both accounts — but it was the guitar that
brought us back soon together in time to share his death. And although I
miss him, wish I could talk about baseball and football with him — he
missed the Bears super bowl season, missed watching Ryne Sandberg
and Michael Jordan — he only got to sling his dry sarcasm at Reagan for

two years and he missed the Washington administration and all the crap that followed it—he would have kept me laughing during those years— yes, although I wish he were still alive, I'm glad to have shared his death with him. I can't imagine a better source of inspiration than a dying man who meets his end with dignity, grace, and laughter. He never never lost his sense of humor and I think I needed to write this and I'm grateful for the experience.

Writing this piece was easy. Everything just seemed to flow together. Thinking about my dad is something I guess I try to avoid sometimes. We wasted so much time being angry with each other—it hurts to think about that. Here I am, a grown man, and I feel like crying—not only now but sometimes when I hear a joke that reminds me of my dad or see a great defensive play in baseball. Writing about him brought a whole bag of emotions to the surface—I can't really articulate what I'm feeling right now but I know it has been good for me. I think I hit the keys harder when I thought about the things he's missed—the sports and the politics. I feel like there's much more to write about in regards to my father but right now, I think I'd better quit. I feel like kicking at the cat—don't worry, he's much too fast for me and I always miss—and besides, I think he feels like he's doing me a favor by letting me at least try—he sure gets in the way enough.

If you do sit down to write during your most energetic time, you will probably discover that the time has flown by. You may think what a joy it was and resolve to try it again. More power to you.

Or you may say to yourself, "Aaargh. The morning's gone. All I've done is write." In that case, try to commit to spending just one or two more best-energy periods writing. If you spend a little more good time writing, you may find that you value writing enough to spend still more. You'll be surprised at how much satisfaction you get looking back over what you've written.

It may feel unnatural at first if you are used to going running, attending class, talking to friends, or listening to music during those hours. But try it. We think you'll find the experience interesting.

Be nice to yourself. Write in someplace comfortable and pleasant. The authors of this book write at home in a sunny office with a view of the garden, but we also sometimes like to write while traveling in a car or on a plane, sitting in a restaurant, or out on the quad. If you feel like it, go to the bookstore and buy an interesting pen or a new notebook.

Don't be compulsive about writing. Don't toil away until you're bored stiff. Just give yourself a chance to focus on some experience you've had, an idea that interests you, a plan you're working on, a feeling you're dealing with, a book you're reading, or anything else that occurs to you. Give yourself time to dream, think, stop, doodle, draw, and start again.

Once you know what it feels like to make writing first, try to spend some of your best time working on writing every week. You won't be sorry.

EXPERIENCE

For this experience, you are to notice and write down what goes on in your mind during the part of your day when you are most wide awake. If you are an early riser and a private person by nature, that may be before everyone else is up. If you are a gregarious night owl, it may be after everyone but the party animals has gone to bed. NOTE: we are not asking you to write during your "best time for writing." We are asking you to *identify your best time, and then use it for writing.* There's a difference.

1. Spend part of your most wide-awake time writing down what is going on in your mind.
   a. Instead of doing what you would ordinarily do, tonight, tomorrow morning, or tomorrow afternoon—whenever is your most wide-awake time—do some writing.
   b. Focus on an experience you've had, an idea that interests you, a plan you're working on, a feeling you're dealing with, a book you're reading, or anything else that occurs to you.
   c. Stop when you feel like stopping.
2. Now spend some time writing to get in touch with the experience you've just had.
   a. Describe the experience.
      • What did it feel like to put the words down?
      • Was your experience like one of those we've described in this chapter, or was it something else?
      • Can you compare the whole experience to some other experience?
   b. Now try to get hold of some of the details of the experience.
      • Concentrate on the sensations of your skin and muscles as you drew the letters or struck the keys. Then work out from the point of contact with skin or muscles. Where else were you conscious of sensation? In your head, your heart, your stomach, your abdomen?
      • Describe the sensation. Is it pleasurable or painful? Do you feel tension, release from tension?

      Record as much as seems interesting.
   c. Describe your emotions.
      Record as much as seems worthwhile.

After you've written as much as you feel like, just stop. You may find that you feel full of energy.

Give yourself a reward. Go have a cup of coffee with friends and show them what you just wrote, go shopping, listen to music, play a sport, watch a soap opera, read a book, call up everybody you know and have a party. If your imagination supplies something more interesting, do that. (You could even write some more if you felt like it.)

3. Discuss your response with members of your class. If you found that this experience led you into writing with unusual interest, ask your classmates what parts of your entry interested them most, what questions they have about your entry, and what kind of writing project they imagine this might turn into.

4. Use your responses to the experiences in Section 1 to compose a description of yourself as a writer.

   a. Write the description to give your teacher and classmates a picture of yourself as a writer.

   b. Review all of your journal entries to identify those which convey the most important information about you as a writer.

   c. If you feel that any of the experiences have changed your attitudes or processes, describe the changes.

   d. Organize them into a sequence that will present a clear, complete description of you.

Part II
Discovering
Writing Projects

Sometimes ideas for writing come easily. Examples are school assignments and the projects people in business are assigned by superiors. When you're given the subject, discovering ideas involves devising creative approaches to the project at hand.

Other times, however, you will want to search your own interests and experiences to discover your writing interests, rather like a good feature writer for a magazine. This process involves working by yourself and in groups to draw from the whole scope of your experiences. In working with personal interests, it helps to spend some time stepping back to look at who you are and where you come from. Thinking about your identity as a writer can help you to get beyond surface "interests" you've written about for school, to find ideas for projects which will reward you.

Discovery also means looking into the world of sources around you: library searches, interviews, surveys, and current magazines and newspapers. Part of this sort of discovery may be knowing what topics may make a good paper and how to focus those topics so that someone else will want to read what you have written.

Finally, discovery means finding writing partners, people to help you to deal with projects that can benefit from collaboration. Peers and teachers with whom you share the inspiration for a project may make the difference between an imagined project and a completed one.

Chapter 3
Discovering
Topics

INTROSPECTION

Many ideas for writing projects can be discovered through **introspection:** contemplative reflection on your experiences in various contexts of time and place. This book's authors often find what we want to write about when considering the following list (Fennick, 1991). Writers' own experiences suggest a number of different starting points for discovery of writing projects. This list is helpful to us and will help you find direction and purpose, as well as topics, for writing.

- Previous writing you have done
- Emotionally charged experiences
- Travel
- People—especially close friends and family
- Work experiences
- Childhood experiences remembered as an adult
- Dreams
- Journals

As you read on, you'll see that these starting points often lead a writer to follow an interest far afield in the quest for a writing project. But before you can follow an interest, you first have to find it. You can get a clear sense of where your interests lie by working with some of the starting points in our list. You can evaluate which possible projects will contribute most to your personal development, and you can follow an interest until it leads you to a piece of writing that will be valuable for a reader.

Previous Writing

One place we like to begin, which may seem off limits to some students, is the file of work we have done before. Updating or expanding the research we have done for a writing project often leads us to reconsider the whole project. Papers can be rewritten, or ideas may have been getting more focused in our minds since the last time we tackled the topic.

Students always seem surprised when we suggest that they rewrite a paper from high school or another class. Experienced writers do this all the time, as Janice Neuleib learned when she wrote her doctoral dissertation on C. S. Lewis, the famous writer of children's books. Lewis, like Shakespeare, didn't do much revising. He did, however, rework ideas and whole sections of papers into new stories and essays. Likewise, the famous novel *The Great Gatsby* has parts of several short stories that Fitzgerald wrote earlier in his career.

If you think about it, reworking an idea from your history as a writer makes sense. If you chose to write on a subject once, you can probably reawaken the interest. A student paper usually can use considerably more time and development than you have time for in one class. Also, you likely have grown in your understanding and perspectives—and in your use of information sources—since you wrote that high school history paper or that report on your science project.

The places where you stopped writing recently are often a good place to start as well. Perhaps the essay test you took in history this week asked a question you could study in greater depth. You could write a researched essay and study for the final history exam at the same time. Perhaps the paper you wrote for your literature class could use a fresh start. Gwen Silbergleid, a student, had written an analysis of a story called "The Astronomer's Wife" by Kay Boyle. The story hints at an affair between the astronomer's wife and a plumber. Gwen had argued that the story gave the reader clues that the affair had actually taken place. She revised the essay to strengthen the argument by finding more evidence in the text and in the critical analyses people had written about the story.

Emotionally Charged Experiences

Usually you can expect to find that emotional charge is connected with *change* in people. Sometimes the emotional charge is the cause, and sometimes it is the effect, of the change. For example, Martha Buchanan recalled a tragic change. She wrote about a friend whom she met nine years ago when the friend was newly divorced and quite well off, living in a new house and surrounded by her many friends and possessions. In the intervening years, the friend has developed multiple sclerosis, become homeless, lived at a mission, prostituted herself in exchange for a place for her and her son to live. In the end, the friend has found that the administrators of shelters for homeless people are unwilling to admit her because they fear the complications of men in her past (she has lived with a violent man who waves guns around) and her present (she has a thirteen-year-old son).

As Martha wrote the journal entry on this woman, the woman had no place to sleep that night.

If you choose to write about an experience with an emotional charge, positive or negative, you'll probably experience strong motivation to write. It turns out that writing is one of the most effective methods of discharging emotional energy. The pencil and paper operate like a lightning rod to ground the energy. So you can expect to feel both excitement and relief in writing about events like your first day at school, your parents' divorce, or winning a prize you wanted badly.

Clearly this sort of material provides a strong motivation to write and has the potential to produce powerful writing. But we need to give just a word of warning. This kind of writing about personal experience has a bad reputation for producing sentimental soap opera, trivialities about someone's summer vacation, or gossip about family issues that don't interest anyone because they happen to everyone. The reaction from a reader may be, "So what?"

If you begin such a project, you will have to be willing to take steps to avoid so-what treatments of emotional experiences. Specifically, you should plan to broaden your perspective by doing research into the issues you bring up. For example, the woman Martha discussed in her journal entry could serve as the central case in an essay illustrating the plight of homeless people. Martha could organize some general factual information around the homeless woman's case and write an article that might well have an effect on people's attitudes.

People who write about emotional events must beware of emotionalism, which is to say excessive emotion. Sentimentality and ranting are the two most common forms of emotionalism; fact and humor are the two best cures for those excesses. As you begin writing about an emotionally charged event, you should make an agreement with yourself to accumulate every available fact from every person you can ask regarding the incident. Facts help you to avoid oversimplifying. You should also ask yourself what is funny about the event. If you absolutely can't find or appreciate humorous perspectives on the event, you're likely to rant and rage in a tiresome way. You'll bore your audience, and they'll care less, not more, about your issue after reading your work.

Travel

A few years ago the authors of this book had an unusual experience—from our perspective at least. We went to evaluate a writing program at another university and somehow ended up observing a music class. The teacher explained to the class that a motif or theme in a musical composition is something like an individual on a trip. The theme goes out from the beginning of the piece, gets transformed, and comes back as the same set of notes, but new and different. He said that the same thing happens to people when they travel.

Like the emotionally charged experiences, these inspirations usually require some shaping. A diary of what we saw, heard, felt, tasted, and smelled won't do. An intellectual reaction to new places and customs will do quite nicely. Consider the example of Brendan Ratliff's trip to Ireland. After he was graduated from high school, Brendan decided to go to Ireland, the place from which his ancestors had emigrated to the United States. His experience of the friendliness of the Irish people led him to begin a project on friendships. He wondered why people would be so kind to a stranger like himself. Using himself and one of his friends as examples, he compared his friendships to the family relationships he had left behind when he went to Ireland and then to college. He later realized that he was interested in the process of becoming financially independent from his parents. He began a second project. He wrote a questionnaire for his friends about the problems of financing college and reported the results in a project that examined the process of separating from parents. Both these projects grew from his reconsideration of travel experiences.

People

Family are so close to us that they become part of the furniture of our minds. Mark Twain used his own parents, his childhood friends, and nearly everyone in Hannibal, Missouri, to create the characters in *Tom Sawyer* and *Huckleberry Finn*. The town drunk became Huck's pap; Twain's father was the judge.

Many writers use family members when they write fiction, but we all use our families in the narratives we write in nonfiction work as well. And our family and friends provide a great many of the ideas and attitudes that inform both our writing and our everyday thinking. In fact, it's hard to avoid illustrating a point with a child or parent. This book's authors find that whenever we set out to write about any kind of social or ethical issue, we use our friends and family to show how people either should or should not act, think, or believe. Most people believe stories and narratives long before they will believe an argument, so the narrative of a person's actions in a troublesome situation can often be the best way to emphasize a point in a paper.

A student writer named Corrine was interested in censorship, particularly of art works. She strongly opposed censorship in any form. She had already done some reading on the subject and was curious about why anyone would want to punish people for creative work. As she thought about her views, it occurred to her that her relationship with her mother might have some bearing on her interest in censorship. She had grown up feeling that she had to censor her own speech because of her mother's frequent bouts with depression. This insight led her to begin a project on a drug called Prozac, which physicians frequently prescribe to treat depression and which Corinne was convinced had adversely affected her mother.

Work Experiences

Everyone has had some kind of work experiences, though maybe not being a riverboat pilot or a carnival assistant. Even working in a fast food restaurant can provide rich resources for writing if you ask yourself the right questions about the experience. What are the rules for the job you did? What skills were required? What kinds of people did you work with? Will the job connect with your career plans, or did you take it just for the cash? Did you develop any convictions about working conditions?

As a student, the first author of this book had many part-time jobs, among them the following occupations: loading trucks at a warehouse, doing maintenance on a drilling rig in an oil field, selling books, guarding the exhibits at an art show, handling tax returns for the Internal Revenue Service, making cheese in a dairy, canning vegetables in a cannery, managing a restaurant, editing computer documents, and managing inventory teams for retail sales chains.

Those experiences and others like them gave him some opinions about the value of work experience. In some ways, the book you are reading grew out of his desire to experience different jobs to find out what satisfactions people derive from their work.

Your own work experiences may be interesting to those who will never have such jobs. A writer named George Plimpton has made a career of taking unusual and exotic jobs temporarily and then writing books about his experiences. *Paper Lion*, for example, was written about a brief period during which the Detroit Lions football team allowed him to practice and play with them.

Childhood Experiences Remembered as an Adult

Popular psychology emphasizes the need to understand your childhood experiences. Most writers draw on all the parts of their personalities to develop their ideas and to discover what they want to write about.

Here's an example. The second author of this book has a vivid memory from her childhood: The boy who lived across the country road disobeyed his stepfather by taking a horse from the barn unsupervised. The horse was badly hurt by a car. The stepfather beat the boy with a horsewhip in front of all the neighbors. Whenever she reads or hears of child abuse, that scene comes to her mind.

Childhood experiences will tell you something about where your strong interests lie. For example, some people think that Charles Dickens was a sentimental writer, especially when presenting the plight of children. He himself had a difficult childhood and spent much of his career writing about those childhood experiences. You may find a subject about which you have passionate concern by looking into your childhood.

FROM THE JOURNAL OF Jon Neuleib

The water makes a sound against the rocks that only lake water can make. Rivers and oceans sound very different from the quiet lapping that sounds against the rocks and shore. I can remember feeding the fish balled bits of white bread that we bought at the Red Fox food store across the lake. The fish would come out from under the dock and catch the balls before they would disappear in the water beneath the end of the dock. The tranquility of the scene is perfect with the sense that both the fish and I have that no one is going to try and eat anyone today. They move quickly through the water and only appear for a moment as I focus on the sinking bread. Being able to see the fish was the thrill of the game. Even when we would go fishing, we could not see the fish until it was pulled into the boat gasping and thrashing against us. Looking into the darkening water I was able to catch an image of the fish as they wanted be and as I was happy to let them be.

The connection of this to something that I might write about as an adult is a bit more difficult. For a different activity, I have been reading about a philosophical debate between ecofeminists and "deep ecologists." The deep ecologists claim that having sentimental feelings about the environment is problematical because people have too subjective a viewpoint about nature if they compare it to personal experiences. The ecofeminists tend to argue that the individual's connection to the natural world in the form of feelings about a particular stand of trees, or a stretch of beach, or even individual animals and plants is a basis for broader interest in environmental issues. Although the debate is actually more detailed than this, the basic idea that the ecofeminists are supporting might influence something that I would write as an adult. Even the fact that I feel that I can not really express my remembrances of the lake without dropping into cliches would be noticeable in this way. It is hard for me to describe the scene vividly because I do not have words that describe the scene in the manner that I remember it. Additionally, it is hard to see why anyone would find this little scene interesting and most of the rigors of adult writing demand that the subject be interesting. In this way I can see the ecofeminists' argument in practice: there is a connection to those types of scenes that I have to express in different ways if I want people to understand my opinions and read my writing.

If you return to Chapter 1 to reread Jon's journal entry on his earliest writing experience, you'll see how remembering and reconsidering an experience can lead you to an understanding of how your past and present fit together. A sense of your personal history helps you to understand how your ideas are rooted in your experience, and that understanding helps to motivate and guide you as you write.

Dreams

Most people think of dreams and daydreams as fantasy areas that provide entertainment and sometimes a bit of a fright. Professional writers use their fantasy lives to provide many of their ideas. A famous example is Mary Shelley's *Frankenstein.* Her account is that she dreamed the story and rose from bed to write the novel. Whether we believe that the story is an exact account of her dream, we can believe that the tale is the stuff of nightmare.

A student writer named Gennie dreamed repeatedly of a man whose face she could never see. The dream always started the same way, with the man picking her up at her house—a combination of her house and her boyfriend's house—and taking her to the movies, the park, or the beach, acting as her guide. Sometimes in dreams she found herself running from something scary or someone threatening, and the man appeared to save her. Once he drove up on a motorcycle and helped her get away from a monster. Once he helped her to run faster and climb over walls and around buildings to get away from something scary that she couldn't see. When she expressed an interest in interpreting the dream, her instructor suggested that she follow up with some research in the psychology of dreams, beginning with the work of the psychiatrist C. G. Jung, who developed a theory that certain strong dream images (*archetypes*) represent important truths about a person's psyche.

You may have a daydream or dream that keeps coming back. Try to imagine why the idea keeps interesting or pursuing you. Most good students have a recurring dream having to do with missing a test, being late for a class, or, worse, discovering at the end of term that they had registered for a whole class and never attended. A good paper could develop from a study for the reasons for this dream. Below we will talk about survey research. In a survey, you might ask a group of students about this kind of dream, whether they have had it, and how the dream relates to the rest of their school lives.

Journals

Experienced writers keep notes on topic ideas. Some even keep systematic notes on information and events that could lead to essays or stories. All the information sources we have listed above could easily become materials for a journal or notebook. You will be keeping a journal of all these ideas as you develop them, so you will be following the pattern of the pros as you work.

If you look back over the journal entries you made for Part I of this book, you might find that you have material you could use to compose an autobiography of yourself as a writer. Donna Svob, some of whose entries you read in Chapter 2, found when she re-examined her journal work that she could describe a process of change in her attitudes. Using her responses to the Experience assignments and her instructor's comments on those responses, she described how she had lost much of the anxiety with which she faced the writing process and how she had developed the confidence to experiment with new projects and new ways of working.

EXPERIENCE

Choose and write about one or more of the following starting points.
1. Find some papers you have written for other classes.

    Bring copies to class, and ask your teacher or peer group to look over the papers. Decide which one might be most promising for you to use as a starting point for a revised or new paper. The revision should involve a complete overhaul of the paper, not just correcting a few surface problems.

    Try one or more of the following suggestions.
    - Rewrite your paper with a new audience in mind.
    - Expand a minor point to make it the focus of the project.
    - Compose a much larger project of which your old paper becomes a part.
    - If the old paper didn't involve research, plan to develop it with research.
    - If you elect to use an old research paper, rewrite it as if you were explaining your results to someone with little or no background in the field.
2. Recall and describe an emotionally charged event that occurred in your life or the life of someone you know. Focus on the changes which caused or resulted from the event.

    In preparation, you may want to draw a map of the world before and after the change. Graphically depicting your viewpoint of places and people, their positions, and their importance may help you to see the way your perception of the world altered after the change.

If the change happened to someone else, you may try drawing and redrawing a map of the world as that person saw it, but you need to be aware that you probably will impose your own viewpoint on that person.

You may also consider the following questions.

- What forces caused the change?
- What good and bad consequences for the people involved followed the change?

3. Describe a trip you have taken.

- Why did you go?
- What did you learn?
- Would you go again?
- What kinds of people did you meet?
- How did you travel?
- Did you expand your world when you traveled?

Be careful to talk about how you were affected by the trip and whether you were changed by what you saw and did. Remember the point of this activity is to think about how you felt and reacted to the trip as well as about what you did. Connect these experiences with your interests now.

4. Recall an experience in your childhood that has left a vivid picture in your mind.

Describe the scene. Then connect that scene with an area you might write about now as an adult.

Childhood experiences may surface in your adult life as the college or major you choose, as the political party or religion you belong to or reject, as the courses you elect to take, as the books you like to read, as the friends you choose, as the person you decide to live with, or as the person you can't abide.

If you look, you can find the roots of everything important to you in a childhood experience.

5. Describe the most important lesson you have learned from work.

To help you to explain how you learned your lesson, try keeping notes on the people you work with, the ways the job could be improved, and the good and bad features of management. Take notes on the kinds of people you meet in connection with work and the connections of that work to the rest of your life.

6. Write about a member of your family or your circle of friends.

Sketch a picture of that person's face. Then describe the person so that people in your class can get to know some details of the person's looks and character. Then explain what influence you have on the person or the person on you.

- How did you get to know the person?
- What interests and attitudes do you have in common?
- Have you ever had a conflict? Over what?

Describe at least two people you remember well from your home town or from your school. Try to pick people who have had an impact on you in some way or who others might consider noticeable "characters."

7. Describe a dream or daydream that you have had repeatedly.

Try to imagine what kind of topic might develop from that dream idea. Ask your peer group to discuss the possibilities with you and discuss whether the dream is peculiar to you or whether, like the missed test dream, it's common to many people.

By the way, if a dream continues to disturb you, you should talk with a counselor or trusted friend about it.

CONVERSATION

One of the best ways to discover topics is through group interactions. Why work in groups? In your writing course, you'll find people with whom you share common reading or viewing interests. You'll also find people with whom you share life histories or ambitions. You belong to a community of minds with those people, and you can be very useful to each other as writers. Even one other person in a class who has interests similar to yours can help you to develop the writing ability latent in you. Recent writing research emphasizes the social nature of writing—that a basic function of writers is to teach and learn in collaboration with one another (Bruffee, 1984; Lunsford and Ede, 1990).

You'll start a conversation, listen to what the other person says, and respond by asking a question, arguing a point, or volunteering some other information. Once you know something about community members, you'll think it is "easier" to talk, listen, read, or write about your interests. Of course, speaking, listening, reading, and writing haven't really gotten any easier. Your contact with the people has simply given you motivation and guidance you lacked. Your communicative competence has been given a focus.

Getting to know members of your community helps you to understand the core interests, values, abilities, and motivations for communication among members of your group. Do you belong to a community of music lovers? Perhaps you'll find someone who shares your interest in blues music, someone who, like you, has been longing to write review articles for an insider's music magazine.

It also might be that the immediately available music lovers are interested only in eighteenth century classical music, or in head-banger rock-

and-roll. In order to communicate, you'll have to find some common ground: say, acoustic music with the classical music fan or electric music with the rock-and-roller.

Or suppose that you're a science fiction fan and you meet a science fiction writer in your class. You might interview the science fiction writer about where her story ideas come from or how she develops a character. You might write a study of one of her stories. You'd have gotten some inside information from which you might develop a study of the creative process. She'd have gotten an intellectual view of her work which might help her to focus on revision or plan the next story. You'd both have been taking advantage of each other's experience with the subject.

In short, the people in your immediate environment can help you find and develop your communicative ability. But first you have to tell them about yourself.

What happens when groups work together? Here are some examples.

A group of four women discussed child development; two of them were interested in their own childhoods, one was a mother interested in her child's development, and one was the daughter of a pastor who was interested in family from psychological and religious perspectives. Charlene, the mother, argued that children ought to have the right to pray in school. Quite involved in the topic, she sat down and dashed off a draft, which she showed to the rest of her group. The draft resembled the sort of article you might see in an inspirational religious magazine. Charlene found that since the members of her group did not share her strong convictions on the issue, her essay didn't inspire them. Their lack of response cooled her own interest in the project.

Still interested in the subject of children, Charlene became drawn to the idea of writing about teaching children to read. Her interest sparked interest in the other members of her group, and she found the project gaining momentum so that she was able to compose an interesting essay on a technique called "Whole Language Instruction," which is currently gaining favor among teachers of language.

Coincidentally, Cindy, the child of a Protestant minister, decided to write a paper on the problems of growing up as a PK (Preacher's Kid), and Sameera became interested in writing about the school prayer issue herself.

We can pick up some important tips about writing from the conversation of the four women. First, the fact that you have strong views on a subject does not necessarily assure you that others will share your views or your interest. Like Charlene, if you care about the people you are writing with and for, you'll adjust your focus to take their interests into account. Their interest will help to sustain you as you work through the project. Second, the subject and the approach to the subject that occur to you first may only be the way into your real writing project. Charlene's interest in children and prayer turned out to be an interest in teaching children. Third, what appears to be a person's lack of interest in a subject often turns out to be a lack of information. Until the group conversation occurred, it simply had not occurred to Cindy that she or anyone else in her environment might be interested in the problems religion poses for children. Likewise, Sameera's initial lack of interest in the subject turned into curiosity as she gained knowledge from her conversations with her peers.

This group became a writing support group that lasted throughout the course. Among the other topics that developed from their conversations were the effects of the Gulf War on the children and mates of those involved in the conflict, women's medical issues, and the psychological development of women in American culture. These topics grew from the personal interests discovered in the Introspection assignments the writers had previously worked through. Meanwhile, other support groups were taking on topics as diverse as those which follow.

- Why I own a quarter horse
- Don't go to see the latest James Bond movie
- Sports cars and the poverty-stricken student
- The academic benefits of exercise during exams
- Taking on an elderly friend
- Taking a course in England
- Don't diet: reform!

Someone has to take the first step in beginning this conversation. If you've done the work in Part I, you have already engaged in some group interaction and have begun to know the people in your class. At this point, you need to escalate your discussions to move them to a more serious level. The process of knowing other people and being known by them creates surges of energy and interest in communication, among many other benefits. The basic technique is remarkably simple. You just ask a question. Nothing interests most people more than a skillful questioner.

"What's your major?" is probably the favorite conversational opener for college students. That question may lead to "Oh really? Me too," and the conversation may grow from there. But other questions provoke more interest. "What's your favorite book?" or "What's your favorite movie?" often will get you involved in a discussion of life and art, the sort of conversation friends have over a cup of espresso at 3 A.M. A variation on this opener is "If your life were a novel, what kind of novel would it be?" If you ask someone, "What do you think is the most dangerous idea in society?" you can quickly become embroiled in a spirited political discussion. "If you ran the college, what would you change right now?" will start a discussion of the weaknesses (and strengths) of your immediate environment.

Asking questions implies a willingness on your part to answer questions too. People build interest and trust in each other by self-disclosure. This is not to say that you immediately confess your deepest secrets to a person you just met. You will decide to maintain a relationship or escalate it based on what makes you feel comfortable, but you absolutely need to know one another at some level to work together in a writing class.

EXPERIENCE

1. Use the following questions (or others that you think of) to start a conversation with members of your class.
   a. Your classmates can help you to generate ideas for papers. Move into a group and answer the following questions for each person in the group, trying to discover as you talk what experiences and interests you share with others in the group.
      • What do you read, watch on TV, choose to see at the movies, talk about with friends, think about when you're alone?
      • What's your favorite class?
      • What are you majoring in and why?
      • What's your political persuasion?
      • What do you think is the most dangerous idea in your society?
   b. Introduce yourself to people who share your interests and push your desks together. If the group grows beyond eight people, divide it.

      You'll get a sense of the people with whom you form a community of interest. Note that by the term **community** we don't mean "people who agree with you." We mean "people who share your interest." The authors value intellectual opponents as highly as supporters (though we sometimes wish they'd keep quiet).
2. Continue the conversation on paper.

   Remember that writing is conversation with other speakers and writers. A good approach to a draft of any writing project is to write to someone you know or to some text you've read.

   The authors of this book usually like to produce four or five hundred words before we stop to ask someone to admire what we've done. If you want to stop sooner or go on longer, feel free.
3. When you have a text, return to the group and trade papers.

   After you've read one another's work, start the discussion again, continuing for as long as you can. Keep notes on your discussion and use them as a starting point to continue working on the paper.

RESEARCH

Too often inexperienced writers think that **research** means going to the library with an outline of a research paper and a very specific agenda to dig through stacks of books or magazines to fill out lots of note cards. While everyone should understand the processes and appreciate the rewards of formal, traditional library research, everyone should also learn about the many other forms research can take. Of course, you can (and usually should) conduct research to develop ideas you discover through introspection or conversation. Like introspection and conversation, research can also uncover interesting projects.

To use research creatively, you need to broaden your definition to include some techniques you may not have tried before. Here are a few possibilities.

- Use personal reading for academic research
- Browse in the library
- Interview people who are experts in the field
- Do a survey of concerned participants
- Observe activities relating to your topic
- View videotapes, films, or other media presentations

We haven't, needless to say, begun to list all the possible kinds of research people conduct. We've restricted ourselves to kinds of research that you can attempt with relatively little technical training.

We won't pretend to try to teach you the research techniques that people spend their professional lives acquiring and honing. Professional research techniques are best learned in the context of professional training. People who teach courses in your major will train you to conduct research exactly as your potential profession requires.

But we can give you a taste of the research experience. The tips that follow will get you started in that direction. Where we leave off, you can pick up assistance from librarians and your teachers.

All forms of research require that you keep records of where you got your information. Some forms of research involving human subjects require getting permission from campus authorities. Ask your teacher if you need clearance to do the research you want to do.

How to Use Personal Reading for Academic Research

Don't think that researching a topic always means doggedly heading for the library and following a lock-step pattern. Most experienced writers keep a clipping file of feature articles and articles that interest them. These articles then turn into their own research and stories. In the papers of

Flannery O'Connor, a southern story writer, is a newspaper clipping of a story about a mass killer, named the Misfit. O'Connor adopted this character for her story, "A Good Man Is Hard to Find."

The authors recently read an article on hate suits in Illinois. We didn't know that people can sue other people for hating them if no action is taken on the hatred. We thought that the topic would make a good paper, given the pros and cons of free expression versus freedom from harassment.

If a subject keeps coming up, you probably should learn more about the topic. When you zip your eyes over the newspaper, notice where you usually stop. Do you always read a columnist like Mike Royko? Do you always read about a sports team or the stock market? If you read something regularly, then you have an area of interest that may be a good place to begin a paper.

Linda Hindahl spent a week observing her own reading of the newspaper and developed the following analysis.

FROM THE JOURNAL OF Linda Hindahl

Analysis of the *Peoria Journal-Star*

List of parts of the paper that I read:
- Front Page
- Editorial Page
- Comics
- Local and State News
- Ann Landers
- Personalities Section
- Accent Section
- Entertainment Section

Possible topics from these sections:
- *Front Page*
  –A research paper on an important news story
  –A piece of fiction based on a news story
- *Editorial Page*
  –A persuasive paper on an interesting issue
  –A research paper on an issue people are concerned with
- *Comics*
  –A piece of fiction based on a cartoonist
- *Local and State News*
  –A research paper on a local or state news story [e.g., nuclear power, education budgets]
  –A piece of fiction based on a news story

- *Ann Landers*
  - –A research paper on a human issue [e.g., divorce, manners]
  - –A piece of fiction based on a letter sent to Ann
- *Personalities Section*
  - –A paper based on an interesting personality [e.g., a local politician]
- Accent Section
  - –A humorous paper on a universal aspect of life [e.g., cooking]
- *Entertainment Section*
  - –A paper based on the way a film is made

Linda's clippings led her to think about the people and events in the small town where she lives, which in turn led to a project on small-town life. You can see a draft of her project in Chapter 9. The process of clipping over a week helped her to see which subjects she returned to again and again. In the process she also gained some information about the subject of small-town life, and she verified that the subject interested other people enough to warrant her doing some work on it.

The authors of this book often find that, because we read widely, we stumble over information while browsing that will help writers we know, ourselves included. Recently, we were having trouble with a paper that involved observing student writers at work on writing tasks. Coincidentally, we read an article on bird research in South America.

The paper on student writers suddenly fell together as we were reading the ornithologist's description of how South American Indians failed to identify birds with which the ornithologist knew they were familiar. He was using dead carcasses of birds, and as far as the Indians were concerned, a bird and a dead carcass were two different things entirely. We realized that we needed different kinds of information than we had been gathering before our study would have meaning. We thought that the birds were like the writing that students do, and that when we studied student writing, we tended to ask questions that were dead issues, as far as the student writers were concerned. We went back to the research resolving to try to ask questions which took the student writers' viewpoints into consideration more directly.

Part of the trick of good research is looking for connections that will change or enrich your paper. We recently noticed an article in a science newsletter that talked about latchkey children. Research has begun to indicate that latchkey kids do just as well in school and in social situations as children who have a parent awaiting them after school. We thought that that subject would make a good topic for a paper, especially when combined with the previous research in the area, which had been conveniently noted in the article.

Magazines and newspapers don't provide information in the same highbrow style that more scholarly publications do, but you shouldn't rule out these sources. You can often use them in the same way as you do the more familiar books and articles from the library. Actually, intellectual disciplines such as history use popular sources to understand the culture of a given period.

If you wanted to understand people's attitudes toward an important event, you might use newspapers to obtain different points of view. If you go back through days and weeks, you can find information that reflects how a newspaper story unfolds. As we write these pages, a mass murder case has been unfolding in Milwaukee. We have followed the story in the *Chicago Tribune*, noting the various perspectives that the paper has taken. Today, the *New York Times* has an article that traces not only this case but others that have similar methods of operation. A fascinating project lies already researched in the pages of these two major city newspapers.

One important shortcut for research is always to check your source's sources. Usually some of the research trail will be laid out for you, especially in the sciences or social sciences. Most journals or newsletters will provide enough information that you can follow the sources without starting at the beginning.

Records to Keep

Title of article, author(s), name and volume number of journal or publication, date the article was printed, page numbers of the article.

How to Browse in the Library

Libraries have changed in the last few years, but we still find students, even graduate students, who follow just one set route for finding information. They go to the card catalogue (or the computerized version of the catalogue) and then to the periodicals index. Then they dig through a set number of articles and take notes. This method will certainly work for writing papers.

However, we don't personally know any experienced and currently publishing writers who use the library this way. We certainly don't.

Actually, most of our trips to the library don't happen until we begin to revise. (See Chapter 6 for more information on using library research to revise.) Sometimes, however, we do go to the library while we are developing ideas for a paper. It happens something like this.

We might have an idea for a paper on the kinds of information that appeared in very old rhetoric books, those from the eighteenth or nineteenth century, for instance. By a lucky chance, we remember that we glimpsed such books while in the rare books room for another reason. We would then head for the rare books room to see whether those old books might really be a resource for a new essay.

Sometimes we try to get lost in the library. We are interested in psychology, but we don't subscribe to the professional psychology journals because it's not our field of research. One day we were in the library looking for articles on children's writing and discovered several psychology journals lying where they had been left at the copying machine. We discovered that the journals had valuable articles that we wanted to read for our own work.

There's no great trick to it. You simply learn to keep your eyes open in the library. It really is a delightful place full of strange and wonderful resources. Take advantage of lucky accidents.

Records to Keep

Title of article, author(s), name and volume number of journal or publication, date the article was printed, and page numbers of the article

How to Interview People Who Are Experts in the Field

Many times writers forget that experts may be as near as our telephones. If you are writing a paper on a topic that you have discovered through searching your own interests or through group discussion, chances are you or your classmates know people who know much more than you do about your chosen topic.

For example, one of our students wanted to do a paper on athletic injuries. She discovered that one of the trainers for the university football team was an expert on causes of injuries and ways to avoid and treat them. Our student thought she knew quite a bit about the topic but soon discovered that the expert could really help her expand her knowledge.

The second author of this book has directed writing centers for many years. She recently gave a young man a long interview on how to run a writing center. He followed up the interview by sending her a draft of an article he was preparing for publication. Her expert interview formed the core of the article, giving inside information that the writer could not possibly have found in the library or in magazines or journals.

Here's a simple interview procedure.

1. Make an appointment first, letting the interviewee know what your purpose will be and how long you will take.
2. Have a list of questions prepared beforehand. Be sure to plan how to get what you want to know as quickly and courteously as possible. Different questions will be appropriate for different purposes.

If the interview is for information from an expert, then the questions will be factual and practical. If, however, you want to find out something about the person's life and experiences, you'll want to ask more personal and sensitive questions. We know an old cowboy who will tell you anything you want to know about the West if you ask him a few questions about his personal experiences.

3. Take careful notes and tape the conversation if the interviewee will permit taping. Get permission from your interviewee to quote or paraphrase any information you use in the final draft of your project.
4. Follow up with a thank-you note and send a copy of your finished paper to the interviewee.

Records to Keep

Time, date, and place of interview; name of interviewee; any additional questions you think of during the interview; and personal notes about the interviewee's behavior while responding.

How to Do a Survey of Concerned Participants

When you take sociology or communications courses, you may find that they have strict methodology for survey research, so this advice is only a beginning.

First, develop a list of questions you want your respondents to answer. Writing good questions requires a lot of premeditation. Try your questions out on some volunteers and ask them for suggestions for revision.

One way of simplifying the survey process is to use *yes* and *no* questions. Another simple tactic is to use questions that can be answered on a scale like this (called a Likert scale).

4	3	2	1
agree strongly	agree	disagree	disagree strongly

You can tabulate the results of a Likert scale with a three-step procedure:

1. On a blank copy of the questionnaire, enter a hatch mark (/) under the appropriate response for each answer from each person.
2. Count the total number of responses for each question, and record that number next to your hatch marks.
3. Examine the resulting numbers for patterns.

Suppose that you choose a group of twenty college students to evaluate the student newspaper. Reasoning that you need experienced students, you restrict yourself to juniors and seniors who have been in the school since their freshman year. You choose ten women and ten men. You give them the statement, "The *Daily Planet* provides accurate newsreporting," and you ask them to respond with *Agree Strongly, Agree, Disagree,* or *Disagree Strongly.*

You may find that your subjects favor one response. If fifteen of the twenty *Agree Strongly* and the other five *Agree,* you can suggest that the newspaper is probably doing a good job for its audience. Of course you can't know for certain that these people's responses accurately represent the responses of all the juniors and seniors. In order to achieve scientifically significant results, you would have to follow very scrupulous procedures for taking random samples of students. Statistical research doesn't often prove anything, but it can give you some interesting information to think and write about.

You will find the results easier to tabulate and interpret if you have some quantitative information. Of course, you may want free-response questions as well, in which you simply invite people to give their opinions on your issue.

If you decide to write on subjects having to do with attitudes on issues, such as male/female relationships, movie rating, or (in our case) whether to teach grammar, a survey will likely be the right choice for developing your ideas and expanding your perspective.

If you promise to keep respondents' identities confidential, you may find people more cooperative. Don't break your promise to them. Researchers have to abide by a strict code of ethics.

Records to Keep

If you send out surveys through the mail, you may want to attach an identification number to the survey so that you can follow up with people who don't return them. In any case, you need to record the number of surveys you give to people; the number people actually fill out; and significant demographic data such as gender, race, age, and major.

How to Observe Activities Relating to Your Topic

Currently, a kind of research used in anthropology called "participant observation" has become widely used in other fields, like sociology and writing research. Participant observers choose a place or group to observe and then become a part of the environment in order to be able to write about what they have seen and experienced. Participant observers take careful notes each day as well as doing interviews and collecting other kinds of information from the group observed.

You might decide to write a paper on the kinds of people who eat at a fast-food restaurant. You would need to eat there yourself for a few days in a row, noting what you eat yourself, what kinds of other people come in, what they tend to eat, and what times of day different kinds of people tend to come to eat. You might also strike up conversations with patrons or with the help. At the end of each visit, you would write up your experiences and begin to develop some speculations (hypotheses) about what populations the restaurant serves most often.

Sometimes participant observers go to a country and live among the people or take a job in a particular field to see how people in those situations really live and work. You could become a participant observer in some situation where you already spend much time—your campus job or your favorite student hangout.

One of our students wrote a fascinating participant observation paper about the women in the office where she was a student worker. She eventually tied her own observations to books she read on women in positions of little power, like secretaries and nurses. She then wrote a paper on what women do to compensate for powerlessness and feelings of futility. Her observations showed the women in the office setting up little power territories—like how to use the facsimile machine—and letting no one else have the knowledge.

Another of our students tried a more traditionally scientific form of observational research. She wrote a delightful paper about pigs, of all things. An older student married to a farmer, this woman had often observed the behavior of her husband's pigs. Her husband believed that pigs were calmer and less likely to harm one another in their pens if they had some form of entertainment. So he put a bowling ball in the pen with his pigs. They rolled the ball around and, according to the student, appeared quite happy while doing so.

She tried to create a scientific experiment to test the truth of her husband's belief that a pig who could bowl was a happier and less warlike pig. Though she lacked scientific training, she followed a simplified version of experimental procedure, creating an **experimental group** of pigs who had a bowling ball in their pen and a **control group** of pigs without a bowling ball.

She took notes on the behavior of both groups three times a day, for twenty minutes in the morning, at midday, and in the evening. She kept track of the number of aggressive incidents in each of the groups, and, sure enough, discovered that pig warfare diminished among the bowlers. While her research will probably not appear in next month's *Nature,* she had great fun doing the research and writing up the results, she entertained her classmates, and she gave herself a chance to imagine what it feels like to be a scientist.

Records to Keep

Times, dates, and places of observation; names and significant demographic data of people you observe; facts and figures of specific behaviors your research targets; and separate notes that record conclusions you draw from your facts and figures.

How to View Videotapes, Films, or Other Media Presentations

You're probably familiar with film reviews through newspapers and television. The reviewers are people who watch movies for a living, so they see a lot of movies, which gives them credibility to their audience. If you're not a movie buff but you want to do a review, you should choose a movie to which you can bring some experience and credibility. You might choose a film by a director whose work you know, a film starring your favorite actor, or a film which is an example of your favorite genre (science fiction, film noir, western, or rock video).

Your purpose, to evaluate or to analyze the film, will control the sort of information you gather. If you plan to evaluate the film, you'll be comparing it to some standard. You might compare a *Star Trek* movie to the standards set by other science fiction movies, or you might compare one *Star Trek* movie against the standard set by the series. So you'll need to have access to other movies for purposes of comparison. If your purpose is to analyze the film, you'll be looking for meaningful patterns in the movie.

You need to have control over the circumstances in which you view the film, so it makes sense to work with a videotape if you can. If you decide to write about movies on a particular subject—the Vietnam war, for example—you'll want to check out the appropriate films and review them to get the right perspective for your paper.

Or you might want to write on a kind of music and want to watch videos or listen to recordings. An even more creative approach might be to combine various kinds of resources, looking at books on Vietnam as well as the films, then interviewing veterans for their perspective. Discovering good ideas for a paper should always include creative thinking about resources.

Records to Keep

Titles, dates of release, names of director and significant cast members, and publication data on book or article versions of films.

EXPERIENCE

Use one or more research techniques to investigate one or more of the subjects you discovered through introspection or conversation.

Refer to the discussions above for directions on how to
- Use personal reading for academic research
- Browse in the library
- Interview people who are experts in the field
- Do a survey of concerned participants
- Observe activities relating to your topic
- View videotapes, films, or other media presentations

Chapter 4
Discovering Writing Partners

PEER COLLABORATIVE PARTNERS

You never write alone. As you sit down to work, you're joined by people whose books you've read, whose classes you've taken, whose behavior you've emulated or avoided, whose ideas you've loved or hated, and whose writing advice you've taken or rejected. The space you work in is crowded with other minds, and recent research in the ways people formulate and carry out writing projects has emphasized the social aspects of developing ideas (LeFevre, 1987).

An important part of some discovery processes is finding and building a relationship with another writer who will **collaborate** with you on a project. People who write for newspapers, literary magazines, newsletters, political organizations, businesses, advertising firms, school committees, or any other sort of group are quite likely to encounter this sort of writing. Collaborative partners share authority for formulating the project as well as responsibility for executing the research, writing, and rewriting necessary to complete the group project (Gere, 1980).

Participating in and observing the group project can give you the joy of seeing a project completed relatively quickly, the satisfaction of doing what you like and of showing off your skills, and the opportunity to observe and learn from someone else's expertise.

Some projects seem to invite taking on a collaborative partner. Suppose, for example, that you had an idea for a paper on "The Changing Face of Marriage," "The American Family," or "Sexuality and College Students." To do the work on papers like those, it would be helpful to have writers who represent various viewpoints. Both sexes, at least, should be represented. Having another writer along would mean that you would have another pair of eyes to do research and read copy, another pair of hands to compose and revise, and another person to encourage you and help you create something worthwhile.

Or suppose that you've always meant to write down the stories your grandmother tells. You might arrange a visit with her, take along a tape recorder, and ask her to cooperate in telling you some stories about her life. Oral versions of stories need a lot of revision before they can become interesting to someone other than a family member, so you would have to do a significant amount of filling in, rearranging, clarifying, and cutting. Still, when you were finished you might have to consider yourself your grandmother's ghostwriter. It might be appropriate to list her as an author. Your collection of "Stories of the Beartooth Mountain Country" might turn out to be "by" your grandmother "as told to" you. You could write an introduction and check out the historical facts behind her stories.

Like any successful relationship, group writing depends on your establishing and respecting sensible boundaries. Before you and your partner(s) commit to this relationship, you need an agreement *in writing* about how to divide both the work and the credit.

Team Building

Why the formality? An important part of the discovery process is finding out what collaborative partners can do and what they want to do. This is team building. Time spent exploring those issues together will be more than repaid later in the efficiency with which people work together.

Perhaps the discovery process will reveal that people want to divide the project horizontally, so that Person A writes Section A, Person B writes Section B, and so on. Or they may want to divide the project vertically, so that the person who loves to go to the library does much of the research, the person who is good at outlines does the organization, the person who can write a quick first draft cranks it out, the person who knows how to summarize and use sources helps to plug in the research, and so on.

Often, one person has responsibility for writing the first rough draft, gets final revision rights, and has his or her name listed first on the title page. The other people contribute certain sections of the paper, read the whole paper to make suggestions for change, and have their names listed in the order in which they work on the paper. The person who revises the first rough draft (and, presumably, does a lot of conceptual work) is listed second. The other authors bring the project closer to completion, making smaller and fewer changes, such as adding informative details and proofreading.

In another form of collaboration, everyone contributes equally and has an equal say in revision. The names are listed alphabetically. Of course, people may have different ideas about what constitutes "equal" participation, so that should be explored.

There are many other possible ways of forming an agreement based on the preferences of the people involved. You can craft the agreement to suit you. It's important that everyone involved think through the whole project and try to plan for such eventualities as the need to change the topic, the need of one person to move out of the role of first author, the possibility that the project may not turn out at all, and the necessity to revise after the project has been turned in. You need to make these things explicit before you begin.

Giving Credit Where It's Due

The authors of this book have occasionally found that student writers have had unfortunate experiences with collaborative projects. Some people reject the possibility of collaboration because they don't believe that everyone will share appropriately in the work and the credit.

Formal arrangements help avoid such motivational problems. People enter any writing group with unspoken assumptions about writing and about group work. Take a seemingly simple issue like whose name is listed first on the title page. One person thinks, "The paper is my idea. I should get to put my name first." Another person thinks, "If I end up putting a lot of work into this, I deserve to have my name first."

If neither person brings up the issue of order of names until the last minute, each can feel that the other is trying to take advantage when the issue finally does come up. Both people feel that their personal boundaries have been violated and that someone is trying to steal from them.

The same thing can happen if one person does much more writing than the other. One person might be thinking, "I've done nine-tenths of the work on this. I don't think he deserves any revision rights or credit. I'm not going to wait around for him to get going. I'll just finish this." The other person might be thinking, "When am I going to get a turn at writing? He is so self-involved he can't see he's not sharing. I'll just wait and see how long it takes him to realize that he's being unfair."

People can feel competitive over the project and feel petty about their competitive feelings. People can feel guilty about what they did or didn't do during the work on a project. They can maintain a conspiracy of silence until they either have a blow-up or simply finish the project with bad feelings.

This sort of tension is not necessary.

If people will put their expectations on the table as they begin, they stand an excellent chance of getting satisfaction out of the working relationship. At worst, they'll find out before they begin that the relationship isn't going to work. In any case, collaborative agreements clarify the task at hand and the resources available.

Lisa and Jim were both interested in a Stephen Sondheim musical play called *Into the Woods*. The play follows characters such as Cinderella and Red Riding Hood after the happily-ever-after endings of the fairy tales in which they star. Lisa and Jim agreed to take on a paper which described the play in a way that would make a potential audience want to see the play. They agreed to share the writing and research. As a music major, Lisa would supply knowledge of the theater and of music. Jim would supply an English major's skill with language for the drafting and revision process. Together they produced a 4900-word paper that summarized and reviewed the play.

Often collaborative partners encounter problems they did not anticipate, and they have to be prepared to alter the terms of their agreement. When the authors of this book agreed with each other to write the text you are now reading, we decided that the first author would compose the first draft and the second author would read and revise the first draft, contributing anything she felt was necessary. In practice, it worked out that the first draft needed substantial reorganization, and the second author suggested the organizational format of the final draft. The first author reorganized the text, and as the final form approached, the two authors often actually wrote together, looking at the manuscript, discussing changes, and entering them on the computer. After further revision and editing, the first author read the manuscript one last time, correcting errors and changing words here and there. Later on, the reviewers and editors whose names appear in our acknowledgments continued to suggest useful changes.

In collaborative work, each word represents both people, no matter whose fingers struck the keyboard to enter a particular word or sentence. An ideal agreement affords each person the opportunity to do some interesting creative work and to share in the less interesting detail work. While you cannot hope to anticipate all the events that will occur during the composition of a collaborative writing project, the time you spend at the beginning of the project to build a relationship will help to bring the project to satisfactory fruition. The main goal of this process is opening communication between you. We'll say that again. The main goal of this process is opening communication between you. Absolute honesty about your preferences is the only workable basis for collaboration.

EXPERIENCE

Using marriage, family, or some other topic you prefer, work out an agreement to collaborate on a project with a classmate. For the sake of this exercise, you can choose a topic and a partner without actually following up and completing the project. This exercise should give you a sense of the experience of finding a collaborative partner. If a project and a partnership emerge, so much the better.

1. Begin by cooperating with your potential partner to create a list of the tasks you anticipate having to complete to finish your project.

   Use our Table of Contents as a checklist to be sure you haven't forgotten anything. When you have finished the list, make a copy of it so you each have one.

2. On your copy of the list, put your name next to the tasks you would enjoy doing.

3. Cooperate with your partner to create a new list with each of your names next to the tasks you would enjoy doing.

4. Negotiate an agreement to share tasks you both want to do. Then agree to divide or share any remaining tasks.

   Each of you should make sure to mention whatever is on your mind. *Don't agree to give away a task you want to do or to do a task you want to give away unless you know you can carry out the agreement CHEERFULLY!*

Work together to organize the details: what subjects you'll cover, what the final form will look like (one long article, magazine, short book, or series of pamphlets), how you'll study the audience to learn how to approach them, how you'll divide up the work, and how you'll produce the copies of your work to distribute to the rest of the class.

Review each other's work to help meet the goals of your writing plan.

THE SHADOW PARTNER

Shadow partner? We're sure no one has suggested to you that you have a shadow partner for your writing, but we've never met a writer who didn't. The shadow partner whispers quietly to you, draining your energy and self-confidence by telling you to avoid risks. Don't attempt a project that will lead you into new territory. Don't try that idea you've been thinking about for so long. You'll upset someone if you write about that. Don't try to write for that audience. Don't criticize that person or group. Don't begin writing a project that may take longer than the semester to complete.

The shadow partner may speak in the voice of a teacher, a parent, a friend, or even in your own voice, saying, "I know that looks interesting, and you've had it in the back of your mind for a while, but really, it's not for you—not yet anyway." The voice may be right. But the voice may be repeating a warning that is years old and not applicable to your present situation. The shadow partner gives voice to your fears, especially fear of commitment.

Committing Yourself to Do What You Want

A commitment implies that you have invested yourself, not just something you have. You have taken authority. You have crowded out teachers, parents, friends, classmates, and anyone else who can take responsibility for your work. You have acknowledged the truth of your situation as a student and a writer: "This is mine. I own it. If it succeeds, I am entitled to most of the credit. If it fails, I am obligated to accept most of the blame." Writing research suggests that taking authority over your writing is an important step in learning to write more effectively (Brannon and Knoblauch, 1982).

When you commit to a course of action, you put a significant part of yourself on the line, and that's a bit scary. A graphic example of this experience is getting on an airplane or agreeing to undergo surgery. You are handing your safety over to a lot of people you've never met. It takes a lot of trust to do that. You think everything will probably come out all right, or you wouldn't make the decision. But you never know.

Even a positive commitment like the decision to do something you want can stress you. You've decided to risk going after your own rewards rather than relying on someone else to define your work and your reward for you. But it may seem like a better idea to play it safe—write something someone else has assigned to you, something that doesn't put your real interests out where people can evaluate them.

Playing it safe does cost you though. A study of young children (Lepper, Green, and Nisbett, 1973) found that rewards other people give you may undermine your interest in something you care about. The researchers gave one group of children tokens as a reinforcement for drawing and merely asked another group to draw for the fun of it. The children who got tokens worked hard to win the tokens. They continued to work hard until the tokens stopped coming. After that they did less drawing than the children who hadn't ever gotten tokens.

If you were a writing teacher, what might this study suggest to you about giving your students rewards for writing? You might conclude that you would be serving your students' long-term best interests by withholding external rewards and focusing their interest on the intrinsic rewards of writing.

Students in writing classes often give themselves the goal of finishing a certain number of papers with a certain grade point average. In so doing, they are putting themselves in the same position as the children who got tokens. They may find it easier to work hard and get the papers written. But they may find that after they have left the class they have motivational problems. If they don't get their token right away, they may get discouraged and stop writing.

Risk Taking

Finishing the work and earning your tokens may seem like the goals of a writing course, but they are not. The goal of a writing course is to create changes inside of you—to make you a committed, motivated writer who continues to grow by seeking out challenges and accepting help after you leave your writing course. Your part in achieving that goal involves agreeing to take a few risks. What kinds of risks?

As an example, when you're trying to decide about a topic, you might ask yourself whether you need to get a good grade on the paper, in order to write about the topic. If you answer "yes," you have already decided that you're going to ignore the satisfaction of the writing process to concentrate on the product, the grade.

Going into a project with such an attitude, you're not likely to give yourself permission to take the risk of doing something you want or trying something new. In short, you've decided to sacrifice both fun and personal growth to your need for achievement.

Research has shown that people who have a high need for achievement set themselves middling problems to solve, reasoning that a middling level of difficulty gives them a good chance for a reward, while people who have a fear of failure tend to choose either very difficult or very easy problems to solve, reasoning that success is certain with the easy problems and failure is no disgrace with the difficult problems (Atkinson and Litwin, 1960). As a student, when you orient yourself mainly to the rewards and punishments of the system, you may choose to write something that's no great challenge to be sure that you can get your reward. You do what you can do, rather than experimenting in order to learn.

We can't deny that people do get hurt taking risks. No one can give you assurances that everything you think of will always get As or that you'll live happily ever after. But if you develop the habit of writing only about what you're sure will bring you rewards from other people, you'll miss one of the greatest pleasures of life—the joy of following your interest and creating something you care about.

Learning is the first payoff of risk taking. Suppose you like to sing or play an instrument. You get one kind of satisfaction from singing in the shower or playing guitar with your friends, and a different kind of satisfaction from performing successfully in front of a crowd of strangers.

When you perform for a crowd, you're mainly interested in applause, so your satisfaction increases as the quality of your performance improves.

You're careful to choose something that's within your ability. You don't want to get stage fright and embarrass yourself. You want to achieve.

When you perform just for the fun of it, you take responsibility for your own actions. You aren't performing because someone told you to but because you, all by yourself, decided that this activity would reward you. If you're used to getting permission from other people to do what you want, or accepting other people's opinions about what is and isn't worth doing, taking all that responsibility can be stressful.

If you agree to take on the responsibility, you open yourself to new kinds of pleasure in learning and performing. You feel the satisfaction of learning a new song. You try new techniques if you feel like it. You goof off if you feel like it. You don't expect yourself to be perfect at what you're doing, so you are more satisfied by your little achievements during the activity and less dismayed by your mistakes.

Likewise, when you write on subjects that interest you personally, you concentrate on the satisfaction you are experiencing at the moment rather than worrying about the grade you're going to get.

Satisfaction with yourself is the second payoff of risk taking. Joseph Campbell spent his whole life studying the accumulated wisdom of the world's civilizations as it is reflected in their mythologies. Shortly before his death, he summed their messages up in one bit of advice: "Follow your bliss." That's the best piece of advice anyone can give you about writing. Whether we succeed or fail as far as readers are concerned, we're most satisfied if we write about what we care about—following our bliss.

Of course you'll always want to be successful with your writing. Everyone feels the desire to achieve, and we all hope that each piece of writing we produce will bring us praise from other people. We all know that we won't always succeed.

When you feel discouraged, the best medicine is the knowledge that you are doing what you believe in and growing from the experience. One of the stories often told about Martin Luther puts the same idea another way. He was working in his garden one day when someone asked him what he would do if he knew that the world would end tomorrow. He replied, "I would plant a tree." If you are truly doing what you want, you are living in the moment, not longing for the past or the future and not hoping for reward or fearing punishment.

Don't be surprised if you feel isolated at the moment you decide to follow your interest. In *Huckleberry Finn*, Mark Twain describes such a moment. Huck is debating with his conscience whether to turn in his friend Jim, who is an escaped slave.

All of Huck's training in the society of pre–Civil War America tells him the right thing to do is to write a note informing the authorities of Jim's location. Huck must betray either his friend or the whole white American society. He writes the note and struggles with the decision of whether to send it before deciding he cannot turn his friend in. His decision seems transparently "the right thing" from our late twentieth century perspective. But Twain captures Huck's feeling of isolation beautifully with a single line. At the moment of his decision to help Jim escape slavery, Huck says to himself, "All right. I'll *go* to hell then."

A decision to follow your interest often results in a surge of writing energy. This book's authors can speak from personal experience on that issue, for we have risked time, money, and career advancement to work on projects having to do with writing instruction that led us into anthropology, psychology, religion, philosophy, language theory, statistics, and often into the details of personal experience. Many of our students have undertaken the same risks to follow their own interests. Those are the students we remember.

Martha Buchanan is one student we'll remember. A successful writer of the usual college essays, she took a personal risk in writing about her direct experience with a man she called Chuck. As you read her journal entry, ask yourself whether you have a writing project waiting in the background that it is time to begin. As you'll see when you get to Part IV, Revising, Martha wrote quite successfully on this subject. She did further work on the subject in her journal and wrote several drafts of the project. Although she benefited from the assistance of other writers, her teacher included, the project bore the unmistakable stamp of her experience and personality.

When you've finished reading her journal, go on to the experience which follows. If an idea comes to mind immediately, write about it. If nothing comes to mind, try sleeping on it and writing when you get up the following morning.

FROM THE JOURNAL OF Martha Buchanan

I'd like to write about Chuck, but so much holds me away from becoming so intimate with his story. Do I really want to again feel the intensity of my anger and outrage? To write about Chuck, I can't hold myself safely distant from my subject. Do I want my heart to be evaluated?

I was taught to write away from myself. The personal had no place in writing. Yet, Chuck's story is intensely personal. My senior English teacher would tear me apart for turning in a paper based upon personal experience. My parents taught me never to speak of anything unpleasant. If unpleasantnesses existed, we were above noticing them. Chuck's story is not supper table talk.

Again, the dichotomy between personal writing and writing for evaluation gets in my way. Yet, the strongest voice is my own. I'm afraid.

I'm afraid that I'm not good enough, that my insights are the insights of a bleeding heart (being laughed at?).

Yet I feel responsible to Chuck. I feel I owe him more than an entry in my journal. But I am overwhelmed by that responsibility. I've never written a story before. What if I don't tell it well? What if I fail to touch the hearts of my readers?

The flip side of the fear of failure is the fear of not even trying. Can I die without guilt if I don't even try?

EXPERIENCE

1. Think of an "impossible" topic, one you're sure your shadow partner (a teacher, a parent, a friend, or someone else) would not approve because it's too broad, too narrow, too controversial, too easy, too frightening, or too embarrassing.

   a. Think about who won't allow the topic.
      - If it isn't your present teacher, who is it? Are you remembering a former teacher who had opinions on choice of topics? Is it a parent? A friend?
      - Is it your own opinion? If you won't allow yourself to write on the topic, what are you afraid will happen? Do you think you'll waste your time?
      - Are you afraid someone won't like what you write? Are you afraid you'll find out you can't do it? Is there some other reason?

   b. Think about who would be delighted if you wrote about this topic.

2. Try writing a couple of sentences, maybe even a paragraph on the topic.
   - Do you begin to feel interested and want to go on? Do you begin to think of other ideas to put in? Go ahead and continue writing until you feel like stopping.
   - Look at what you've written. Do you now believe that you could write on this topic?
   - If you still think you couldn't, how might you modify the topic to make it a suitable subject for a writing project for your class?

TEACHERS AS WRITING PARTNERS

It's great fun to write something challenging that you thought up entirely by yourself and that you finish on your own. It happens now and again, and there's no pleasure like it.

You get a similar kind of fun when you start a conversation with someone, discover that you know something he or she needs to know, and find that you have written something in which you trade your effort for the reader's approval. "I loved your article. You said exactly what I think about the men's movement, but you said it much better than I could." You were the sponsor of both those writing projects, so you enjoy the satisfaction of ownership when they go well.

However, the world is full of writing assignments someone else sponsors. This is especially true of the student writer's world, so it's important to have a productive way of dealing with those assignments.

Assignments provide two obvious advantages.

The person who gives the assignment has already announced a desire to read what you have to write, which is a trait we, as authors, find endearing in people.

And the person who gives you the assignment has taken the trouble of finding a topic, often the most disagreeable part of writing.

But we know that assignments can cause motivational problems too—a certain passivity. A famous study of student writers (Emig, 1971) noted that writers may distinguish writing they do for school from writing they do for themselves. This study suggested that a writer would give self-sponsored writing more intense and involved attention than school-sponsored writing. In this section, we'll describe a way of collaborating with your teacher so that you can take a personal interest in your assignment but still enjoy the advantage of the teacher's advice and involvement. By the time you've finished reading this section, you should also be able to propose your own idea for a writing project and receive a teacher's assistance in taking a workable approach to your idea.

Asserting Your Authority

Suppose that your teacher assigned you to write a paper on addictions. You might say to yourself, "That's a dull topic. I don't use drugs. I don't smoke. I'll do a typical five-page research essay with five sources. My roommate can proofread it for spelling. I'll get a plastic folder to put it in. That's what the teacher expects."

You know where this is leading, right? If you decide that an assignment is school-sponsored, that it belongs entirely to someone else, you can fall into a state psychologists call **learned helplessness.**

You feel helpless to take responsibility for the work. You want the person who gave you the assignment to tell you exactly what to do—how long the paper should be, whether you can use contractions, how many footnotes you have to have, whether you have to type it, and whether spelling counts.

It doesn't sound like much fun, does it? And you're not learning much, either, if someone else makes all the decisions for you.

Are all writing projects either self- or school-sponsored then? We doubt it. You've probably had experience with assignments you were able to **cosponsor,** that is, to share ownership and responsibility with someone else, perhaps a teacher, an employer, or another writer. Even when someone else invents an assignment, you can usually find or make a personal stake in the assignment.

By **personal stake,** we do not mean the ego satisfaction of getting the best possible grade or writing the best possible paper. We mean finding a connection between your experience and the assignment. To return to the example of the paper on addictions, you might say to yourself, "I don't know much about addictions. I'll look around a bit to see if I can find some way that addiction relates to me."

Having done some reading, you might find that addiction is a much broader phenomenon than you first knew. People can be addicted to drugs, alcohol, gambling, and tobacco. They can also be addicted to food, work, sex, exercise, emotions, or even other people. You might realize that you, a friend, or a parent is touched by addiction directly and daily.

Having found a personal connection with the assignment, you would suddenly take a new interest in it, the interest of ownership. You could do research to find answers to questions you have personally. You might visualize the addicted person as your audience and try to write to inform or persuade that person. Instead of dutifully going through the motions to please the teacher, you would take an interest in making the paper well-researched enough to be believable and long enough to be clear and persuasive. You'd decide for yourself whether contractions were appropriate and whether spelling counted, given the writing task you were trying to complete.

You'd probably end up working a lot harder and spending a lot more time than if you just did the usual research paper, and there's no guarantee that you'd get the best possible grade or write the best possible paper. You'd be taking a chance that your teacher would value the personal perspective you took on his or her assignment. You learn from taking such chances.

Your teacher may also work with you to modify an idea of your own to increase the likelihood of its success. Girard, a student who wrote sociological papers about subjects such as leaders and advertising executives, composed dull and general sentences such as "A leader must be someone outstanding whom other people will want to follow." He had decided that writing was something one did for teachers and that his own interests were irrelevant. If he wrote in an "intellectual" style, he seemed to think, he was fulfilling his responsibility. His teacher read a few such papers before she assigned Girard a subject that was within his immediate experience. He decided to do a scientific observation of people's behavior at a college party and was able to write much more clearly and interestingly.

A teacher can help you to shape an idea you develop in a journal entry, a conversation, or a rough draft into the beginnings of an assignment for a writing project. In Girard's case, the teacher recognized that he was writing without either information or conviction. When she asked him what point he wanted to make about leaders, his responses were all obvious and trite, and when she asked him what new angle he planned to take on a subject that had been worked so often, he couldn't identify a new approach. So she suggested that he work within the scope of his experience, which would give him both information and a perspective with the stamp of his personality.

Heather had written a journal entry detailing the events leading to the remarriage of her boyfriend's mother. She was trying to present the reasons why the remarriage had forced her boyfriend to move out and had created a rift between her boyfriend and his mother. Her teacher, reading her journal entry, suggested a couple of ways to develop the entry into a project, both of which involved examining the boyfriend's part in creating the problems in his mother's marriage. Heather, who saw her boyfriend as the victim, did not want to consider that viewpoint. Her teacher asked if she might be too close to the subject to be able to work through criticism and revision of the project. After thinking it over, Heather decided that she wanted to continue. Her teacher felt that she needed some objective distance from the subject and assigned her to do some reading about divorce, remarriage, and blended families. Heather was able to use psychological research to explain how some of the events were part of a pattern many people experience.

In Heather's case, the teacher recognized that she had not considered a reader other than herself and a few close friends, so he asked her to think about who might be interested in such a discussion and where it might be published. As you collaborate with your teacher on the details of your writing projects, you'll begin to be able to visualize the final form your idea may take and anticipate problems that may occur in your approach to the subject. At this stage, you may change much of your project before you have finished, but you'll have some vision of the final product to follow.

Four Questions to Help You Write Your Assignment

Experienced writers learn to anticipate the questions and problems Girard and Heather encountered. At this stage the project may seem misty to you, but if you think about it in consultation with your teacher, you'll probably discover that you can glimpse the final project through the mist. Try asking yourself the following four questions.

- "What point is this project going to make?"
- "Who would benefit most from reading what I have to say?"

- "How will my project differ from other writing on the same subject?"
- "Where would the sort of reader I've described expect a project like mine to be published?"

These four questions will help you to begin to define the **information** you want to convey, to imagine a **reader** who might be interested in your information, to establish your personal **perspective** on the subject matter, and to identify a **forum** (that is, a publication) in which the reader might encounter information like yours. Your teacher can advise you whether you've sufficiently defined your project. He or she can also give you some good advice about the sorts of problems you'll need to solve on your way to finishing the project.

Linda Hindahl proposed an article on small town life.

FROM THE JOURNAL OF Linda Hindahl

Small Town Life Article

This would be an account of an experience I had moving to a small town and trying to fit in. It would focus on a basketball game my son played in but would also include my earlier experiences with trying to find a place in the town. The point would be to show how I finally came to feel a part of it all.

This would be written from the perspective of someone who has learned to like the Midwest. I think that it would appeal to people who have moved from a large town to a smaller one. It will have a family orientation, so the reader would probably be someone with a family.

There are lots of articles about subjects like this but none that I have read talk about how a high school athletic contest helps the *parents* to feel more at home in the small town. I think that would be different, especially for a woman to write.

Outlets for this would be magazines such as *Midwest Living* or possibly the Parade magazine that comes with the Sunday *Peoria Journal-Star*. It would help if people already knew something about the Midwest and had an interest in it.

Linda's teacher suggested that she begin by telling the story of her experiences with the small town. He urged her to be candid in describing her reactions to her new environment. In first-person accounts of experience, the writer's thoughts and feelings—especially those she isn't certain she's supposed to have—create much of the interest.

As an experienced reader and writer, your teacher has often been over the terrain you are about to cover in developing your idea into a writing project. Taking advantage of your teacher's ability to foresee problems, you can begin to map out a direction for your ideas that will enable you to satisfy both your own and your teacher's expectations.

EXPERIENCE

Use the format below to propose an assignment for your next writing project, and collaborate with your teacher to anticipate problems OR use the format described below to build a personal stake into an assignment your teacher gives you.

1. In a paragraph or two, describe the project you plan to complete. Your description should take into account your teacher's requirements and should include
   - a summary of the **information** you plan to convey (ask yourself, "What point is this project going to make?")
   - a description of the sort of **reader** who would be appropriate for your project (ask yourself, "Who would benefit most from reading what I have to say?")
   - an explanation of **how your project differs** from other published writing on the same subject (ask yourself, "What is my personal angle on the subject?")
   - the names of one or two potential **published forums** for your work (ask yourself, "Where would the sort of reader I've described expect a project like mine to be published?")
2. Discuss your proposal with your teacher and revise according to his or her directions.

Part III
Drafting

Drafting is part science and part art.

Planning is the "scientific" part of the drafting process. In planning, writers analyze their own writing projects to build a framework they can work in comfortably, with some assurance that their writing is building toward a goal. Some kind of planning usually begins the drafting stage and continues to change and grow as the paper takes shape. Some people love to plan out each detail before writing. They may act out planning by tidying their environments before beginning. Some good writers we know plan with the traditional sentence outline. Others seem to simply plunge in with a main idea in mind, preferring to watch the plan emerge from the writing itself.

Once a plan is set and the actual writing begins, a writer has to be prepared to monitor how well it's going and to adjust the plan if the necessity occurs. This is the "art" of drafting. As you draft, you often operate on instinct. Words and ideas may come from out of the blue. You may find that you experience euphoric feelings, uncomfortable feelings, or uncertain feelings. You may experience impulses to change your plan or to follow a new lead. An important part of learning to write is learning to take advantage of sudden inspirations, to interpret feelings, and to distinguish productive from unproductive impulses.

Chapter 5, Planning a Draft, details some of the analytical aspects of drafting. The time you spend working on the plan may not seem to be real writing, but we can assure you that planning time is time well spent: the more you are able to plan, the less you'll have to revise. Chapter 6, Composing a Draft, details some of the more artistic, synthetic aspects of drafting. In these activities you have to be prepared to get your hands messy, to operate sometimes without a certainty of where you're going.

Chapter 5
Planning
a Draft

_____

_____

_____

PLANNING TO CHANGE THE WAY YOU WRITE

Before you work on the particular plans for writing projects, you need to bring to mind the larger goals for which people enroll in a writing course. As you become preoccupied with the thousands of details involved in producing a writing project, you may lose sight of the fact that completing writing projects is only a means to an end. The real goal of a writing course is changing the way you write—increasing your skill, your comfort, and your commitment to writing.

In the romantic fantasies of some people, writers are stubborn individualists who live reclusive lives and scorn human contact, communing with a spirit of inspiration. Indeed, as a writer you must draw heavily on inner resources, but you must draw just as heavily on the advice and assistance of editors and other writers. Your teacher acts the part of the editor who helps you to turn a concept into a practical reality. In a writing class, much of what you learn also comes from class members. You must commune with the group around you. Your contact with the group will change both what you write and how you write.

Writers' Communities

A willingness to observe and emulate the productive techniques of others often separates the successful writer—the one who learns, grows, and changes—from the person who never reaches an audience and who sleepwalks through a writing course. Many famous writers learned from writers' communities (or "peer groups," as they are often called in writing courses). Hemingway, Faulkner, Fitzgerald, and the rest of the "Lost Generation" met in Gertrude Stein's Paris apartment to talk about life and art. J. R. R. Tolkien, C. S. Lewis, and others formed a similar group which called itself the Inklings. Many writing classes are now set up on the studio, or workshop, model, so that writers bring their drafts to class, read them, and exchange comments. Learning to write has become a communal experience, like learning to dance or to draw. Each writer involved in the studio becomes both a student and a teacher.

The great advantage of studio work is that you gain so much experience so quickly. Involving yourself in someone else's work enables you to learn from that work. Your growth as a writer goes on fast-forward.

We have two guidelines for making a writers' community work. The first is that each writer should have good, personal reasons for joining the community. Jennifer Rasso wants to improve her ability to produce **academic discourse,** the scholarly sort of writing required in most college courses. She is aware that a writing course will help her but that she will have to overcome some personal resistance to change. She has strong opinions about how a writers' community should operate.

FROM THE JOURNAL OF Jennifer Rasso

I'd like to be able to write more "scholastically." I think my writing is too free form and has no construction. When I was in 8th grade I went to college for kids and took a class on poetry. That is the only experience with a workshop atmosphere. I'd like to attend and experience the environment if nothing else.

I like a lot of privacy when I write on a computer. This stems from the fact that if I am in a classroom atmosphere and am not typing all the time I tend to feel inadequate. Five minutes to two hours is about my time limit for private writing. After that I crave human companionship.

I like group sessions during class, but only if everyone in the group talks and adds to the conversation. It irks me no end when a group gathers and one person just sits there. I like group critique sessions. I feel that this is a good alternative to teacher critique because it allows your peers to see what you have written and to give insightful advice. I would love to experiment with writing. I'd like to have guidelines to help.

Jennifer has set an excellent personal agenda for herself and has tried to anticipate the problems (such as, liking to keep her writing processes private) she may encounter in achieving her goals. In addition, she has enunciated some reasonable expectations for group work. Most students share her attitude that groups work best if everyone participates.

The authors of this book strongly agree with Jennifer's sentiments about involvement in the group. If you want or need to learn something about writing, you must be able to commit yourself to take part in the group with the intention of learning from its members. Once you commit to your group, you'll begin to accept its members' influence on you. At that point, you begin to change the way you write, to observe how other people work, and to pick up some of their habits. You notice how carefully one person listens to the assignment, how another is able to relax and enjoy writing, how a third asks for help in the middle of a draft, and how a fourth composes at the keyboard. Perhaps the person next to you listens well when you ask a question. Someone else works steadily, persistently, even stubbornly, until a problem is solved. Yet another person writes with a sense of humor.

Our second guideline is that you have to be willing to take other people's projects as seriously as you take your own.

A class, especially a writing class, is much more than a delivery system for information. If you just want information about writing, you can get it from books about writing, just as you can read about sports or music. But doing sports, doing music, or doing writing requires other people. You have to be able to trust those people to do their part.

People who are faithful about class earn the trust of class members. Trustworthy class members know that they owe it to each other and the teacher to plan to be there physically whenever possible, to be there emotionally by explaining necessary absences, and to be there intellectually by keeping up with the work. Skipping class, skimping on the time you spend on your work, or falling behind in your work sends a strong message that you don't care about the people.

Taking others' projects seriously also works in your own self-interest. You put yourself in a position to learn a great deal more if you are involved in the composition of several projects besides your own. It's as if you were suddenly turned into fifteen or twenty different people writing fifteen or twenty different pieces at the same time. As you work in class on studio days, you'll want to notice the person who writes next to you, to get involved in that person's work, to ask how it's going, and maybe to offer to talk about how you handled similar problems. Go ahead. Studios are public spaces. If you find someone struggling with something you know how to do, it's okay to offer help.

It's okay to ask for help too. If someone else has an idea about how something of yours should be written, it's even okay to get out of your chair and allow the other person to write at your computer or in your notebook for a moment. Taking down the fences for a while as you write enables you to get a sense of how other people read your work as well as how other people write.

It's simple. If you plan to change, you'll take part in a writers' community.

EXPERIENCE

1. What would you like to change about the way you write? Can you accept help from others? Are you willing to try some experiments in writing?

2. What are the goals of the writing course in which you are now enrolled? What are the methods? Examine your teacher's syllabus or the notes you have taken in class for explicit or implicit goal and method statements. Ask your teacher if you're not sure. You need to get this information straight.

PLANNING FOR YOUR AUDIENCE

Your project will have at least three kinds of readers. You, of course, are the first reader for anything you write, since you must construct your meaning by reading back and forth through your text as you write. Writers need to keep in mind two additional types of readers, real readers (actual people who pick up the paper in any circumstance and who can read it if they know the language) and intended readers (people like the writer who have something to learn, debate, and/or enjoy when reading the paper). As a writer you may find that thinking of your intended reader as your **audience** may help you to focus what you have to say.

The audience for a paper is not quite like the audience for a speech because you cannot look out and see how people are reacting to your message. What you can do, though, is imagine a reader as someone who has chosen to come to your paper as an audience would choose to come to a movie or a concert. The intended reader would not be there if he or she had no interest in your topic. As a writer, you have a right to assume an interested reader as your audience, but you have many tasks to do to find the interested reader and maintain the reader's interest.

Your immediate writing community comprises people whom you can directly **address.** Beyond your immediate writing community lies that imagined, intended community composed of people who read the sort of writing you can do or can learn to do. These are people whom you haven't met yet, but whom you can influence with the power of language. You can't address them directly as you can the members of your immediate environment, but you can **invoke** them—that is, imagine who they are and what they would be interested in—by thinking about people you *do* know.

To **invoke** someone is to call on him or her, and, indeed, writing for the wider community resembles making a phone call. To reach someone at a distance, you first do some research in the phone book to find out who and where they are. You dial them up, and, if your research was adequate, you make contact with them. You may have any of dozens of purposes, from the trivial to the crucial, for making the contact.

Since you initiated the contact, you have the responsibility to identify yourself, to make your agenda clear, not to waste the person's time, and to end the call when you have accomplished your purpose. Throughout the call, you have to guess how the person is responding to your message because, unless you know the person very well, you will have trouble visualizing what is happening at the other end of the wire.

Readers' Expectations

General Assumptions You Can Make About All Readers

You can assume some things about all readers. They will all expect you to make it clear to them why they should bother to read your writing. They will all expect your writing to have a recognizable beginning, middle, and ending. They will all expect your writing to be perfectly proofread. It's safest to assume that you need to follow the reader's interest, provide a very clear structure, and mind your spelling and punctuation. No one will criticize you for those qualities.

You may also assume that the invoked reader isn't around while you're writing. That may sound like a silly thing to point out, but some writers don't seem to be able to remember that writing is different from talking in that respect.

Not having the reader around while you write hinders you in that you have to make some guesses and supply some information that is not necessary in conversation. Writing to the invoked reader helps you in that you can write in your own way, at your own pace, in your own room, and make any changes necessary for the reader at your own convenience.

Specific Information You Need to Discover About Readers

You need to supplement your assumptions with some more specific information about readers.

Advertising provides a good example of how to plan for the invoked reader. Advertisers conduct market research to find out what people like, need, or want. Perhaps you've been phoned or given a questionnaire about your buying habits. The people who designed the research were trying, in their mercenary way, to get to know you. It's in their best interests to do so because they want to find out who might be willing to buy what they have to sell.

Using the information they can gain from a few people, advertisers create a picture of a larger audience they guess may be out there. No one can guarantee that the invoked audience will respond predictably, which is why some products succeed beyond expectations and others fail despite the best efforts of the producers. As a writer, you can learn to spend your effort as carefully as companies spend their dollars on advertising. The time spent in sorting out receptive readers from the crowd will be well worth it in the success and satisfaction you gain from your work.

You can also help to clarify the picture of the invoked reader by imagining who would not be interested in your subject.

Suppose you were writing about the educational uses of television. Who would not be an appropriate part of that audience? People who think television fosters illiteracy? They probably wouldn't like what you said, but they might be very interested. What about people who prefer to get their information and entertainment from print sources? Indeed that group might not even own a television, so you might more profitably spend your effort on people with whom you have at least some interest in common.

Constructing the Reader's Context

Once you have focused on a particular group of readers, you are ready to plan more specifically to meet their expectations. You can understand those expectations by examining the printed contexts—the magazines, newspapers, pamphlets, and books—in which you are likeliest to meet your readers. Your goal is to dig beneath the surface of the context to understand the people whom this context represents. In a way, understanding the reader is like an archaeological dig (Foucault, 1966).

Suppose you were an archaeologist from Mars who dug in the ruins of an Earth city and found only one piece of written material. You returned to your laboratory with it, and, using fantastically clever decoding techniques, you deciphered the words on the cover. "Hmm. *TV Guide*. I wonder what that means?"

Suppose that you tried to reconstruct Earth society using facts from the *TV Guide*. What "facts" could you obtain? You'd learn that we have a twenty-four-hour day, and a seven-day week. If you happened upon an issue that had the end of one month and the beginning of another month, you'd get the idea of months. You'd have to look pretty closely at the publication information in the front to learn that *TV Guide* comes out fifty-two times a year. You'd note that we have two seasons, Fall and Reruns, and that our major agricultural product was something called "programs."

You'd be able to list our interests: entertainment, news, shopping, education, and so on. You'd notice that the articles were short, that we liked our reading to be light and brief, and that we liked pictures and bright colors, especially in advertisements. You'd become aware of the frequency and variety with which we mention love: who is sleeping with whom on the soap operas, how we can become more attractive on the talk shows, why God loves you on the religious channels, why you ought to love the the arts and the environment on the educational channels, and so forth.

Having noted all the facts, you as Martian archaeologist might feel warranted to draw some conclusions: that the elaborate schedule indicated that we valued order and system in our lives, that the prevalence of sports and movies suggested we were more interested in them than in learning, or that the brevity of the articles suggested a short attention span.

You might decide that the television governed every moment of our lives and that we never slept. Some of your facts and conclusions as a Martian archaeologist would seem clearly true to earthlings, and some would seem false, or true only in a metaphorical way. As earthlings we consider it a fact that the year has fifty-two weeks, but we teach children there are four seasons, not two, and so on.

The Meaning of Printed Contexts

Using *TV Guide* as a metaphor for America, we get a new way of looking at both television and American life. We get a creative mixture of understanding and misunderstanding from such comparisons, just as we get information and misinformation from a statement such as "O my luve's like a red, red rose, / That's newly sprung in June." Love may seem sweet and beautiful like a rose, and it may wither and die, but obviously love is not just like a rose. Love doesn't grow in the dirt. You don't spray it for aphids. Love doesn't have green stems and thorns. Or does it? The point, at any rate, is that the Martian perspective on symbols such as roses can wake us up to some truths about people and their purposes.

Popular Magazine Readers' Expectations

Information acquires its meaning in large part from the context where you find it. Looking at a rose in a garden gives it one meaning; visualizing a rose as a symbol for love focuses your attention on different qualities of the rose, thereby giving it a different meaning.

Each magazine you read represents a self-contained world, a different context for information. For magazines you know, you can probably name special sections that you like to read, and you can predict what will be written and how.

In *Time*, for example, the last page of the magazine often contains an essay written in a familiar, rather private style about some issue of importance to the writer. Whether the issue is political, social, medical, artistic, or educational, the writer will assume an easy and informal relationship with the reader. More public writing is contained in the "Nation" section of *Time*, where news currently important to Americans is presented and analyzed. But nothing in *Time* is as public as the front page of most newspapers. In *Atlantic Monthly*, the personal essay we find on the last page of *Time* occurs in extended forms, composing the greater part of each issue.

Editors help build a context and expectations for the reader by the choices they make about format, language, subjects, graphics, advertisements, and everything else that you see when you pick up a magazine.

These help to form the context by providing a set of features that readers of the magazine recognize as characteristic of that magazine.

Suppose an article entitled "Love: American Style" appeared in ten different magazines. *Time* and *Newsweek* readers might expect politically liberal opinions about gender issues and an energetic prose style. *Cosmopolitan* and *Playboy* readers might expect a chic, sexy, chatty article or story focused on sexual technique and experience. *New Yorker* and *Atlantic* readers might expect urbane opinion and literature about the vicissitudes of the modern urban "relationship." *Reader's Digest* and *Prevention* readers might expect down-to-earth advice about the relationship between a sound marriage and a sound cardiovascular system. *Scientific American* and *Natural History* readers might expect discussions of chemical changes in the body during infatuation or the evolutionary advantages of polygamy.

Each shift in context places the subject in a different light. As you become more and more aware of how context changes meaning, you begin to see how important small details of presentation can be. The best way to understand an audience's expectations is to analyze a piece of writing that has met those expectations. And the best place to begin your analysis is with writing you read voluntarily.

Jim Husfield reads a film magazine called *Cinefantastique*. He wrote a detailed analysis of the magazine to help him plan a writing project on "Star Trek." He discovered that in this magazine for science fiction and horror genre films the articles are short, informal, and focused on the people who make the films.

FROM THE JOURNAL OF Jim Husfield

The magazine *Cinefantastique* is a bimonthly publication that appeals to fans of science fiction and horror genre films. The in-depth research and interviews with the people either acting, directing, or creating the special effects for these films is what interests the readers and is why this magazine can command a cover price of over five dollars an issue. In the October '91 issue, I was attracted to the thirty-six pages (over half the issue) that were dedicated exclusively to "Star Trek: The Next Generation" as it ended the fourth season and prepared for the fifth. This issue was not only of interest to me and Jeff Alfano; but also Rob Festestine, Kris Knudsen, Eric Curl, and a host of other Trek fans. People who do not attend many special effects laden films and have no real interest in science fiction (I'm trying to describe my step-father) would have no desire to purchase this magazine.

In *Cinefantastique* there are nine articles listed along with three regular features (movie ratings, reviews, and letters from readers). The magazine comes out bimonthly (in February, April, June, August, October, and December). The magazine is almost devoid of ads but the inside covers at both the front and back boast full page color ads for an upcoming film. The first article is a two and a quarter page analysis of the character Hannibal Lecter [from the movie *Silence of the Lambs*] as the new horror star of the '90s and the entire article was written by Thomas Doherty. Any and all sources of information are cited immediately upon reference within the text, there are no footnotes, the writer uses first person style, and avoids contractions except in quotes and to make a point three fourths through the article. Nowhere is it made very clear how to submit an article to be considered but the mailing address is given along with all the other typical publisher's information at the bottom of the contents page.

From this analysis, Jim could draw three conclusions about people interested in reading about science fiction and horror film. First, the potential readers would prefer a focus on the personalities of the actors, directors, producers, or writers of science fiction and genre films. Second, a successful project for these readers would use an informal style to create a sense of having a conversation with the subject of the project. Third, an interview would be an appropriate research method for this project.

This information was definitely worth the trouble it took him to develop it. The editors of successful magazines must work out approaches to their subject matter that appeal to potential readers. Since the money of a magazine's financial backers and the jobs of the magazine's employees depend on selling magazines, you can rest assured that the approach to the reader works. You can learn a great deal about how to win the attention of a reader by analyzing an approach that has stood the test of the marketplace.

Intellectual Magazine Readers' Expectations

People who teach in colleges and universities are accustomed to reading very technical magazines (often called "journals") which print the work of scholars in their fields. You may be familiar with journals such as *Journal of the American Medical Association, Nature, College English,* and so on. Each of those journals requires its writers to follow a certain relatively formal style, but each journal presents a different version of formal style.

The expectations of intellectual journal readers gave rise to the term paper style you may have learned to use—in which first person isn't allowed; you can't use contractions; you feel that you should use learned words and long sentences; and you have to follow certain rules about notes, works cited, and the layout of the page.

Writers for academic journals follow the rules of the formal academic style appropriate to their professional audience. Academic style sounds awfully stiff and formal to some people, and that sound may obscure the fact that writing to academic audiences is a little like telling stories to a family member. In a family, you have a way of talking to each other that you understand, and you can assume that you share an interest in the subject matter.

But if you think about writing in college, you realize that you spend most of your time writing for exactly that audience. Your teachers took their training from people who assigned reading in those journals, and, in all likelihood, your teachers write for such journals themselves. In their minds, articles for intellectual journals are the model for college writing. The more you can write like a journal article, the more likely you are to earn the respect of college teachers. The longer you remain in the academic environment, the more its idiom will become like the language you learned as you grew up. You'll find after you have left college that the intellectual approaches you learned to writing will continue to be something you share with other people who have your experience.

The same basic criteria apply whether you are telling a family member the story of your cousin's wedding or writing up the details of your research on American wedding customs in a term paper for your sociology professor. Both audiences ask themselves some basic questions as they consider the story you're telling: Do I like this story? Does it tell me something new? Does it make sense based on what I know about the people and circumstances involved? Is it presented the way I'd expect it to be? It's important that they answer each of those questions, "Yes."

Read the following journal entry by Jon Neuleib (whose writing you saw in Chapter 1 in a journal entry about debating with his teacher over whether a sentence could begin with "Because"). In this entry Jon, a college debater, focuses on an intellectual reader's expectations. He asks himself three questions about a journal called *Foreign Policy:* What would interest a reader of this journal, who would not be interested in this journal, and how can he tailor a project for the readers of this journal? The first two questions help him to focus on visualizing the reader. Once he has visualized the reader, he can begin trying to frame his knowledge in terms the reader would like.

FROM THE JOURNAL OF Jon Neuleib

Many of my friends read a magazine called *Foreign Policy.* The journal is a good example of the kind of things that students read and then talk about with other students. My friend Eric got me a free subscription to the journal so he makes a great figure for this example. Eric is a political science major and he reads the journal to make sure that he can keep up to date on what is happening in his field. He reads the journal to get ideas for timely papers and also because he is truly interested in many of the issues that are discussed regardless of their applicability to his current classes.

I read the journal primarily to keep up with my work on the debate team. We have to keep a close eye on the trends in policy discourse to make sure that the arguments we make in debate rounds are consistent with the way that the government's policies are going in the real world. In this way, Eric and I use the journal for many of the same reasons. We also like to read various articles and then talk about them with each other if there is no other outlet for our opinions on various issues.

The group of people that are described by the criteria I used to describe Eric is a large one. There is a whole group of scholarly but popular journals that people with similar needs and experiences read as well as this journal. Magazines like *Current History* and *Dissent* all take various approaches to what might be broadly considered politics. All these journals take a position that critiques the current policy choices that the government is making with approaches that fill the spectrum from ultra-conservative to socialist.

People who choose not to read magazines like this fall into two basic categories. The first one is the people that simply do not care about what goes on with the government's actions. While it might be too simple to say that all these people do is to watch T.V., their level of interest does not seem to be much above the sound bite they get on the evening news. The second group of people are those who care about the government's actions but who do not choose to spend their time reading about alternative approaches to politics. These people get what they need to know from newspapers which report which policies the government is currently pursuing. These people are usually involved in some other area of scholarly discourse so they have little time to spend weighing the various alternatives. While being far from the apathetic non-readers, they still have very little interest in the specific issues that these journals raise.

A paper that I am working on that has to do with the multitude of problems that exist with the government's current policy on the ocean could probably be of interest to this journal. The paper includes a broad overview of the problem area that needs to be addressed and then offers solutions for the problems that are identified. The journal's articles are not exactly similar to the paper that I am working on, but the general approach and the area of interest is quite similar to pieces that appear in the journal.

I also think this is true because the people that I know, such as Eric, who read the journal have talked with me about issues that I am raising in the paper and seem interested by the problem area. The paper's criticism of the government's stance on things like ocean dumping is pretty consistent with what most people think about the harm that is being done to the ocean. What makes the paper interesting is that no one seems to agree on what should be done about the problem. The journal would probably not even consider my paper in the shape it is in now but I think that the problem areas and solutions are very similar to ones that the journal prints.

You don't have to be a college debater to write for an intellectual audience, nor do you have to interest yourself in politics. For any subject you can imagine, someone, somewhere has probably produced intellectual writing. Is your subject television? Try the *Journal of Popular Culture,* or talk to someone in the communications department who teaches radio and television production. Would you like to write about sports? Look up *bio-mechanics* in the card catalog or talk to someone in the athletic department who teaches *leisure studies.* We don't mean to rule out the more traditional intellectual interests, but we want to emphasize that you can explore any interest from an intellectual perspective by focusing on analysis of the interest.

As you prepare to write a draft, making yourself aware of readers' expectations can give you a clearer vision of the final product than you began with. Knowing whether the project you have in mind is suitable for an intellectual or a popular magazine, you'll make informed choices about both information and style. The intellectual reader will expect and tolerate a much higher level of technical information and a more formal style than the popular magazine reader.

Having the magazine or journal in mind, you write more efficiently and more pointedly. This is not to say that you can solve all your reader problems in your first draft. Having decided that you are writing for either the popular or the intellectual reader, you still have a range of magazines and journals with differing expectations. You may even change your mind in the midst of your writing—decide that you want to change your reader and printed context.

Experience

➡WARM-UP

1. Name a magazine that you read. Describe someone you know (besides yourself) who also reads the magazine.
    *   What in the magazine interests each of you individually?
    *   What would interest both of you?

2. Decide whether the two of you represent a larger group of people you know. Name a few names if you can.
   - What other magazines or books would you suppose these people would have read?
   - Can you think of other qualities or experiences they may have in common that are relevant to your purposes as a writer?
3. Now think of someone you know who probably would not be interested in the magazine. Explain why you think the person would not be interested.

➥FOR YOUR WRITING PROJECT

4. Think of a magazine you like to read which might be interested in publishing a writing project you are working on.
   a. Find the magazine in your library or bookstore.
   b. Photocopy an article from the section of the magazine where your project might be published. Use the copy as a model for the form of your writing project.
   c. Describe the expectations of readers of the magazine. (Answering the questions listed below will help you to find the relevant information.)
      - How many articles are listed in the table of contents?
      - How often does the magazine come out?
      - Does the magazine have advertisements? For what?
      - How many authors are there for the first article?
      - How long is the first article?
      - How many sources are cited in the first article?
      - Are there footnotes? How many? Do they include content or just bibliographical information?
      - Does the first article use contractions? First, second person, or third person?
      - What instructions does the magazine give to people who want to submit an article for possible publication?
      - What kinds of research has the writer used for this project?
      - In what ways does your world already resemble the world of the magazine? In what ways does it differ?
5. Examine the following list of *journals* (the usual term for intellectual magazines). It represents the major subject headings found in many lists of undergraduate requirements.

The Arts	
Art in America	*Dance Research Journal*
Artforum	*High Fidelity*
Ballet News	*Musical America*
Dance Magazine	*Musical Quarterly*
	Studio International

The Humanities
American Historical Review
American Literature
American Philosophical Quarterly
Classical Bulletin
Classical Journal
Classical Quarterly
Current History
International Philosophical
  Quarterly
Journal of American History
Journal of Biblical Literature
Journal of the History of Ideas
Journal of Modern History
Journal of Modern Literature
Journal of Philosophy
Journal of Religion
PMLA
Theology Today

The Natural Sciences
American Scientist
Conservationist
Environment
Nature
Science
Sierra: The Sierra Club Bulletin

The Social Sciences
Amerasia Journal
American Indian Culture and
  Research Journal
American Behavioral Scientist
American Journal of Psychiatry
American Journal of Sociology
American Psychologist
Aztlan
Feminist Studies
Journal of Black Studies
Journal of Ethnic Studies
Journal of Social Psychology
Resources for Feminist Research
Society
Women's Studies

**Professional and
Technical Studies**
Administrative Management
American Educational Research
  Journal
Artificial Intelligence
Byte
Harvard Business Review
Harvard Education Review
Journal of Higher Education
Technology Review

a. Choose a journal that seems likely to be willing to publish an intellectual version of the sort of writing project you're working on.
b. Find the journal in your college library.
c. Photocopy an article from a section in which your project might be published. Use the copy as a model for the form of your writing project.
d. Use the questions in step 4 to analyze the context of the journal. What can you tell about the expectations of the readers?

PLANNING YOUR ROLE TO SUIT YOUR PURPOSE

An important part of developing a plan that you can write from is finding a **role** as writer you're comfortable with. By the term **role** we mean the part you act with respect to your reader and your purpose for writing. Communicating with a parent, you may act the part of child, with a teacher the part of student, with a friend the part of confidante, with a younger sibling the part of substitute parent. You'll know that you've found a comfortable role because the writing seems genuine, fluent, and convincing. You find that the words come easily to mind and that it "sounds right" when you read it back to yourself. If you're not comfortable with your role, your writing may become slow and painful and sound awkward to you as you read it over.

Of course your comfort is only half the problem. Your audience also has to feel comfortable. For example, you might take on the role of authoritative elder brother or sister when you write a letter to a sibling, with the best intentions of offering helpful advice. Your sibling, reading your letter, might think, "What I don't need is this kind of pushy interference. I'm not a five-year-old." Likewise, you might strike a comfortable, chatty tone with a paper for a teacher, intending to convey that you like the teacher and enjoy the subject matter. The teacher might look at your work and wonder, "Doesn't this person know the rules about how to write an academic paper? This sounds flippant."

In short, role implies rank. You have a rank with respect to any audience. You write as an equal, as a superior, or as a subordinate. Most people learn about rank as we deal with people of different ages. We treat our elders with respect and formality. We treat our juniors with affection and intimacy. We deal with our peers straightforwardly, with little variation because we perceive writing to peers as similar to writing to ourselves. It won't do to try to use one strategy with all audiences. If you treat everyone as a respected elder, your writing becomes timid. If you treat everyone as a junior, your writing becomes pompous. If you treat everyone as a peer, your writing becomes presumptuous.

Letter writing provides you an example of a kind of writing with a clearly defined role. When you write a letter, you may write as a friend, a dutiful niece or nephew, a graduate thanking someone for a gift, an applicant for a scholarship or a job, a complaining consumer, a person regretfully breaking off a relationship with someone, a child, a parent, or any of dozens of other possible roles.

You find some letters easy to write, while others stress or bore you so that you procrastinate. If you have just discovered that the new sweater you bought through a catalog has a rip in the collar, you can write a letter quite quickly. You feel disappointed, perhaps even wronged, so you write quickly, with confidence that you are doing the right thing. You like the role of "wronged consumer." You can write a letter accepting a job offer just as readily. You are pleased that the employers like you enough to hire you. It's easy to write from the role of "valued new employee." But you may take more care with the letter of acceptance. You still want to impress your new employers.

It may take you longer to write the letter home to tell your parents you have decided to change the major or college they want for you. How much should you tell them? What will they say or do? It's not much fun to write from the role of "child who wants parents' money but doesn't want to take their advice." The letter you write to the friend who moved away last month, with whom you used to spend all your free time, feels awkward, and you don't know whether to send it. You don't like the role of "friend who is trying to pretend that distance doesn't make a difference."

Unfortunately, some of the writing we have to do will make us uncomfortable because some roles are tougher than others to fulfill. If you are uncomfortable in your role, the words don't come easily. You can't say what you think, so you don't know where to begin. A comfortable role enables you to use your knowledge; an uncomfortable role may demand that you do more work to compose and think through what you must write. It's worthwhile, then, to spend some time planning your role.

Role as a Function of Subject, Audience, and Context

If you chose, for example, to write about the adolescent identity crisis (a psychological process during which people in their teens strive to discover who they are and how they differ from their families), you might first decide that an audience of teenagers would want to read about a subject that concerns them so nearly. Your audience would dictate the context for which you wrote: you'd have to find some magazine teenagers read that would be interested in publishing a piece about the identity crisis.

Suppose you decided to try to write for *Rolling Stone*. That decision would define your role pretty clearly. Your role would be "hip commentator," someone who presents the information in an entertaining tone. You would have to be someone who has expertise and experience in the music world. If you can't fit that role, you have two choices. The easier choice would be to reject the topic, but a more satisfying approach would be to find out what you need to know and to play the role of this particular type of commentator. Your readers would expect you to be one of them but with a bit more knowledge and experience. You'd have to approach them as a peer, neither a superior whom they can tune out nor an inferior whom they have no reason to believe.

When deciding whether you have the expertise to write from a given role, you might try imagining a conversation in which a friend has asked you a question like, "Should I wear this?" or "Should I go out with this person?" or "Which college do you think I should go to?" or "Do you think I can get that job?" Questions like those are requests for information about how the questioner looks to you. It's important to have the right kinds of information to answer them as factually and accurately as you can.

Notice how the audience and context define your role. It's easy to rule out "preacher," "psychological expert," "parent," or "just one of the kids." You might get away with taking on the role of the "advice columnist" if you were willing to do some psychological research on the kinds of questions people ask such writers. You'd have to establish that you knew enough about the concept to write about it.

Changing Roles and Changing Purposes

You can see too that your role defines your purpose. Given the subject of adolescent psychology, the teen-aged audience, and the *Rolling Stone* as a context, the most natural purpose becomes to entertain or to inform. Preferably you would entertain your audience by informing them.

Most of us pick a topic first without knowing what role we unconsciously play in relationship to that topic. You may have a great interest in fishing or a particular kind of music and want to discuss some part of that topic. In order to do so, you must decide who you are in relation to the topic. Could you write an essay that would inform *Field and Stream* readers? Could you find enough information so that you would be able to write to those readers? It would not do to try to write to your classmates about fishing since those who love it would not need persuading and those who do not would find your role as fishing expert out of their fields of interest no matter what you said.

Writing about a more generally popular topic like music sounds easier, but again you have to be careful in sorting out your role. Once again, you must be an expert or be willing to become one. No one wants to read about your reaction to last night's rock concert unless you can establish your role as musician or at least as expert on the groups who played, one who has knowledge of other concerts by the group and musical innovations displayed in the concert and who can make informed recommendations about purchasing disks or tapes.

The most dangerous kind of role involves writing to general groups who are older or more experienced than you. Everyone, of course, has to write from this disadvantaged role frequently; we write to teachers, editors, employers, and project evaluators.

Imagine a classroom writing activity that would mirror this kind of role problem. Suppose you decided to write to parents about the identity crisis. That would, of course, put you in the position of writing to a fairly general group who would not tend to trust your authority unless you could present yourself plausibly as an adolescent speaking for other adolescents going through the crisis. Your audience would be immune to appeals to understand the teen-aged viewpoint unless you could demonstrate how such understanding could assist them in accomplishing their own purposes with their children. You'd have to ask yourself, "Do I know what purposes parents have? Do I respect those purposes? Can I help parents without feeling like a turncoat?"

You'd have to think about where such a piece might appear, and you'd immediately run into two problems. First, you might not even know what sort of magazines most parents read. Second, even if you found out what your own parents read, say, by going through the magazine rack at home, you would have to formulate your paper on identity crises to fit the kinds of articles your parents are accustomed to reading. You have to ask yourself the question, "Am I comfortable with the role this topic puts me in as a writer?"

You might be able to refer to the context of your own discussions with your friends' parents or with teachers about identity questions to decide whether you can be comfortable with your role as younger writer to older reader. Your own parents could give you some insights, too, if they and you are far enough from the issues to talk meaningfully about how you acted as an adolescent.

The point is that you must look carefully at whatever role your topic tends to lead you toward and decide whether you can write in that role. Ideally, your role should provide you a strong and safe point from which to write your first draft. In first drafts, your first priority should usually be simply getting your ideas into words, sentences, and paragraphs. If you have two conflicting purposes—for example to tell what you know but to decide what your reader knows too—you may find the drafting process to be slow and painful. A comfortable role allows you to write with a unified sense of purpose.

As you write you may find that you want or need to redefine your role. You may discover that your curiosity drives you to do some original research, perhaps using interviews or questionnaires to discover what adolescents think about separating from their families. Since subject, role, context, and audience are inextricably connected with each other, your new subject matter would require reconsidering the whole approach.

Scientific information might imply an audience of scientists, teachers, or other people who deal with adolescents professionally. Your hip commentator role would go right out the window, and you'd have to get used to wearing a white lab coat. You'd have to familiarize yourself with some intellectual journals, keeping in mind conversations, especially arguments, you've had in intellectual contexts such as classes.

Instead of treading carefully to avoid offending people's feelings, you'd be concentrating more on explaining clearly how you had obtained your information and how you had drawn your conclusions. In your role as expert commentator you would want to establish the accuracy and value of the new information you had discovered.

All writing roles imply a certain relationship with your reader. The question becomes, what role will best facilitate your communicating with the reader? Usually you can answer that question by synthesizing the important elements of your situation as a writer. You can derive your role from the combination of your subject matter, your audience, and the context you've imagined—almost as if you were adding up a column of numbers or solving an equation.

Consider the examples of Corrine and Martha, who both are planning projects which relate to gender roles (the social expectations we learn for typically female and typically male behavior). Each of them writes three letters on their projects or on an experience relevant to their projects. Corrine wants to write an essay on flirting to inform girls who are interested in learning flirting techniques. Martha, an older student with children of her own, comes from a radically different point of view. She writes about the problems of trying to rear her daughters outside the expectations for female behavior that Corrine is trying to teach.

Corrine writes three letters about her twenty-first birthday party. The experience seemed relevant to her project because it involved males and females in a social setting and some risqué behavior. Her first letter—to Kate, her boyfriend's eleven-year-old niece—exemplifies a role in which she writes to an audience of lesser rank. Her second letter—to Brian, a friend her own age—exemplifies writing to a peer. And her third letter—to Lisa, her forty-year-old aunt—exemplifies writing to a superior.

FROM THE JOURNAL OF Corrine Holke

Letter 1

Dear Kate,

Hi there, how are you doing? I am doing fine, and I had a really good birthday last week. Jim got me lots of presents and threw me a surprise birthday party. He convinced me to go out to eat when I wasn't even hungry—but I didn't figure out the plan. When we got home from dinner all of my friends were in my house. It was really neat. Then we went out again and had a lot of fun.

You might like some of the presents that your uncle Jamie got me—he got me three coloring books, crayons, sunglasses, and some perfume. We should play with these things the next time I come home from college. Did you get any fun presents for your birthday? If so maybe we can play with those the next time I'm home—O.K.?

I have to get going—I miss you—

Corrine

Letter 2

Dear Brian,

Hey sexy guy what's happening in good ol' mundane Milwaukee? It can't be as exciting as neurotic Normal, now can it? You do have that maniac up there, but we have the English renegades here—top that! Have you heard about what happened on my birthday yet? If not, you are about to hear about a very strange evening.

It started as a regular typical 21st birthday—you know, presents of champagne, Jack, and Rumplemints. I went to the bars with my usual crowd of men (why bother with women?). Well, about an hour after I got home I was disturbed from my coma (you know how difficult that is itself) by my neighbor Russ—a frat boy who I go out to parties with. He was telling me that the police were here to see me. What in the hell was going on? I just wanted to sleep, but I had to get up to talk to the cops. So I throw on my grandma robe and see what's up. Well, I walk out and see two cops—one Normal cop and a state cop—and immediately think that I am busted for something that has to do with buying alcohol for minors (which I hadn't even done, but all of my roommates were loaded!). It turns out that someone had called 911 from the apartment next door—a female—and they were questioning me about making the call. Well, I hadn't even been next door, so I was confused. The cops were confused too, because they said that the neighbors said that I was with them. Well I was with them, but not in their apartment—at the bars. So I got off the hook, but they arrested my roommate Lynn because she was the only female that was in their apartment. She was freaking, but I didn't know this because I went right back to bed after I was off the hook. She is a really innocent girl and she didn't do it—one of the guys was trying to sound like a girl being assaulted and he didn't even fess up to the crime when he saw Lynn being cuffed.

All in all everything turned out fine. Russ fessed up about a week later, but Lynn still has to clear her name in court. Pretty wild isn't it, but what else could you expect from me?

Love ya,

Corrine

Corrine noted the obvious differences in these two versions of her story. The version for the young child differed in almost every respect from the version for the friend. It may appear that one version was censored and one was not, but in fact, Corrine was merely displaying sensitivity to the interests of her two audiences. She observed, "I felt more comfortable writing to Brian because I know him a lot better than Kate. I like Brian more and have more things in common with him. These feelings enabled me to write more honestly to Brian—not that I lied to Kate, but she would not follow the arrest story, so I just omitted it from the chain of events. Likewise, Brian would just tease me about a surprise party so I didn't tell him."

Corrine's third letter, to her elder aunt, was complicated by her respect for her aunt and her desire to win approval from an older person she respects. After briefly describing the party, Corrine went on to discuss her school work, which suggests that she regards her aunt as a mentor. Corrine comments, "This letter was also easy to write, but I was not quite as comfortable as I was when I was writing to Brian. I look up to Lisa, and I like her a lot, so I didn't want to sound too ditzy when I was writing her. Brian's letter was the easiest to write because I know that he doesn't always judge the way I write—he just likes to hear from me. Comfort with the audience helps the writer feel more at ease when that person is writing."

Letter 3

Dear Lisa,

How are you? I'm doing well. I just turned 21! Your old alma mater is doing fine—still enabling me to get into enough trouble to make me happy. How's Denver? And Gary? And the kids? Good, I'm glad to hear that.

My birthday was really memorable this year—so many things happened! I got a surprise party with lots of champagne, a bottle of expensive cologne (really wasted at the many fine establishments that downtown Normal has to offer) and then my roommate Lynn got falsely arrested for a crime she didn't commit (she was accused of making a prank call to 911 from my neighbors' apartment). The police even came and questioned me about the crime—after I had passed out in my lovely bed! It was quite an interesting evening to say the least. What happened on your 21st birthday? Was it really fun—and were you with Gary? Just curious.

How's teaching going? You will be (or should be) proud to know that I am following in your footsteps and becoming an English teacher. I student teach next Spring (1993) but at this point in time I am not sure where I will be placed. Next semester I teach in the local schools two hours a day for nine weeks—that should be really fun. I have only officially taught once, and that was last spring when I taught *Hamlet* for three weeks at University High School here in Normal. That was fun and scary at the same time—but at least my initial nervousness about teaching is gone. Well, I just wanted to let you know how I was doing since I haven't spoken to you in so long—I'll talk to you at Christmas maybe, until then farewell!

Love,

Corrine

The experience of writing the three letters helped Corrine to define the role that she could assume most comfortably for the project she had in mind, a role that combines aspects of her first two letters, of someone writing as a friend to someone younger. She notes, "The role that I have for a project that I have in mind is advisor to a teen-aged, female audience. I plan to write a paper on flirting and want to direct it towards a magazine like *Seventeen* or *Sassy*. It would be in the form of an advice article on 'How to Improve Your Flirting Abilities.' I will have to take on the role of an experienced flirt, about age 17, who is very good at what she does. I will have to take into consideration that the girls who read this article are probably not good flirts, have low self-esteem, and want to meet lots of boys. This implies that I am sort of an 'expert in the field of flirting,' but I am, so this should not be a hard role for me to take on."

Corrine has taken on, quite honestly, a project which leads her to an audience she likes and a role she finds comfortable. Such articles abound in popular magazines which hew to the typical social expectations of young girls in America. She is aware that she may appear "ditzy" to some people, but she rightly estimates that those people are not part of her audience. Her teacher suggested that the role she took on in the second letter probably was *too* comfortable for her. She needed to recognize that she was also writing for an editor and to use some of the respect she felt for her aunt in writing the third letter.

Corrine's views and the roles she finds comfortable differ in almost every detail from Martha's, as you will see. Martha has rejected virtually every part of the traditional female role. Her three letters concern haircuts for her daughters. She writes the letters to a friend her own age, to her mother, and to a family member half her age.

FROM THE JOURNAL OF Martha Buchanan

Letter 1

Dear Vonnie Mae,

Mary took Laura and Kate out to spend the day. I kissed the girls good-bye and proceeded to use the day (ah, solitude!) as I wished. I trust Mary completely. She and the girls have developed quite a warm, wonderful relationship now that they no longer live together.

Hours later I noticed some strange children playing in my side yard. I was a bit irked; I really don't like the neighborhood children playing in the yard or on the porch without the girls.

A few minutes later, Mary came in. I asked where the girls were. She said they were outside. I looked, but I only saw those strange kids I'd never seen before.

I kept asking where; she kept saying there.

The girls came in, and I'm sure my face fell to the floor. She had taken them to have their hair cut. Fine. She often takes them for a haircut. This time she really took them for a hair cut. They each have about half an inch of hair sticking up from their heads.

The most shocking thing of all is my reaction. You know me, Vonnie. Whatever they want to do with their bodies is their business. They own themselves; I have no right to tell them how to dress or how to present themselves.

Radical Mama. Teach the girls to question, to be themselves, to reject any cultural norm that they feel is wrong.

It's worked pretty well up until now. They make wonderful choices. I don't want my daughters to be unthinkingly, stereotypically female.

I almost cried. It wasn't so bad with Laura. She's never been anything but herself. She's refused to wear dresses since she was in the fourth grade.

But Kate has always been the other side of the same coin. She's been the daughter who chose what we consider more feminine characteristics. She looks like a little boy.

Beyond that, my baby is gone. The small child disappeared with one haircut.

Even as I was laughing at myself and telling myself to practice what I preach, I was so aware of my loss. Kate kind of balanced Laura and me. When I thought that my ideals were being challenged as she wanted to have Barbie dolls and play with make-up, I was totally unaware that she was fulfilling a need within me to conform.

> Love,
> Martha

Letter 2

Dear Mother,

The girls decided that it was time that they did something different with their hair. It is really short. They don't have much time in the morning after delivering papers to get ready for school, so I guess it's all for the best.

It would be nice if you could tell them that you like it when you see them. I know that it will be a little shocking, but there isn't a thing that they can do about it now, except wait for it to grow out.

I really didn't react well when I first saw them. Maybe you can do better.

> Love,
> Martha

Martha comments, "As I wrote to Vonnie, I wanted very much for her to see the irony and humor of my reaction to the girls' haircuts. Because she shares similar values, and has known the girls for a long time, much doesn't need to be said. We've laughed in the past at the girls' ability to call me on my shit.

"As I wrote to Mother, I wanted only for her to not give me a hard time when she sees the girls, and for her to not insult them. I knew that she wouldn't find it too funny, regardless of how I presented it. Her fear (unspoken, of course) is that I'm raising the girls to be that L word."

Martha's letters, as honest as Corrine's but coming from quite a different world, illustrate the same need to select information appropriate to the relationship she enjoys with the audience. The warmth, humor, and irony of the letter to the friend clearly suggest the role of confidante. As she writes to her mother, she experiences the same pressure to select her information that Corrine experienced in writing to the younger niece of her boyfriend. She knows that a parent or grandparent reads with an agenda much different from the agenda of a like-minded friend.

Martha's third letter is written to a young relative, Sherry, who has entered seminary training. Martha knows that the younger person may respond uncomfortably to the subject of the letter, but Martha also knows Sherry well enough as a person to trust that she can write with some of the candor she uses in writing to a close friend.

Letter 3

Dear Sherry,

Hi Sweetheart! How are your classes going? It's funny to think that you're in school to learn to be a minister.

It doesn't seem like so long ago that you were twelve and visiting the girls and me for the summer.

Remember how you idolized Sherrie S.? You thought that she was perfect. She was so pretty; she did everything just right. You wanted to be just like her.

Laura and Kate don't. In fact, they couldn't care less how they look. My friend, Mary, took them out for the day recently and brought back two strange little androgynous children I'd never seen before. In other words, she let them cut all their hair off. I mean all.

Well, they're not exactly bald, but almost. Each of them has about half an inch of hair sticking up.

Remember the talks we had about how you were just as wonderful and just as attractive as Sherrie, but that you were different from her? Remember how I said it didn't matter if you fit into that narrow mold of the perfect woman? Be yourself, I said. Don't try to be Sherrie. Hair and make-up don't matter.

Well, maybe I'll revise that to make-up doesn't matter.

Sherry, my baby left and a grown-up came home. She even moves differently.

You know, Laura and Kate have never idolized Sherrie S. They do think she's pretty, but you've always been the cousin that they wanted to be like. And it's not because of the way you look. It's because of the way you think.

You care about other people tremendously, yet hang on to yourself in the process.

I'm thinking about you. I hope that you have a healthier term than you had last spring.

Love,

Martha

Martha thinks of the third letter as ". . . an affirmation of all four girls. Writing to family is always difficult. I'm not sure of how much muck they have to get through before they can hear what I'm saying. I know that Sherry has listened to a lot of BS about me and my lifestyle. The disapproval is tremendous. Now that she's reached adult status, I hope that she can see through the fear of difference and remember who we were to each other."

Martha's letters are a warm-up for a paper she wants to write about her experiences over a nine-year period with a man named Chuck, someone she met when she was a nursing home administrator, someone who was rejected for being different, and who learned he could call on her when no one else would help.

She plans to tell the story of how the governmental and private social agencies charged with caring for people like Chuck failed him when he needed them most. With such a writing project, she could not assume the very comfortable role of confidante she assumed in writing to her close friend. The people who need to hear her message are people who do not already share her views and experience. Neither could she assume the relatively uncomfortable role of child to mother. She would find she had little to write to someone who she feared would judge every word. She found that the role of advisor she assumed in writing to her younger relative suited her. She could assume that her audience was her junior in terms of knowledge about the situation, but her peer in terms of reasoning ability and moral development. If she took an intellectual stance on the subject, she might write for the audience of one of the journals in sociology.

You can see from our two examples that defining a comfortable role is a critical step in taking on a writing project. Your role can either smooth the path for you and allow you to write what you think, or it can slow you down and force you to soft-pedal and select. Martha had a complex problem. She knew that her audience would be accustomed to the usual arguments concerning the poor in America, and she knew that most people who disagreed with her would have ready rebuttals to the logical arguments she might present. She therefore planned to circle around logical arguments by presenting a case that illustrated her views and letting the case speak for itself.

Oddly, Corrine's role problem is just as complex but for entirely different reasons. Corrine has to be aware that a college teacher can probably read Martha's work and debate her views without questioning the value of discussing them. But many college teachers would advise Corrine to attempt some other subject or to take a more critical view of the assumptions she brings to the subject. In Corrine's case, the subject of flirting dictated a younger audience and a lighthearted role for her to play. Her teacher supported her decision to continue with the project in the interest of giving her some room to develop a sense of herself as a writer and in the context of Corrine's plans to work with some more "serious" projects. Corrine proposed another project involving risqué subject matter—the issue of censorship of art forms. This more intellectual project would balance the one on flirting and help her establish credibility as a writer.

EXPERIENCE

1. Write three letters about an experience relevant to an idea you have for a writing project.
   a. First, think of three people—one half your age, one your age, and one twice your age—to whom you might write a letter about your writing project. Then write letters to two of them.
   b. After you have written the second letter, describe the differences you notice in the ways you approach your two readers. Pay particular attention to your responses as they indicate differences in rank and social expectations. Describe your feelings as you wrote the two letters.
      • Were you more comfortable writing one of the letters? Which one?
      • Did the different feelings cause you to write differently? How?
      • If the two letters were substantially the same, which reader will find the letter more to his or her liking?
      • Why didn't you adjust your information to take your audience's preferences into account?
   c. Write the third letter. When you have finished, once again describe the differences between this letter and the other two.
      • Did the letter turn out the way you thought it would?
      • Which of the three letters was easiest to write?

- Can you explain how your role hampered or helped you to write easily?
    d. Make enough copies of your three letters to distribute to the members of your class. Discuss the following question: Which of the three letters presents the subject matter most appropriately?
2. Define your role for a writing project you have in mind.
    a. Describe the subject matter and audience.
    b. Describe the printed context in which the audience would be likely to read about your subject matter.
    c. Describe the role you would have to take on to write about this subject for this audience in this context. What purpose does this role imply?

PLANNING THE FORM OF A DRAFT

Imposing or Finding a Form?

In the finished and printed draft of a writing project, the form seems obvious. In fact, it looks so final and premeditated that you forget all the messiness that preceded the form. You may wonder why you didn't just look the form up in a book and pour the content in.

We can find forms existing apart from content: application blanks, outlines, tables of contents, and formats for writing assignments. In writing classes, you may have learned to write by imposing certain forms on information: the five-paragraph essay, the process analysis, the research paper, the short story, or the technical report. The people who invent these forms intend them as tools to solve particular writing problems.

For example, the five-paragraph essay helps high school teachers solve the problem of teaching people to be organized and specific. Five-paragraph essays probably serve no useful function beyond the classes in which you are taught to use them. The short story, on the other hand, appears in many different settings, in oral and written forms.

Some writers can write comfortably with a pre-established form in mind. If you know the form and the subject well, you can write efficiently, filling in the outline step by step. But you lose something when you decide on a form before you begin writing. The problem with imposing strict pre-established forms is that you have to sort the information, possibly a number of times, before you know for certain which form works best for a particular subject and reader. If you try to force an idea into a pattern before you are certain the pattern will work, you may find the process of writing to be tiring and more drawn out than you want it to be.

On your way to finding the final form of a project, you should feel free to tinker with forms to see which one works best. You may brainstorm, list ideas, doodle, draw in your notebook, write whatever comes to mind, or draw up and modify a series of outlines. These are all ways of dealing with an idea with varying levels of structure. It's unlikely that the final form of a paper you write will emerge from a beginning plan, but you have to start somewhere.

Two General Kinds of Form

Early in the drafting process, you can begin to see which of two general directions your draft may be taking: toward either the **story form** or the **essay form.** Early in your work with a project, you will find yourself making a decision to head in one of those two general directions.

The story form (also called "narrative") follows a chronological sequence. Under that heading we can include not only fictional works such as novels and plays but also the nonfictional news stories you find in newspapers and magazines, practical descriptions of processes like repair and instruction manuals, textbooks that teach a process (like this one), and anything else that is ordered by sequence in time.

In oral forms of storytelling, the person who tells the story usually holds the floor without interruption until he or she has finished telling the story, assuming that the audience's main question is "What happens next?" In practice, the choice of story form often implies that the writer intends a **monologue.**

The essay form (also called "exposition") follows a logical sequence. Under that heading, we can include many textbooks and scholarly articles; the opinion articles you find on the editorial pages of newspapers and magazines; and anything else that is ordered by logical sequences such as general to specific, abstract to concrete, or more important to less important.

If we are having a debate on an issue with friends, we often stop to respond to their questions or challenges. Think of logical essays as **dialogues** in which friends assert ideas and question and answer one another. When someone using essay form states an idea and then backs it up with proof, imagine that someone in the conversation has responded to the idea with "How do you know that's true?" Likewise, when someone using essay form makes a point and then follows with an example, imagine someone asking for clarification: "Wait a minute! I don't understand. Example please."

The form—story or essay—of a writing project often emerges as you draft and revise a piece of writing, keeping in mind the ideas you have to work with and the audience who will eventually read your work. As you begin, you make a guess about which will work better, a chronological or a logical structure.

Finding Form in Experiences

For example, suppose you've just returned from college to visit your hometown. You've been someplace new, and when you tell your friends about your adventures they listen, even if they've been there, because they're interested in seeing the college through your eyes and hearing about it in your voice. You have memories of facts, ideas, opinions, stories, people, food, and language all mixed together.

Perhaps you took along a diary, and you recorded some impressions. Perhaps you write a letter to absent friends about your experiences. Your friends probably aren't interested in reading your diary, nor are you necessarily willing to let them have a look at the most private part of your reminiscences. So when you write your letters, you choose the parts that you think will interest your friends and that will present you as you want them to see you.

You use story form to tell them about the parties you attended and the person who flirted with you in the sidewalk cafe. It seems natural to quote dialogue, to describe physical appearances closely, and to adopt a familiar, intimate style with your reader.

Your trip has also given you some more intellectual information about college. You present the intellectual information in more intellectual ways. In your letter you use essay form to lecture about the high expectations and the competitive classes; you report a debate about politics you had with someone in your economics class. It seems natural to present logical arguments. You find yourself using words like *furthermore* and *obviously* to introduce your arguments.

The story and the essay both grow out of the same experiences. When you process your experiences, you are constantly making the choice to present information in a relatively personal or impersonal, concrete or abstract, practical or intellectual, emotional or logical way. However you decide to present the fruits of your experience, you know that everything that you say grows from the same root. Behind the stories you tell lie intellectual opinions on which you might write essays. Behind your essays lie the feelings on which you might write stories.

Academic ideas are rooted in experiences we have had. That point is illustrated in the journal entry by Shelly Sellers that follows. Like most students, Shelly has considerable experience writing in the essay form. She likes "grasping for an idea and then searching for evidence to prove it." In one of her classes, Shelly has read an essay which argues that schools should concentrate on teaching "useful information" and abandon their efforts to deal more broadly with social problems. Based on an experience of hers, she has decided she would like to write an essay rebutting the article.

FROM THE JOURNAL OF Shelly Sellers

I have begun to plan an essay based on my rebuttal of an article written on what schools are for. I plan on trying to prove that, based on the problems in our society today, some of the facts in the article are out-dated. I plan to recap the article's highlights, list what the author believes schools are not for and then state facts and my own observations as to why there is a need to rethink some of these notions. I then want to list what the author thinks schools are for. I then plan to cite contradictions in the author's essay.

The experience that has sparked my interest in doing this essay was not a happy one. In high school, a male friend of mine began a trip down the wrong road. He skipped classes and did not bother much with homework. He was a smart kid though, so his grades were still average. The school presented the problem to the boy's mother, who was raising him on her own. The boy's mother tried to discipline him, but it did not work. He got into more trouble at school, but not as bad as some others that I knew of. He was not damaging property, or hitting teachers or anything. His mother wanted to start him in counseling, but she could not afford it on her own. Before she could ask the school for a recommendation, they had expelled him for not serving his detentions by the end of the week. The kid is intelligent, but now living at home without a high school diploma. The school offered the boy no encouragement or help. They got rid of what they perceived to be a troublemaker. In the meantime, the kids who did drugs at lunch time and smoked in the lockerrooms during P.E. were allowed to graduate. I am not saying that the "druggies" do not have the right to their diplomas, but I think everyone should have an equal chance. The schools have to make an effort to get and keep all kids in school, rather than just the model students.

Shelly believes she has observed some practical consequences of the idea that schools should simply transmit information. Her experience with a school that failed to educate a bright child while it graduated a number who just slid by persuaded her that the situation was more complex than the writer had suggested. While she has much work to do, her decision to begin with an idea that grew out of firsthand experience increases her commitment to the project.

Martha has decided to tell the story of a man she knows personally who she feels was victimized by the systems that handle old people. She has a strong argument to make, and she wants to make the argument primarily through telling the man's story. In her journal she recalls a series of incidents involving the subject of the essay she will write.

FROM THE JOURNAL OF Martha Buchanan

Richard Kelley was victimized because he was old, poor, and proud.

If he had had financial resources, he never would have been in a nursing home. Moreover, if he had needed long-term care at some point, he would have been respected by the staff (private pay), and would have had his own bathroom. If he had been a sacred cow, the staff never would have done more than whisper about his sexuality. "Is he or isn't he?" If he had had his own bathroom in his room, he never would have been in Nick's room in the first place.

If he had been a younger man, he would have had the resources (physical and emotional) to live alone. If he had been a younger man, he would have still had value. Public aid recipients in nursing homes are basically throw aways. They receive $30 a month to pay for all their personal needs. How much does a pair of shoes cost?

If he had been less prideful, the staff would not have resented him so much. His pride was a barrier that refused easy access to his thoughts. He was degraded by being in a nursing home, but he wasn't totally destroyed. He rarely shrugged his shoulders in resignation at a situation that he felt was unfair. He made straight for the administrator's office. He was known as one that got you in trouble by the lower staff. If no one was answering call lights, he'd ask why not? If the food was burnt, underportioned, he'd ask for more and better for Helen [his sister].

He made enemies. Many enemies. Yet, he never did anything out of malice. His concern was for Helen. If something happened, he didn't name names. He asked that it not happen again. Unfortunately, part of my job as management was to find out why it had happened in the first place. It is impossible to assure that a situation will never come up again. The most you can do is assure that the event has been investigated and that necessary measures have been put into place to do better. The staff knew that if Richard was unhappy with the food one night and one week later a new procedure was begun, that Richard was the only one who had the self-esteem and the knowledge to have said something.

Balancing Form

Both Martha and Shelly have begun with experiences, and both have planned to make argumentative points. But they have envisioned different courses of development for their ideas. Martha wants to use the story of one particular old man to make her arguments. By telling the story of how the "system" mistreated her friend, she plans to try to invoke anger or pity or sorrow—some form of caring in her audience. Shelly, on the other hand, plans to argue the schools' issue directly. By analyzing and criticizing another point of view, she can set up a kind of debate between herself and the author of the article.

Each of these approaches—the chronological story form and the logical essay form—can accomplish the purpose of bringing about changes in people's attitudes. But once you've chosen either a story form or an essay form, it's important to plan to balance your writing with the form you didn't choose. Martha will have to remember that, after all, she is writing to make an argument. While she is telling the story of her friend, she will have to keep in mind that her audience will want some logical analysis and explanation of the problems in the system that neglects or abuses old people. When writers forget that experience has an intellectual dimension, they produce mindless, egocentric, step-by-step monologues. Stories without ideas don't satisfy the mind.

Shelly, on the other hand, will have to remember that ideas alone do not satisfy a reader either. When writers forget that their ideas are rooted in their experiences, they produce abstract and general, overintellectualized and undersupported lectures, which bore almost everyone. In developing her essay on schools, Shelly will have to keep in mind the original experience that prompted her concern. She may elect to tell part of that story in the process of making her arguments, or the story may remain in the background. Whichever is the case, it will be important for her to keep returning to her motivating experience to remind herself of what reactions she wants to invoke in her reader.

As an example of the way story and essay form go together, consider this book. The general outline of this book follows, chronologically, the authors' version of a college course in the writing process—from warming up, to discovering resources for writing projects, to drafting, to revising, to editing. You could say that we're telling the story of how the writing process works.

But within our roughly chronological form, we often make logical units because we want to encourage you to consider learning as an active experience of conversing in dialogue as well as a more passive experience of listening to a monologue.

The small explanation you've just read begins with the point that each form contains the other. It continues with examples to explain the advantages of telling stories within essays and inserting little essays within stories. We developed the section logically, by making a persuasive assertion and then using examples of two students' writing, assuming that some writers would prefer, perhaps from force of habit, to write straight essay form or straight story form.

We intended to convince writers of the value of crossing from one form to the other, but we knew that some writers would not need convincing. They would probably try what we suggested if we explained it clearly enough. So we added the section you are reading now, using a slightly different logical form, stating our main point in the one-sentence paragraph that begins the section, giving examples of our main point in the next three paragraphs, and concluding with the paragraph you're now reading.

As a final example of this process, consider the following plan Scott McCullough developed for a project on motorcycles (an idea that grew out of a journal entry in Chapter 1). He writes an extended entry (we have printed about half of it), partly because he likes his subject and partly because he knows that the work he does planning will streamline the process of working on this project.

FROM THE JOURNAL OF S. Scott McCullough

What points do I want to cover?

1. Early awareness of motorcycles and the people who ride them, especially after seeing *Easy Rider.*
2. A declaration of my identity as a biker, even in the face of public condemnation.
3. The bikes I have owned and the hardships and pleasures they have brought me.
4. The sense of family among bikers, and how the reality of that subculture differs from the public's misconceptions.
5. The joys of riding: the smell and rush of the air, especially just after a rain; the sting of the rain pelting my face; the gratifying sound and sensation of a strong, willing engine; the triumph over gravity and inertia while slicing cleanly through a curve at speed; the transcendental experience of actually riding into a sunset.
6. The accompanying difficulties of riding: riding at night in a cold rain; baking under the sun in slow traffic; the implicit negative social connotations; the limited accommodations for cargo and passengers; being cut off by idiots in station wagons; the potential for accidental injury.

I want to define the appeal of riding in terms that non-riders can understand. One of my primary goals is to challenge media-reinforced stereotypes and misconceptions about riders and riding. I think a chronological, conversational approach would accomplish this best— not necessarily either a straight essay form or a straight story form, but an introspective narrative along the lines of E. B. White or Thoreau. I want to sneak around my readers' potential biases and charm (?) them with my opinion, not bludgeon them with it. Perhaps a personal account of my riding experiences would express that message without seeming dogmatic. I want to avoid shocking my readers and turning them off, but I also want to appear confident in my beliefs.

The subject is riding; or more specifically, the joys of riding. How can I summarize that subject? Hmmmm . . . maybe: Motorcycling is one of the most satisfying (legal) activities I have ever experienced.

I envision some puritanical control fanatic rebuffing that statement. I know who: The Church Lady from *Saturday Night Live*. What self-righteous pule would drip from that pouting mouth? I can hear her annoying sanctimonious whine now:

"Oh, yes—aren't we just the self-indulgent young miscreant, always recklessly flirting with disaster on the public highways? Don't we realize that those noisy things are *sooo* dangerous? Vicious swine! Terrorizing poor old ladies in their sensible sedans! Oh, you dirty, nasty Philistine!" Some people are just like that—their fears and prejudices will cripple them for life. No matter how hard I might try to sell them on riding, they'll never come around. I accept that. But if I can convince even one person to open their horizons my efforts will have been rewarded. That's all I hope this piece will accomplish: if that one person reads it and shares the joy I feel, I'll have written it well.

I think Robert Pirsig's book *Zen and the Art of Motorcycle Maintenance* was the best pro-motorcycle propaganda ever. Pirsig didn't glorify recklessness or portray his machine as a phallic extension of his ego. He simply wrote about the motorcycle as an extension of his being, as a vehicle for his own self-delivery. I believe he wrote something about the motorcycle he was actually working on being a motorcycle called himself. That's an important realization. His quest for quality and simplicity would have been impossible in a modern luxury car. The very idea seems ludicrous. But since a motorcycle is stripped of everything unnecessary and frivolous, it is a perfect metaphor for the human condition. Its operation depends on the quality and compatibility of its essential components. Humans are no different—if any of the components of a person's psyche are imbalanced or flawed, the person will malfunction. Pirsig's motorcycle functioned while he came apart, but the machine's integrity inspired him to discover a renewed internal balance.

Although I intend to approach motorcycling from a different perspective than Pirsig, I hope to achieve a similar effect.

Scott's reflections on the subject have produced two important results: a potential form for the subject and a context in his intellectual and emotional life. With boundaries set, Scott is now prepared to begin drafting officially. In fact, his plan has shaded over into drafting already. Like

Scott's motorcycle, a good plan makes you want to turn the key and press the starter.

EXPERIENCE

➡WARM-UP

1. Think about whether, in general, you prefer to write the story form or the essay form.
   * What makes you prefer one medium or the other?
   * What experience do you have with the medium you like less?

➡FOR YOUR WRITING PROJECT

2. Plan the form of a project you are about to draft.

   Your plan may take the form of an outline, a list of the points you plan to cover, or a paragraph describing the main idea you hope to convey. Once you have laid out the plan, decide whether its form is logical (essay form) or chronological (story form).
3. Provide balance for the form you have chosen.
   a. If you have planned an essay-form project, describe the experience that, so far as you can tell, is most directly responsible for your interest in writing this essay.

   For example, if your essay happened to be on a political issue like sending American military to the Middle East, you might write about political conversations you had with someone, a debate you heard, or a book you read (yes, books and classes count as experience).

   Try to describe the experience vividly, so that someone who wasn't with you could see what you saw, hear what you heard, and feel what you felt. Don't think that you have to present the information impartially. Feel free to emphasize the parts of the experience that support your opinion.
   b. If you have planned a story-form project, name the subject of the story. Then make a statement about that subject.

   For example, if your story had to do with a love affair, you might say, "People have to listen to make love work," or "You don't know someone until you meet his or her parents," or "Money really does matter."

   Imagine someone you know who might question your assertion, and try to anticipate and answer that person's questions.

   Then explain your reasons for believing what you believe. Feel free to use your experiences as support for your opinions, but try to find outside corroboration for your experiences, such as other people's opinions and books and articles.

PLANNING A WRITING SESSION

If you've had part-time jobs, you know that managers come in all kinds. There's the kind that stands over you seeing to it that you get the work done in exactly the right way, the kind that tells you to do the job and then disappears, the kind that gives you as much responsibility as you're willing to handle, the kind that likes to work alongside you, the kind that yells, and the kind that encourages. All of them have one responsibility in common: they plan the work you will do.

As a writer, you have to be your own manager much of the time. You have to plan your writing sessions in order to make them productive. As your own manager, you have the advantage of knowing a good deal about what makes your employee happy and productive. You also know all about your employee's sneaky tactics for putting off or getting out of work.

Time Management and Setting Composing Rhythms

The manager's first responsibility is to establish and protect your writing time. As a writer, you mustn't allow yourself to schedule classes, work, or social activities in your writing time. You have to think of writing time as the time you have reserved just for you to think your thoughts and get in touch with who you are, a private part of your day that you don't have to share with anyone.

You should protect your time and be ruthless with people who try to steal it. No rule of etiquette, family loyalty, friendship, or romantic passion says that you have to allow people into every hour of your day. If you protect your writing time, you'll find that when you have finished writing, you're ready to talk to people, you're glad to see them, and you have something to share with them. If your friends are used to having twenty-four-hour access to you, they'll be annoyed at first when you tell them that you're busy, but they won't abandon you. Remind them you're not a public utility like the telephone or electric company. You'll probably find that they'll pursue you and value your company even more, since any commodity is valued according to its scarcity.

Another managerial responsibility is seeing to it that the work starts punctually and flows efficiently. Each time you begin writing, you engage a complex series of logical and emotional operations, so you mustn't expect always to be able to sit down and begin writing. In order to get started, you have to get focused, which means finding your place in your project.

It's okay to do a bit of desk-clearing or pacing to help you get started if you're on a regular writing schedule. You can write a quick list or outline to give yourself a sense of how far you've come and what the next step is. You can write a brief letter to someone about what you're working on. Explaining your project to someone other than yourself is often a good way of getting focused.

If you're a good manager, you'll often sit down to begin writing and discover the words there at the ends of your fingers ready to pour out. You'll probably find a rhythm that feels comfortable. Writing rhythms are made up of various combinations of the phases of the writing process. Think of the writing process as consisting of several phases which may occur in any order. In the getting-started phase, you settle into your writing time and place. In the discovery phase, you tinker with ideas and plan out what comes next. In the drafting phase, you translate thoughts into sentences and paragraphs. In the revising phase, you make relatively major changes such as adding and deleting material. In the editing phase, you change small details such as spelling, punctuation, and word choice. Any writing session will comprise combinations of those elements—more planning and less drafting one time, more revising and less editing another time.

There's no correct way to combine the phases of the writing process to form a rhythm any more than there is a single correct rhythm for every piece of music. You know that the rhythm is right if it feels comfortable to you and if it's producing what you want it to produce. As you write, you'll plan what you're going to say, perhaps write steadily for a while, and then need some time to think so you'll read back over your work and possibly revise or proofread a bit. You may then find yourself able to go on. If you don't feel like going on, you may shift to planning in order to regain your momentum. Or you may find that you've finished what you had to write for today. It's likely to be slightly different each time you write.

Earning and Giving Yourself Rewards

How long should you continue writing? It's tempting to say, "That depends," and how long you write does depend on circumstances. If your paper is due in the morning and you haven't started it yet, obviously you've no choice. You keep writing until you're finished, even if you have to pull an all-nighter. If you're sitting in a classroom waiting for the instructor, you have fifteen minutes to wait, and you feel like writing, by all means do it. Stolen writing moments are often sweet.

However, one-night stands and quickies are not the right way to build a relationship with your writing ability. You need to make a commitment to some "quality time," as they say in the marriage books. How much? *Two to three hours three to four times a week is probably a fair amount of time to shoot for.*

You don't need to spend all that time writing your English homework, nor do you need to spend a whole session writing on one project. All kinds of writing count (even personal letters), and going to the library to take notes on books and magazines counts.

Sitting and thinking counts.

Doodling in a notebook counts.

Anything counts as writing so long as you can honestly tell yourself the activity will help you get something written. What's important is to block off time and arrange to plug writing projects and writing-related activities into that time.

During your writing time, give yourself small rewards when you have come to a small stopping point. Get up and stretch, have a cup of coffee, pet the cat, go outdoors and take a short walk, run an errand, read a bit, take your writing to some new and interesting setting, listen to some music, open your mail, or make a phone call—whatever you feel like doing.

Save some bigger rewards for bigger stopping points such as the end of the writing session. Go out to lunch. Have a workout, a run, or a game of handball with a friend. Watch your favorite soap opera. Go shopping.

On the days when you finish a project, celebrate with a major reward. You deserve to go out to dinner and a movie, buy yourself something you've been wanting, take the day off, have a party, or go away for the weekend.

When you're in the middle of a project that takes longer than a week to finish, you may feel frustrated when you reach the end of the week and realize that you've still got a lot of work to do. In such situations, it's a good idea to save some small writing task, such as a letter, to finish at the end of the week. Finishing something, anything, feels good as you close out the week, and it allows you to take some time off with a relatively clear conscience.

We're quite serious about giving yourself rewards. Everyone wants a humane manager who recognizes good work and rewards it.

Procrastination

Occasionally, the authors of this book ask writers to compose a wish list of issues they'd like to discuss, skills they'd like to acquire, or problems they'd like to solve. Procrastination always occurs on the lists of several people in a class. Everyone procrastinates sometimes. We can't give you sure-fire tips for persuading yourself not to put off doing your writing until the last possible moment. However, we can describe to you a pattern teachers see over and over again.

In our experience, *people procrastinate when they would rather not know how much work they really have to do.* Procrastinators would rather deal with the unpleasant consequences of underestimating the amount of work they have to do than act and have their fears confirmed. They usually know exactly what they're doing, and they often wish they could overcome their own impulses and get to work.

As soon as procrastinators find out the due date for a writing project, they visualize a time period, often a weekend just before the project is due, when they will "get serious" about the project. For the present, though, they go on vacation. The deadline may be in a week, in a month, or not until the end of the semester.

As hours, days, or weeks go by, procrastinators think periodically about the project, especially if the teacher reminds them, *but they don't write.* They worry instead. When the worry reaches an intolerable level, they act, but they have little time to ask advice from peers or teachers or to do revising on their own schedules at their own paces. They usually underestimate the time it will take, and they often discover that they lack materials they need. Since they believe deadlines belong to teachers, they then beg for extensions of the deadline.

Another kind of procrastinator adopts the motto of *Mad* magazine's cartoon character, Alfred E. Neuman: "What? Me worry?" This procrastinator basks in sublime self-confidence that everything will come out all right and seems able to shrug off every suggestion to the contrary. Past disasters from procrastination fade when this forward-thinking person considers what he or she knows is possible. The next project can be wonderful. Of course, like the worrier, this procrastinating writer has little time or attention to spare for the actual writing process, preferring to dwell on visions of the perfect paper. Both writers come to the bottleneck of the weekend or the night before the project is due with insufficient preparation to bring a writing project to a satisfactory conclusion. By delaying, they rob themselves of the opportunity to experience the satisfactions that writing affords.

Eventually most writers who procrastinate grow annoyed with themselves and make two small changes. *They learn to plan to use the entire time allotted to complete an assignment, and they learn to act in some small way every time it occurs to them to worry.* They have realized that the only way to find out how much work they have to do is to start doing the work to see how long it takes.

If they need a book from the library, they take half an hour to check out the book when they think of it. They carry it around with them and read snippets of it when they can. If an idea occurs to them, they stop and take another half-hour to jot it down. They worry less because they act on the worry. They immediately develop a sense of how long the project will take, and they set a realistic work schedule. "Let's see. Half an hour to get the book. Two hours to read what I need to. Another whole afternoon at the library. And writing out my notes took an hour. I need about fifteen minutes to talk to my teacher to be sure I have the assignment straight. . . ."

You can do the arithmetic. When you see how long things take, you may find it easier to persuade yourself to act. Procrastinators live in a fantasy world. In their fantasies, they will have plenty of time later to do the work. They know they are capable of doing the work, so they can feel comfortable putting it off. When you step out of the fantasy world, you may get to work.

EXPERIENCE

1. Draw a line to represent the next week beginning from this moment.
   a. In a column under the days of the week, write in the start and stop times of one- to three-hour periods during which you might write.
   b. Choose your times and commit to two or more writing sessions over the next week.

	Mon	Tue	Wed	Thur	Fri	Sat	Sun
AM							
PM							

2. After you've completed each of your writing sessions, draw another time line representing the writing session itself (see next page).
   a. Label the ends of the line with the times you started and stopped writing.
   b. Underneath the line, briefly describe the writing-related activity you engaged in.
   c. Then beneath the writing activity, describe any breaks or rewards you gave yourself.

Beginning   **Ending**

Energy Graph

- -

Writing Activity

Rewards

    d. Finally, using the time line as the base, draw a graph of your energy level through the session.

3. Draw a third time line representing the total time you'll invest in the project.

    a. Assume you will spend roughly the same amount of time each week, experience roughly the same motivation, and produce roughly the same amount of writing. Factor in any interruptions in your routine that you know are coming.

    b. Draw a time line beginning at this moment and extending into the future to the end of the project you presently have underway.

    c. Underneath the line, describe the stages of the project as well as you can imagine them.

    d. Above the line, fill in the dates by which you can comfortably complete the stages. Be realistic!

Beginning   **Ending**

Dates

- -

Stages

Chapter 6
Composing a Draft

_____

_____

_____

GETTING FOCUSED

Here it is—the big moment. You're going to begin composing a draft. You've planned and planned—gone as far as premeditation and logic can take you. The next step is art. As you sit down, plan in mind and pen in hand, you need to focus on the task at hand. You're marshalling all the resources you've gathered and beginning to put everything together.

A deep sigh may be in order at this moment. You feel a little like someone about to swim in deep water. Should you slip in slowly or dive head-first?

You may decide to slip in slowly. To delay the shock, you may pace, sharpen pencils, or tidy your desk. If you've written out a plan, you may read over what you've done to focus yourself on the task at hand.

As words come to mind, you censor them. This idea is irrelevant. That word is too plain. Some other idea isn't original enough. You hear the stereo down the hall and get up to close the door. Eventually, you sit down, write a few lines, and scratch them out. Then you find your rhythm, and the words, sentences, and paragraphs begin appearing on the page. While you are writing, the desire to pace or tidy your desk, to censor your words or pay attention to distractions, everything but the writing itself, submerges. You write steadily for a while.

When you lose focus, are distracted, or stop writing, the thoughts and impulses surface again. You were experiencing the satisfaction of watching the words in your head appear on the paper. Now that's stopped and you have to wait for the words to start flowing again.

The novelist Ernest Hemingway once observed that writing resembles an iceberg in that seven-eighths of it is under water. We're not sure about the fraction, but the authors of this book do believe that the text of any decent writing project rests on a base of ideas and experiences the writer ignores, problems the writer works through without writing them down, and various other "irrelevant" submerged material. In the final product, readers see only the "relevant" surface parts the writer decides to show.

Text and Subtext

Often those distractions—the seven-eighths of the iceberg you don't see—are quite relevant to the *process* of writing though they may be irrelevant to the *product*. When we, as authors, sit down to write, we are often too impatient to wait for a perfectly formed sentence to appear in our minds, so we begin writing right away. The writing usually involves a statement of the problem we are trying to solve. For example, in beginning this chapter, the first author sat down to work and wrote the following:

FROM THE JOURNAL OF Maurice Scharton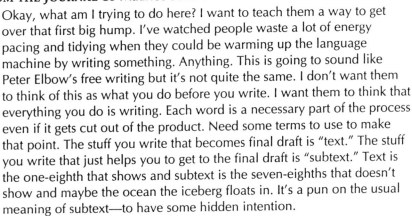

Okay, what am I trying to do here? I want to teach them a way to get over that first big hump. I've watched people waste a lot of energy pacing and tidying when they could be warming up the language machine by writing something. Anything. This is going to sound like Peter Elbow's free writing but it's not quite the same. I don't want them to think of this as what you do before you write. I want them to think that everything you do is writing. Each word is a necessary part of the process even if it gets cut out of the product. Need some terms to use to make that point. The stuff you write that becomes final draft is "text." The stuff you write that just helps you to get to the final draft is "subtext." Text is the one-eighth that shows and subtext is the seven-eighths that doesn't show and maybe the ocean the iceberg floats in. It's a pun on the usual meaning of subtext—to have some hidden intention.

When Maurice had finished with this entry, he shifted smoothly into writing the **text** of the chapter. As he continued to write, he shifted back and forth from writing the very private **subtext** you have just read to writing the more teacherly text you are now reading.

If you try this technique, you may find that you feel less stressed during writing sessions. The worst that will happen is that you'll write more words than you usually do. Putting the pictures and words of subtext onto the page will bring more of your writing process into view and under conscious control. You can **change typefaces,** or hit the [bracket key] or the CAP-LOCK KEY, or change to a different sort of pen to make it easy to find and delete the subtext later.

It may be that your subtext has to do with some problem entirely unrelated to the paper you are working on. If you're mad at your "significant other," you're going to find it hard to concentrate on the article you've been wanting to write about world hunger, and in a case like that, a wise course would be to write about the personal problem that's bothering you in order to get it off your mind. Then perhaps you'll have some attention to spare for the hungry.

You may even find that you're able to make productive use of the energy from something like a personal quarrel to get your work done. (That's all right so long as you don't use work to avoid solving other life problems. You should also be talking to friends or to counselors about life issues that intrude on your writing.)

It may seem like misbehavior to you to take control of the page and write whatever comes to mind on it. Good. A little misbehavior often leads to creative insight. Pretend you're an anarchist. Stage a revolutionary raid on the printed page. It belongs to you.

If you can't think of a word, you can draw a blank line, skip it, and go on. If you want to write something silly, irrelevant, or funny, you can go ahead. If you suddenly become interested in working on something else or in skipping ahead or back to some other point in the present project, you can do that too. You can also abandon drafting per se to do some outlining and listing if you need to stop and sort out your thoughts.

Nonlinear Subtext

Once you decide you own the page, you can use it however you please. You can even use it to express yourself in nonlinear ways. By **nonlinear,** we mean ways of thinking that abandon traditional subject-verb-object, paragraph, and outline structure. Sometimes the familiar mental technology of writing becomes an impediment rather than an enhancement to your thought. At such times, you can close your eyes and jump into the unknown—not without a parachute of course. We have two kinds of parachutes in mind—clusters and matrices.

Clusters

If you're at all a graphically oriented person, you may find that a **cluster** helps you to think more clearly.

Clustering involves starting with a single idea that's important to what you're writing about. The single idea becomes a sun around which you allow a solar system of related ideas to evolve. So, for example, if you were writing about children's literature, the cluster might look like the one on page 139.

Clustering, as you can see, closely resembles doodling. But it's focused doodling. This kind of play serves serious purposes. The central location of one idea represents its importance to the writer. As the writer begins to associate more and more ideas with the central idea, he or she will frequently turn up relevant information that was stuck at the unconscious level.

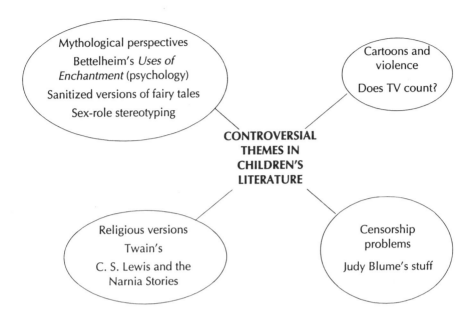

Even more importantly, laying the information out in a graphic format on the page enables a writer to see patterns of association that sentence and paragraph form obscure. With the cluster above, the writer has revealed that a new center is forming around mythological perspectives on children's literature. So the cluster has helped the writer to take an important further step in focusing on (or narrowing) the subject of the project. After you've finished playing with the cluster, you may find that you're ready to compose an outline using the ideas you've generated, write some verbal subtext, or perhaps return directly to writing the text of your project.

Matrices

A **matrix** (singular of *matrices*) is a more logical form of nonverbal subtext. Like a table in a science book, it has both horizontal and vertical sets of important ideas. It's useful for helping you to categorize and cross-reference information. You'll often find that interesting and surprising questions and connections begin occurring to you when you build a matrix.

A matrix takes a bit more thought to set up than does a cluster. Matrix building is a little like planning a party. For a party, you try to put together some people who will be able to talk to each other and generate some interesting and lively conversation. In building a matrix, you are trying to do the same thing with ideas.

You begin with a pair (or more) of related important ideas. For example, if you were working on a project about children's literature, you might wonder about the ways writers deal with sexual themes for children. If it occurred to you that sex was an adult theme, you might decide that adult literature would be a productive aspect of the matrix.

You could generate some interesting ideas by comparing and contrasting adult with children's literature, but you could focus your thought more if you added another dimension to your inquiry. Suppose you guessed that one difference might be how explicitly sex is presented. You might generate a matrix like the one below.

SEXUAL THEMES

	Children's Literature	Adult Literature
EXPLICIT	Ask Prof. Allen?	Romantic novels, erotic literature
IMPLICIT	Rapunzel, Sleeping Beauty	Pre-20th century mostly?

By asking yourself questions, you generate both answers and more questions. Looking at the first **cell** (the upper left box in the matrix), you would ask yourself what you knew about explicit treatments of sex in children's literature. You might decide that you needed to talk to your professor about that question. Implicit treatments of sex in children's literature would surely involve fairy-tale characters such as Rapunzel and Sleeping Beauty.

The cells under the "Adult literature" heading might make you wonder whether *anyone* in the twentieth century adult literature treated sex implicitly instead of explicitly. If you know anything about children's literature, you'll see that we haven't begun to exhaust the questions and answers this matrix generates.

We might expand the matrix to give it three dimensions, and we'd find, oddly enough, that three dimensions would make it more, not less, focused. Suppose we decided to subdivide children's literature into literature for adolescents and true children's literature. We might also subdivide the "explicit" category to distinguish "frank" treatments of the subject from "graphic" treatments of the subject.

That might produce the following matrix.

	Children	Adolescents	Adults
GRAPHIC	Nonexistent?	Rap lyrics	Erotica
FRANK	Beauty and the Beast	Judy Blume	Mainstream
IMPLICIT	Snow White	School library	Pre-20th century

Filling in the matrix was slow work but worthwhile. As a result of the work, the writer can see a new and narrower focus on the subject. The second and third rows, labeled "frank" and "implicit," suggest to the writer the idea of investigating whether present treatments of sexual themes in "school library" adolescent literature resemble treatments of sexual themes in pre-twentieth century adult literature. Do schoolbooks promote nineteenth century sexual values and attitudes? The writer can find out by comparing some representative samples of both periods, perhaps the best sellers of their respective time periods.

Reading to Rediscover Your Focus

Having done some nonlinear, nonverbal work with subtext, you may find yourself ready to begin producing text again. At this point, you may want to read back over what you have read. Reading to get focused has some advantages. You can get your ideas in mind, tinker with your plan, revise for content, and even correct mechanical errors as you go.

Once you've written part of a draft, you may reread to start your next session. In this way, you'll go over the beginning every time you begin writing. The beginnings of most essays would profit from this sort of attention since this is where you either capture or lose the interest of the reader. You also recapture the tone of what you were saying, and, not least of all, you get to admire your work.

Reading to find your focus does cause some problems.

A reasonable amount of time can be spent reading back over your work, but many people squander their best creative energy in the fiddling with words and phrases that inevitably accompanies reading back over their work. There are at least four pitfalls in reading back over a paper to renew your focus.

First of all, you're reading or revising rather than generating new material, so you may arrive at the point where you left off and feel like reading some more instead of drafting. This problem will become more and more pronounced as the project grows longer and longer. If there's no one around, the authors of this book sometimes discreetly talk to ourselves: "All right. This is great fun, but you're not getting anywhere. What do you feel like writing?"

Second, you may get trapped in revising. If you always begin by reading back over the piece you're working on, you will always find some little detail that you can change. You can get started on those details and wake up an hour later to find that you've made no headway on finishing the draft, that you've developed a couple of paragraphs way out of proportion with the rest of the essay, and that you feel frustrated with yourself. In such a case, you have to tell yourself that you would have had to do the revision anyway and perhaps you needed more time to think about what came next. You will sometimes, but not always, be convinced by this argument.

Third, you may find that the material gets stale as you read over it and over it. If writing a paper extends over a week or more of writing sessions, you'll be more and more tired of the paper, and it may begin to sound like nonsense. Changing the job around a bit will help. You can give yourself some other small writing project to do or spend some time in the library doing research.

Fourth, reading to start writing is time-consuming. You will have a tendency at first to overestimate the amount of time you can persuade yourself to work or the amount of work you can get done in a session. If you've been writing regularly the last few days on a project, you may not need to reread simply to get going. Generally speaking, you can pick up the context of what you were saying by reading the page or two you wrote most recently. Then you ought to be able to begin writing.

If you always spend a significant amount of your writing time rereading your work, you should ask yourself whether you're avoiding your real work. Try writing some subtext to express and order your thoughts. Once they are on paper, they will become more controllable.

An influential theorist of language and psychological development (Vygotsky, 1938) has suggested that all language development begins with the inner speech we have called "subtext." As children learn to externalize this inner speech, they develop mature abilities with language. Faced with new subjects, new audiences, and new forums for our writing, we all tend to regress, to return to that muttering inner speech that preceded full participation in communication. But unlike children, we can use our writing ability to work our way back toward clear and coherent expression.

EXPERIENCE

Think of a project you have been meaning to get started on. Start an internal dialogue by focusing the subtext on the problem at hand and use it to help yourself write text.

1. Begin by writing down a pertinent question.
   - What do I know right now about this topic?
   - What do I need to do to write a paper like this?
   - What made me interested in this topic in the first place? or
   - What adjustments do I have to make in my schedule to get this done?
2. Write an answer to the question. As you write, other questions will probably occur to you. Simply put them down as you think of them, and continue writing. Keep writing about a question until you are no longer interested in doing so, or until you have decided on how to take the next step in dealing with your assignment.

3. If you feel like shifting into outlining, listing, clustering, matrix building, or writing text (a part of the actual paper), do so. Once you're back to making progress on your project, you can continue writing until you feel like stopping, or you can shift into subtext again. The important point is that you are in control. You can write as long as you feel like writing.

FOLLOWING YOUR INTEREST

Have you ever done something impulsive which turned out better than you could have hoped? Perhaps you plotted and planned, trying to control all the consequences, before suddenly deciding, "I'm just going to do what I want."

In this section we will deal with the impulses you experience as you write. Our goal will be to help you to notice, evaluate, and act on the moments of inspiration that occur while you are drafting. If you have done your preparatory work properly, you will find that writing usually produces moments of discovery that lead you in new and interesting directions.

An important motivational key to drafting is remembering that, once you have finished your planning process, you can start drafting at any point that interests you. If a middle paragraph of your project pops into mind as you sit down to write, by all means start with a middle paragraph. If you find your mind skipping ahead or back to other points in the project, follow your interest. There will be time to sort out any problems you skip over. You can feel perfectly free to work on a project in the order that interests you, the order that makes it easiest for you, or in any order whatever.

If you are able to write from outlines, you may derive satisfaction from working straight through the outline. But you may also find that writing the outline gives you permission to write the way you want to. Knowing that the concept of your project has been laid out, you may find it comfortable to skip from one part to the next as time, convenience, and, above all, interest dictate. If you prefer to just dive in and write, you can start something and then start something else, skipping around until you find what you're interested in.

Following Impulses

Giving yourself permission to follow your interest helps keep your ear tuned to your internal conversation. As you write you'll "hear" ideas popping up in your head in an all-at-once way (Berthoff, 1981). As words and ideas pop up, they may distract you from the line of thought you're pursuing in a way that's reminiscent of the noise you hear when you're talking in the midst of a group of people. If you have strong powers of concentration, you learn to tune out those noises so that you can stick with what you're doing, but of course in tuning out the noise you risk missing some information, which may have the same effect as turning up the car radio to drown out the knocking sound in the engine.

Especially when you're writing, it's important to keep one ear open to the other voices. One of them might be saying, "I've got a great idea." If you say, "I'm busy right now, but I'll get to you in a minute," there's a good chance that the voice won't be there when you get around to listening. And the voice will eventually stop trying to get your attention.

Another effect of giving yourself permission to write the middle first is that you stay in touch with a certain feeling that tells you you're on the right track. "A certain feeling?" you ask. "What does that mean?"

People who do research into the writing process call it a **felt sense** (Perl, 1980). This feeling guides you in deciding what to do next. You might think of it as curiosity, interest, or impulse.

When you read the table of contents of this book, for example, its order looks natural, as if we wrote it to an outline. Actually, our composing processes involved following the felt sense through a complex labyrinth of associations. The whole journey started on a March morning in 1989 as one of the Experiences. In its final form that Experience is in Chapter 2 under the heading Wanting to Write.

At the time, it seemed that Wanting to Write and a few other experiences might be all there was, but when that experience was written down, we had a felt sense that there was another one wanting to be written down, then several more, then some explanations to lead into the experiences, then some more practical explanations having to do with writing skills, then several sections on evaluating writing, and so forth.

The felt sense would occasionally disappear, but usually stopping for a moment and listening to the internal conversation or engaging in an external conversation with students or colleagues would bring back the feeling.

Following the felt sense is sometimes scary because you can't really tell where it's leading you next, and you're afraid some of the time that you're getting lost. Sometimes you do get lost, but more often you find yourself writing about what interests you.

Of course, giving yourself permission to follow your interest—to listen to the internal conversation or follow the felt sense—may mean that when you have finished writing you have a rather disorderly draft. That is the price you pay for writing about an idea you are still groping to understand. With more familiar ideas, you will probably find that the draft comes out more neatly.

In this chapter, for example, the section you're now reading came out quite readily in one sitting in the form you're now reading it. The preceding section, on Getting Focused, took several sessions and a good deal of rearrangement. We try to be philosophical about following the felt sense down bumpy roads. We tell ourselves that we're doing two things at once—finding out what we think *and* writing what we want. Naturally this process takes work.

To some very good writers, the notion of following the felt sense sounds like madness. Such writers have invested considerable time and energy in developing a set of step-by-step procedures that produce writing for them. When we work with these writers, we don't presume to tell them that they should abandon trusted methods, but we do urge them to loosen up to the degree they find comfortable. If they need to stick to their outlines, we suggest leaping into an introduction where it interests them, perhaps by telling an anecdote, rather than starting with a statement of the topic and then an outline of the paper. We also sometimes suggest writing the conclusion first and building backward toward the introduction. The idea is to stimulate the writer's interest in the subject matter—partly to provide the writer a rewarding experience of writing and partly to provide the reader occasional diversions from the predictable rhythm of main-idea-followed-by-example.

EXPERIENCE

For a project you're working on, identify the part you're most interested in writing. Never mind for the moment whether that part occurs next in your outline.

1. Skip to the point where the most interesting part begins and draft until you run out of interest. If, during the drafting, you think of some other interesting bit of writing to do on this or any other project, interrupt yourself and follow your interest.
2. As you write, try to nurture your interest a bit. Write at a comfortable pace. Slip into note taking, outlining, drawing, or some other method of discovering ideas if you feel like it.
3. Once you've run out of interest, stop. At a later time, evaluate the experience.
   - Did you write more, less, or about the same amount as you usually do?
   - Did you spend more, less, or the same amount of time?
   - Did you find more, less, or the same amount of satisfaction in writing?

RESEARCH DURING THE DRAFTING PROCESS

Someone has probably introduced you to the idea of the research paper. Generations of students have learned that you go to the library, open a box of 3" x 5" note cards, talk to the librarians, and find the bibliographies. Then, on the note cards, you write down the author's name, the title of the article or chapter, the name of the magazine or book, the volume number of magazines and the publisher of books, and the page numbers. If the bibliography summarizes the article, you add a note about the summary.

Once you have found a lot of likely looking sources, you look through them until you find material that interests you, you take notes, and then you start putting everything together to make the research paper.

In this line of thinking, research is like going on an expedition to do archaeological work in Egypt. You hope to find treasure, but even if you don't stumble onto King Tut's tomb, you're willing to do the work because you will profit from the research process. You dig about in some ruins and find artifacts in no particular order, some of them broken into pieces. You're not sure what they mean, so you return with the artifacts, patiently fit the pieces together, and set your findings up in an exhibit in your museum.

This sort of challenge appeals to some people for some kinds of writing projects. You have a vision of what you may find, and you take a detective's pleasure in locating the pieces and fitting them together.

Research to Answer Specific Questions

But some people blend research into the drafting process. To those people, stopping to do research during a writing project feels like having lunch with a friend on a busy day. The information nourishes them, and the change of pace clears their heads.

To the research-as-lunch crowd, doing research is something that happens on any paper, not because you set out to "do research" but because in the process of writing about something that interests you, you find that you need to know something that you don't know now. Writing the paper is like talking through an issue with people you know, and doing the research is simply sitting down with an informed person to ask his or her advice about a specific question you've encountered in working on your project.

If you approach research from this perspective, you find that every paper is potentially a research paper. When you're stuck for an answer, an example, or a statistic, you simply turn to another source for the answer as you would turn to someone who knew the subject matter better than you for advice.

Sometimes it works out that you begin with a paper that you have already done some writing for, perhaps even a completed paper from an earlier assignment, and you do research with some specific goals—a certain point that you want more support for or a section that you need information to write. Having a particular goal in mind has some advantages. It considerably narrows the ground you have to cover when you do the research. You're not doing a general search on a subject, so you won't spend weeks working out your research plans, accumulating materials, and taking notes. You will have a particular set of ideas you want to insert into your project at a particular point, so you will be able to go with a shopping list.

Suppose you were doing a research paper on Roman orgies. "Let's see. I need something that describes the way meals were organized in patrician Roman households during the reigns of Caligula and Claudius. I also need to know what the plebes were like at that time."

"I'm pretty sure that the upper class were not the only ones indulging in orgiastic behavior, but I need to know. I think it'll turn out that a lot of the orgiastic behavior was food-related."

In this case you might go to the library to find historical sources on the Roman Empire. You'd probably run into Gibbon's *Rise and Fall of the Roman Empire.* You might decide to read a novel called *I, Claudius,* written by Robert Graves. Reading fictional treatments of history often helps you to get a better feel for the period. You might then discover that the Public Broadcasting Service (PBS) had produced a series of television programs based on the novel. Your three sources would give you three interpretations of the period for three different audiences.

You might interview a teacher or a librarian to get an expert opinion. In fact, as a student you shouldn't try to choose research materials entirely on your own. You'll need to talk to your teachers and to the librarians to find out not only what sorts of materials are appropriate but also what sorts are available in your library. For an intellectual audience, you should focus on scholarly journals and books that have been published by university presses. The information in those sources is likely to be more reputable than the information you find in popular press books and magazines. A rule of thumb for finding scholarly information is that if your source is listed in the *Reader's Guide to Periodical Literature,* it is probably *not* scholarly. Ask your teacher to recommend scholarly resources, and ask your librarian (not a student helper but a professional librarian) to help you identify the professional bibliographies (also called indexes) that list materials relevant to your writing project.

Some topics require not only reading in the library but also dealing directly with the primary sources of information about a subject. You might acquire primary source information

- by talking with people to get their opinions through *interviews and questionnaires*
- by *attending a concert or play or visiting a restaurant* to write a review;
- by *visiting schools, offices, or dormitories* to find out how they work;

- by *trying out new processes* like assembling a computer or teaching a lesson in order to learn how to perform the process more effectively; or even
- by *trying to set up scientific experiments* to test a hypothesis.

In consultation with one of her peers, Gwen Springman worked some research time into the process of drafting an article on rape.

FROM THE JOURNAL OF Gwen Springman

I discuss in my paper the rape story of Mary Vincent. One point of this that I could possibly expand is the fact that her rapist has filed a complaint against her and is taking her to court. I would like to do more research and find out how many other victims have found themselves in the defending position.

Shelly suggested that I do some research on the role of plea bargaining in rape trials. I like that idea a lot.

I don't believe that I will have much problem incorporating these ideas into my paper. For the first one, I did mention it briefly in my story about Mary so I will just simply add the research on counter civil suits right into my paper. This should be pretty smooth. However, I am not quite sure right now where I would put the information about plea bargaining into my paper.

I could call a rape crisis center and a lawyer to discuss these point with them.

Gwen has set out a tidy and workable plan for using research while drafting. She has accepted a good suggestion from a classmate and has originated an idea of her own. Her potential sources include both printed material and people to interview.

Reading Research Materials to Stimulate Ideas for Drafting

By this time in your life, you will have established reading habits. We therefore need to spend some time considering the sort of information your reading produces. If you like reading, you may want to curl up in the library with your research as if it were a mystery on a rainy afternoon.

That sort of reading is fun, but it may not get you the information you want. The reading you do with research materials is really a form of writing. This form of reading has a social purpose—to help you explain yourself to someone else.

You compose the meaning of the text you are reading in the context of the ideas you are writing about. As you work through a source you have picked up, you are composing your writing project, working your way through the ideas for the paper you are writing, so you need to write down what you are composing.

You can reinforce the sense that you're writing rather than reading if you put yourself in your writing posture.

Instead of sprawling in a comfortable chair or lying down as you do when you read, you can prop the book open; take down the title, author, and place and date of publication in a notebook; read and take notes when you find something interesting; and write down what you're thinking about the reading as you go. You can keep your comments separate from the summaries and quotations as you work by putting brackets around your comments.

When you run out of interest in your reading, stop taking notes and start skimming. If nothing interesting turns up, skip to the table of contents or the index to see if anything there interests you. If you find something, continue. If you don't, stop.

At that point, you can either declare yourself finished for the day or go to another source and pick up the idea where you left off. You'll probably find that certain sources provoke a lot of note taking and commentary on your part. They may be the first ones you read if the subject is unfamiliar to you, or they may be sources written by someone who explains the issues in just the right way. Don't worry about taking a lot of notes from one source and fewer from other sources. There is no recipe for learning or writing. You simply work with what you find.

You may find that taking notes as you read makes you impatient or drowsy. You may feel the desire to jump up and do something else—clean your room, watch TV, make a phone call, or go for a run.

You probably expect us to tell you to stick with it, resist those distractions, and get your work done. We're certain you've heard that sort of advice before, so we won't bore you. Instead of fighting your impulses, we suggest that you interpret them. Ask yourself what it means if reading makes you want to do something other than sit and read or take notes. Why are you experiencing impatience or drowsiness? Why do you feel fidgety or talkative?

It might be that you're avoiding work you need to do. We think you know yourself well enough to know when that sort of thing is happening. But there can be other reasons for those feelings.

Your writing ability may be asking you for some time to process the information you're taking in. If that's the case, the right thing to do is to get up and move around, or lean back and catch a quick nap. When you are ready, do some more reading and note taking.

In short, give yourself permission to do whatever you feel like doing to get through the reading. Yes, it will take longer to get the job done, but probably not much longer than it will take if you reread the same passage three times because you can't pay attention to it. Next time, you'll be a little more realistic about how long it is actually going to take to do your reading.

If, having allowed yourself some distracted time, you still want to catch a plane to Zanzibar when you think about doing your reading, you probably need to consider the idea that you're working on the wrong part of this project. Perhaps you're longing to do some more drafting or to show your work to someone to get advice.

Or it may be that you are working on the wrong project entirely. It's easiest to write the sort of material that gives you pleasure to read. If you ask yourself what you've been reading recently (and don't say, "Oh I couldn't write that sort of stuff"), you may be surprised to find that your reading interests are leading you where your writing ability ought to go.

Gwen Springman tried the reading technique we've described to read an article on the idea that rape suspects should be forced to submit to AIDS testing. She reported that reading in the writing mode felt awkward and distracting at first. Despite the awkwardness, she found that reading this way made her reading more usable in her writing.

Problems and Solutions in Library Research

If you do research with a particular goal, you have a problem to deal with—namely that only a few resources will do. When you go to the library with specific needs or preconceptions about what you're going to find, you have to be prepared to get some expert assistance from your teacher and the librarians, perhaps even from teachers who are specialists in the area. You should take a draft of your paper with you when you go seeking help.

If you can show a librarian or a teacher the argument you're trying to make or the idea you're trying to explain, he or she will be able not only to suggest some places to look for the information you're trying to find, but also to suggest some ways of handling the problem if your source doesn't work out.

Possibly the most disconcerting result of doing research is discovering that you were wrong about something or that you can't find materials to support the case you're trying to build. If you've built up a commitment to an idea only to discover that you can't prove it, you have experienced what everyone who does research of any kind experiences more often than not. Having found that you were wrong, you wonder whether you can finish your project at all. The answer is "yes."

At the core of any research project is the story of your thought about the idea. You begin with certain preconceptions and some evidence. You use those materials to build a guess, a hypothesis about a state of affairs.

Then you do some reading to learn whether anyone else thinks the way you do.

All those imposing-looking references, footnotes, interviews, and descriptions of experimental procedures that you find in scholarly work often simply record the experience that the writer had in discovering some information and in working through what he or she thought about the information. The development of your thought is as interesting to a reader as are the conclusions you are able to reach. So even if you aren't able to support the point you had hoped to support, you can record your response to the sources you found and explain how they altered your thinking on the matter.

By now you're aware that incorporating research sources into your writing increases your credibility as a writer. There are still more important reasons than credibility for working with research. For any subject you can imagine—from Roman history to current gender-related issues on campus—there is an ongoing conversation in print. When you sit down and begin writing, you have entered the printed conversation, and you should make yourself and your readers aware of that conversation by finding out what others say, summarizing it, and reacting to it as you do in normal conversation. Since your conversation is occurring in the context of a college course, you should include the scholarly voices you are hearing (Porter, 1992). As you write in college, you should find it natural to mention the names of philosophers, biologists, psychologists, artists, literary critics, and all the other scholars you encounter day in and day out. If you begin making the effort, you'll eventually find it feels perfectly natural to begin a sentence with a reference like "As the psychiatrist C. G. Jung noted in *Man and His Symbols . . . .*" As you write, whenever an idea occurs to you that you have found in reading, mention the source when you mention the idea. Don't feel that you have to stop and look up the rules for citing sources right this moment (though you can, if you want to, by referring to Chapter 12 of this book). Just mention the source and go on with your explanation. You'll find it's quite satisfying to begin using that education you're spending so much time and money to acquire.

EXPERIENCE

1. Include research in the process of drafting a project. You'll need a draft of a project you're working on now.
   a. Read through your draft noting places where you could write more if you did some outside reading.

      In the margin of the draft, put a plus sign everywhere you can see the possibility of expanding, clarifying, or supporting a point with research. On a separate sheet, explain why you think research would be useful at those points ("I think a reader might wonder whether it's constitutional to force people to take a blood test. Has anyone written anything about that?") and what kind of research you would expect ("I'd expect to see a reference to a heavyweight legal authority here or else to a powerful feminist organization. For the opposition, I would expect some group like American Civil Liberties Union to be cited.").

b. Trade papers with someone in class and add your suggestions for expansion by research.

Again use plus signs to note points in the manuscript thtn might be changed by research. On a separate sheet, explain why you think the research would help and what kind of research you would expect to find.

Mention anything you've read that has to do with the subject of your peer's writing project.

c. Develop a plan for incorporating the information you hope to find into your project. Detail the specific points you will have to expand, rearrange, shorten, or delete. Include the names of people you can call or talk to to get advice about where to find resources.

2. Read some research materials to stimulate ideas for drafting. You'll need a book or an article relevant to the project you're working on now. Consult with your teacher and your librarian to secure a selection you can use.

a. Arrange a comfortable situation so that you are in your regular writing position but can see the source and reach to turn the pages. At the top of a blank page, write the author's name, the title, and the place and date of publication, and then begin reading at whatever point interests you.

As you read, stop to take down information you'd like to remember. When you've taken down something, jot the page number at the end of your note.

When you have a reaction, write it down too, but signal that it's your commentary by bracketing it, parenthesizing it, single-spacing it, or some other maneuver. "This guy is absolutely wrong. I'm positive I read in *Science News* that the apes . . . ." "This is a great idea. I can see exactly how this fits in with the theory that . . . ."

If you feel like returning to your project to do some more drafting, go ahead. Continue writing until you run out of interest and then pick up your reading where you left off.

When you're finished, give yourself your usual reward for writing.

b. At another time, come back to your source and read a different chapter, article, or section without taking notes.

After you are finished reading, answer the following question: What differences do you notice in your interest in reading and your experience of writing about the research material in the two parts of your source? (There are probably advantages and disadvantages for you in both ways of reading. Try to decide what each way is good for.)

3. Read through your draft to incorporate references to research.
   a. Wherever you can recall the source of an idea, add a reference such as "According to _____" or "Studies by _____ have shown that" or "Research in _____ suggests that."
   b. Using phrases like those in step a above, incorporate explicit references to the reading you completed for the second part of this experience. Refer to Chapter 12 for instructions in how to cite a source and create a Works Cited entry.

SHAPING A DRAFT: BEGINNINGS

Your goal with a draft is to get it into shape so you can show it to a reader to get advice about how to revise it. During your early drafting stages, it's probably not necessary to spend a lot of time and energy tidying up misspellings and working on punctuation. Instead, you should concentrate on working through the whole structure of the project you have in mind. The more complete the draft is, the more clearly the reader can envision what you're trying to accomplish, and, of course, it's only common courtesy to give your reader the best draft you can produce at the moment. At a minimum, your draft should have a clearly recognizable beginning, middle, and end.

To help you to create a complete draft, we're going to focus on beginnings in this section and endings in the next section of this chapter. Writers often tell us that they are unsure how to introduce and conclude a draft, so they simply get started and then stop. If you stop and think for a moment, you'll realize that introductions and conclusions occur every day in the context of your oral use of language.

Recall a situation in which you introduced someone. Think through the experience. What did everyone say and do? How did you feel while making the introduction? What did you hope to accomplish with your introduction? Were you successful? Perhaps you were lucky enough to think of just the right introductory tactic. But it's also quite possible that after an awkward moment, some common interest, experience, or attitude emerged from the conversation. At that moment, the real introduction occurred: the two people made a connection with each other.

Now think about your experience of composing introductions for papers you write. Can you see any relationship between introducing people to each other and introducing your writing to someone? Can you see any relationship between your goals in making introductions and your goals in writing introductions? Do you sometimes find your introduction after you've finished the project? Writers often discover their real connection with the reader only after writing for a while. In practice, then, the introduction often occurs somewhere in the middle or toward the end of the draft. This section explains the function of an introduction and presents guidelines for reshaping a draft to locate effective introductory material at the beginning of the draft.

Beginning the Conversation with a Reader

Many people handle the personal greetings and introductions with a recipe—a pat phrase of some kind. "How do you do?" "Pleasure to meet you." "Charmed, I'm sure." "Hi." "What's happening?" "Yo, dude." "I'd like you to meet Polly." "May I present Mr. Tipton." You can bow deeply, kiss someone's hand or cheek, tip your hat, wink, shake hands, hug, smile, nod, stand up, make eye contact, or use any one of a hundred gestures or remarks to initiate conversation with someone.

You can also greet people in problematic ways. On her telephone answering machine, one of our friends, a rather dynamic person, has recorded a message which insists that callers not hang up without leaving a message just because they have gotten her machine instead of her. "Don't be a wimp," she says. "Grow up and join the twentieth century."

When we introduce our friends to each other, we take their peculiarities into account. We don't introduce the "Don't be a wimp" friend without letting the other person know that she comes on a little strong at first but is really all right. A shy friend gets a bit of preparation for the experience. "She likes French films. Talk to her about the film course you're taking."

Writers encounter these social problems when they draft a piece. You have this writing project that you're sure someone would like to know about. But you have to prepare the person and the project to meet each other, so you set up an introduction.

Sometimes everything goes beautifully. Your ideas are clear to you, and you know just the right person. But usually you have to plot and plan to make it work out.

Awkward Beginnings

The first few pages you write may be rambling or painfully slow and disjointed. You may open with a cute remark that falls flat. You may start on one subject and end on another. You may find that a ten-page paper has a four-page introduction, or a two-sentence introduction. You may skip the introduction and get right down to business.

You may decide to use the same device every time. You may rely compulsively on the "funnel-shaped" paragraph which begins with an example and works its way toward the thesis statement of your essay. You may try to tell a joke, drop an interesting fact, draw a clever analogy, tell a heart-warming story, quote a famous writer, or ask a rhetorical question. We cannot begin to list the devices people have invented to make introductions work and to ease the anxiety of connecting with a reader.

The wonderful difference between written and oral introductions is that you can redo a written introduction if you want to. You don't have to walk away muttering to yourself, "I can't believe I said that." You can write a hurried introduction, go on, and come back to improve it later. You can cut to the chase by beginning with what interests you most about the subject, and then build the rest of the project around that part.

Introductions and Your Best Work

Since you have time to work on it, your introduction should include some of your very best writing. You can't know, as you begin writing a piece, when or where your best writing will occur, so it follows that you can't write your introduction until you've written everything else. We therefore hereby give you permission to write awkward introductions to your first drafts. Whatever enables you to start and continue writing will do.

Once you've written and revised your work, you can begin looking for your introduction, which should be your best work. Occasionally you will find that the first few pages you wrote were indeed among the best. More often, you'll find that as you warmed to your subject, you wrote better and better. Your conclusion may turn out to have been your best work. Or you may find that somewhere along the way you used a funny story, a brilliantly clear example, or an elegantly phrased sentence.

You may be thinking, "Wait a minute. There are lots of problems with that idea. Writing that works in the middle or the end might not work at the front. Sometimes you have to start in a certain way and follow a format. If I move my best writing to the front, I'll leave a hole in the middle or the end. Anyway, I like to save the best for last."

Let's deal with those objections in reverse order, just to illustrate that you can discuss ideas in whatever order works best. Saving the best for last works with captive audiences. If people are attending a concert, having paid their money and taken their seats, they will probably stay through to the finale unless the music is absolutely awful. The performers can safely save some of their best work for a triumphant finale. But as a writer you cannot often hope for a captive audience. You usually face an audience who can decide to pay attention or dismiss you within the first few paragraphs. Once you have lost their attention, you have to write twice as well to refocus them, if they continue reading your work at all.

As far as leaving holes in the middle or the end is concerned, you can deal with that problem in either of two ways. Your best writing probably bears repeating, so you shouldn't feel compelled to use it only once. Comedians, musicians, painters, sculptors, athletes, public speakers, and, yes, writers—people who practice any profession whatever—all have favorite tricks that they use and reuse because the tricks work. If you do decide to use your best writing only once, at the beginning, you can simply write something to fill in the blank space. By the time you've written a complete draft or two of the piece, you'll have become expert enough with your subject matter to supply good new material.

Formats don't present very serious problems either. Formats like those for research papers or technical reports often list items you must include in the introduction, but they don't often list items you may not include. The introduction usually works as a free space which allows personal expression. You can simply introduce the introduction or write a preface if you feel that you must adhere to guidelines in your introduction.

Titles

Before we leave the subject of introductions, we should mention that you also need to introduce your introduction; that is, you need a title.

Some people like catchy titles. If you want a catchy title, once you've located your best work and moved it to the beginning, you should take a few more minutes to look through the draft to find your best phrase and use that as the title. If the authors were going to publish this section as an essay we might title it, "Best Work." You can also use a complete sentence as a title: "Put Your Best Work Forward" might work for this section. One of our professors in graduate school pointed out the problem with catchy titles. They work in the context of the article, but if someone publishes the name of the article in an index without a summary of its contents, a researcher may not be able to intuit the subject of the article; this forces the researcher to traipse off to the stacks to look up the article in order to find out its subject. As a compromise, academic articles' titles often have two parts separated by a colon—"Putting Your Best Work Forward: How to Write an Effective Introduction." Although everyone titles a few projects with two phrases and a colon, these titles are a bit pompous, especially if the project is short. The best titles catch your attention and inform you in one pithy phrase or clause. We usually decide to stick with a very straightforward title for written work and save our clever titles for speeches.

You may recall from Chapter 2 that a writer named Scott McCullough had written about his favorite game, motorcycle riding. Picking up on that idea, he produced a draft about being a biker in the Midwest. As you read this draft, decide which paragraph you think is the best work. (We'll number the paragraphs for easy reference.) If you moved the best work to the beginning of the draft, what other revisions would you think appropriate? Scott wants to write for an audience like the readers of *Rolling Stone*.

DRAFT BY S. Scott McCullough

1. Even as a very young child, I was fascinated by motorcycles and craved the experience of riding one. That craving became acute at the age of eight, when my father took me to see *Easy Rider*. At about the same time, I began to notice the people riding motorcycles as much as the bikes themselves. Suddenly, I realized that motorcycling was not merely a physical activity, but that it was also highly social, bringing together people with highly divergent interests and backgrounds who shared the love of riding. Bikers always seemed to enjoy life more fully and expansively than any people I had ever met before. I knew that someday I wanted to be one of them, forever travelling to wonderful and mysterious destinations.

2. Many people are cowed into believing that such a joyous life is somehow evil, or illegal, or a waste of time. What a sad and beleaguered attitude! I believe that life is to be lived as fully and completely as possible without harming others. Those who fear death the most often seem to live the least, while those who love life the most are often most willing to risk it. Bikers are perceived to be so threatening largely because they challenge risks instead of fleeing them, and because they often refuse to succumb to social pressures to conform. Most people spit out "biker" like a shameful label, reserved only for the lowest and most pitiful dregs of society. I have known many bikers, have lived among them, loved them, have ridden and partied and laughed and cried with them, and declare with pride (rather than admit with shame) that **I am one of them!** I could use the innocuous title of "motorcyclist" instead, but it seems to imply a sense of reservation and equivocation that I do not mean to convey.

3. My first bike was a Kawasaki H1 with a bald rear tire, worn swingarm bushings, and no title or registration. It was a wickedly fast machine, but it handled like a cement truck and wobbled drunkenly at speeds over 50 mph. My friend Larry and I would take it out on the country roads after work, gleefully taking turns blasting off towards the horizon. Of course it was foolish and illegal, but although the police never caught us, the riding bug did. In a moment of idiocy, I traded that first bike for a console stereo that didn't work and have regretted it always.

4. My next bike was another Kawasaki, this time a less-violent KZ 650. It was good looking, moderately fast, and cornered like a jet fighter. My friend Scott Bunton, who was separated from his wife at the time, had a Honda CBX, and we would ride at criminal velocities for hours at a time. Although I lacked any formal rider education, several near-disasters taught me how to steer and brake at speed. By the time I sold that bike, I had become a smooth, proficient rider.

5. I then bought two identical 1971 BMWs, one worn-out but still running, the other much better maintained but in need of engine repairs. I rode the worn-out bike for two troublefree years before selling it dirt-cheap to a friend. I then proceeded to go way overboard on the second bike, spending colossal sums of money for high-performance engine parts and machine shop services. You can probably guess what happened next: 3000 miles later, the high-dollar motor went south. Now I'm borrowing the worn-out engine from the first bike, preparing to dump yet more money into my own. The whole engine fiasco has been as painful a lesson as falling down, and I vow never to fall prey to the temptation again (although I probably will anyway . . .).

6. Riding a motorcycle and being a biker are two separate activities. Mere motorcycle riders tend to be novices, dabbling in riding the way they might dabble in woodworking or needlepoint, hesitant to ride in inclement weather or to cross the county line. They feel a vague sense of shame and humiliation when their respectable friends see them riding. "I didn't know you rode one of those things," their friends might say "Don't you know how dangerous they are?"

7. "Oh, I just wanted to see what it was all about," they sheepishly reply. "I don't really ride much, not really."

8. "Well you're just lucky you haven't killed yourself already. Those things are *so* dangerous. Anyway, only dirty scuzzbags ride motorcycles. Didn't you see that movie on TV the other day about a gang of vicious bikers who killed women and raped children and smoked LSD and snorted marijuana and . . . ."

9. After such an embarrassing exchange, the casual motorcyclist usually slinks back home, parks the bike in the garage, and calls the paper to place a classified ad. Their social fears and inhibitions prevent them from ever discovering what riding is all about. They have condemned themselves to a life of passive travel inside a climate-controlled box, isolated from the infinite variety of sensory inputs all around them, doomed to experience the world vicariously.

10. Real bikers, on the other hand, thrive on the constant variety of sensations, exposure to the elements, potential risk, and logistical hardships which motorcycling provides, and preach the joys of motorcycling with the zeal of a Jehovah's Witness on speed. "You've never ridden? Gee, I never knew. Let's go for a ride next Saturday! I know a fantastic road up by Ottawa, you'll just love it. Oh yeah, and while we're up there we could ride through this great state park, then there's a place about 30 miles west of there that has the best barbecue in the world, and then . . ." Their lusty quest for the ultimate ride on the ultimate road and their exuberant desire to share their excitement with others sometimes makes them seem dangerously unbalanced to timid souls.

11. Because they share so many wonderful rides and adventures, bikers come to feel that they are a family, and to address each other as brother or sister. I have gained many brothers and sisters during my years of riding, people riding bikes as diverse as BMWs, Nortons, Harleys, Moto Guzzis, Indians, Ducatis, Triumphs, Hondas, Yamahas, and Suzukis (and some on marks whose names I cannot even recall). Being a biker is nothing at all like what the movies portray; indeed, much of the rest of society seems mean and savage in comparison. The biker society is based upon trust, self-discipline, and respect, coupled with a shared love of riding. The longer I ride, the more impressed I am with the utter honesty with which most bikers address one another. They dispense with the duplicity and evasiveness so pervasive throughout our culture, replacing it with a refreshing truth and directness. The few truly bad people who happen to ride motorcycles are no more representative of that family (also known simply as the brotherhood) than the few truly bad people who drive cars are representative of all car drivers.

12. Riding is like a good clean acid trip or good sex: when the roads are smooth and twisty, the scenery and weather are right (not necessarily beautiful, but harmonious), and I'm completely melded with the bike, I sometimes realize that I've transcended mortal existence. That sense of spiritual connection with absolute reality is so incredibly urgent and blissful, and time passes so deliciously slowly, that any

other sensations or experiences seem shallow and insignificant in comparison. Although I enjoy riding alone, sharing such exquisite rides with a passenger or with other bikers is a unique and tremendously satisfying experience. That supreme spiritual satisfaction, combined with the cameraderie and sense of family between bikers, makes motorcycling one of the most fulfilling (legal) activities I have ever experienced.

Postscript: (I decided not to use this, but I liked it and didn't want to delete it away.)

13. Being a biker in the conservative Corn Belt is tantamount to waving a flag over my head and screaming, "Look at me! La-de-doody-do! I'm a freak!" When I pull up to a stop sign in a car, I'm anonymous; but when I ride up to the same stop sign on my bike, most straight citizens studiously ignore me. They stare straight ahead at the horizon to avoid making eye contact, surreptitiously locking their doors when they think I'm not looking. Children, lacking that ingrained fear and misunderstanding, smile and wave, displaying the same innocent fascination I remember from my own childhood. Perhaps that joyous interaction and fascination is part of what makes riding such a splendidly satisfying experience.

For a title, we might suggest "Look at Me! La-De-Doody-Do!" or "BMWs, Nortons, Harleys, Moto Guzzis, Indians, Ducatis, Triumphs, Hondas, Yamahas, and Suzukis." Both those titles come directly from the draft.

As beginnings go, Scott's introductory paragraph is not bad. However, he could punch up the beginning by moving paragraph 3, or 7 and 8, or 12 to the beginning. Paragraph 3 would begin his essay *in medias res* (Latin for "in the middle of the action"). That would bring up the subject of motorcycles in a more exciting way than the childhood memory. Paragraphs 7 and 8 accomplish the same end using conversation, which many people find inherently interesting. Since Scott has in mind the reader of *Rolling Stone*, a magazine which uses interviews a great deal, this introduction has much to recommend it. Paragraph 12, with its casual talk of drugs and sex, would shock many people, but probably not the *Rolling Stone* reader. One of the favorite games of the young is something the French call *epater les bourgeois*, which is to say "shocking and upsetting the middle class."

Finally, we would suggest beginning with paragraph 3 and following with paragraph 13, which sets the joyful tone of the rest of the piece. We would then follow with paragraphs 4 and 5, which pick up the narrative of motorcycle purchases. Then we would return to paragraphs 1 and 2 to fill in some background and close out with paragraphs 6 through 12. We would do some rewriting of the beginnings of paragraphs 13, 4, 1, and 6 to make them fit logically and stylistically with the new paragraphs they follow. Depending on your choice of the best work in the draft, you might reorder the paragraphs in some other, equally effective way.

We go to the trouble of shaping a rough draft because we know that the more we do, the more readers can see into the future. A reader who looks at a fragmentary and disorderly draft can and should concentrate on suggestions for finishing the draft and putting it into an effective order. If you have already completed some of that work, if you have taken the draft as far as you can see to take it, the reader can open a door to help you to take the next step.

EXPERIENCE

You'll need a completed draft of a paper you're working on.

1. In class, exchange papers with classmates, and read through each other's work identifying what you feel to be the writer's best work. While you're reading, note and underline one or two effective phrases or clauses that might serve as the title.
2. Compare your best work to your introduction.
   a. Now retrieve your own work, copy the passage of your best work and answer the following question: How does your best work relate to the main idea of your paper?
   b. Find the point at which your present introduction stops, insert the passage of your best work, and, once again, answer the following question: How does your best work relate to what follows your present introduction?
   c. Cut your original introduction but don't throw it away (it might turn out to be useful as a conclusion or in some other way).
3. Using your best work and your answers to the two questions, rewrite your introduction.

   Don't feel compelled to stick to the exact original wording except where it's useful. When you've finished, continue reading through the paper to see if the change in your introduction implies other changes as well. Ask your classmates and your teacher whether the new introduction conveys your main idea effectively.
4. Compose a title using one of the most effective phrases or clauses from your draft.

SHAPING A DRAFT: ENDINGS

Writers often simply stop drafting when they run out of energy. They hand a draft to a reader with an apologetic, "I know this isn't finished yet, but would you take a look at it anyway?" You should learn that the moment when your energy flags, when you lose interest in drafting, is the moment to stop and write the conclusion. *Then* you can hand the paper off to someone.

How do we conclude a draft?

T. S. Eliot said it best in a poem called "East Coker." "In my end is my beginning."

Practically speaking, the end of a first draft often turns out to be the beginning. Most of us start out with some wheel spinning, taking a few pages to gather our momentum and our wits before working our way into the subject. By the time we've arrived at a point that feels like the end, we're ready to look back over our shoulder, admire our achievement, and summarize what we've written. When we write that summary, it turns out to state concisely the intentions with which we began the drafting. We look back at the introduction, recognize the difficulties with it, toss it out, and move the conclusion up to the front of the draft.

That strategy usually gives us the core of a good beginning, but we're left with a sense of incompleteness at the end. If we feel that we've written as much as we care to for the moment, we may resort to the old formula from speech class: "Tell them what you're going to tell them, tell them, and then tell them what you've told them." That is, we simply restate the introduction in slightly different words.

The authors of this book probably don't need to point out to you that the speech formula is (how shall we put it?) just the least bit mechanical. It closes out the text but doesn't really take account of the reader. Readers expect to be dealt with more courteously than that.

Endings That Satisfy Reader Expectations

Story-Form Endings

We can explore reader's expectations by returning to the distinction (in Planning the Form of a Draft in Chapter 5) between story and essay form. A draft that follows some chronological, story-like order may arouse expectations of a story-form ending.

As a reader of stories, you constantly expect the writer to tell you what happened next in the action of the story. You usually expect the story to begin moving toward the ending when the conflict that provoked the action in the story has peaked in the climax of the story. In a fictional story like *Romeo and Juliet*, we find various conflicts: loyalty conflicts with love, the old conflict with the young, and family conflicts with family. In a non-fictional story form such as Thoreau's *Walden*, nature conflicts with civilization, the personal life conflicts with social life, and the desire to understand life conflicts with the busy-ness of living life.

As the story ends, you expect a resolution in which the writer brings up and comments on the consequences of the climax. A fairy-tale ending like "and they lived happily ever after" signals, in a very simple way, the resolution of a conflict. As a result of resolving the conflict, the characters live happily. The important point to notice here is that a good ending restricts itself to explaining the direct consequence of resolving the conflict.

In *Romeo and Juliet*, Shakespeare assigns the conclusion to the Friar, who summarizes the events that led to the deaths of the main characters, and to the Prince, who comments on the lessons to be learned. In *Walden*, Thoreau uses the last two sections, "Spring" and "Conclusion," to accomplish the same end by way of a description of the spring thaw and a philosophical discussion of what he learned by living in the woods.

Of course different kinds of stories imply different ways of resolving conflict. If the story is a tragedy, we expect the conflict to result in a death, and we expect the ending to explore the consequences the death will have on the main characters. If the story is a comedy, we expect it to end when everyone becomes friends; the main characters will go off together, perhaps even marrying. If the story is a joke, we expect it to end in a punch line. If the story is a sequence of jokes, like a comedian's monologue, we expect it to end with one of the best jokes.

The end of this book—which follows story form—begins with Part V, Producing the Final Draft. We see the main conflict in writing as that between a writer's and a reader's needs. By the time you get to Producing the Final Draft, you will have experienced and resolved conflicts over how best to deal with your audience in Part IV, Revising. You'll even act out the conflict with peer readers in various situations. Producing the Final Draft simply ties up the loose ends after the conflict is over.

To end a draft written in story form, then, you have to ask yourself where you have resolved the main conflict. Suppose you've written an article that describes a political conflict on your campus, say, over the imposition of a tuition increase. In such an article, you'll pose students against the administration. Someone will win, and the conflict will thereby be resolved. How do you end such a story?

You know readers of stories want most of all to know what happens next. So one natural way to end would be to use personal comments from the two groups about what they plan to do and to close with your own evaluation of the two groups' behavior. "The Board of Regents stonewalls, the university administration kowtows, and the students demonstrate. Thus, in a ritual handed down from previous generations, do we formally observe the imposition of yet another fee increase."

If you were writing about an event that had occurred a certain distance in the past, you might close with a postscript. "The university president who successfully fought off the fee increase subsequently lost a similar battle. Not long after, he took a higher paying job at another university. The Board of Regents members who favored the increase remain in power. The governor whose budget cuts necessitated the increase has begun campaigning for his second term. As we prepare to vote, let us remember."

Essay-Form Endings

A draft that follows logical essay form usually works like a dialogue, a conversation of some kind. The conversation may vary from the formal, ritualized lecture with question and answer period to the informal back-and-forth of a chat.

You can get a sense of how to end an essay-form draft by recalling the ways you end a conversation. Suppose you're talking to someone on the phone. How do you signal that you want to end the conversation?

You can simply tell the person you have to stop and say good-bye, but that's not very polite. "Well, I've got to run."

You can accomplish that end more tactfully by suggesting the person find something else to do. "I'll let you get back to your homework."

You can return to the original subject with an evaluative comment. "Anyway, as I was saying, that was a disgusting concert." A negative evaluation may end the conversation on a rather sour note, ordinarily something you would rather avoid.

On a more positive note, you may evaluate the success of the conversation itself in reaching an understanding between the two of you. "I'm glad we got that cleared up."

Possibly the most positive way of ending a conversation is by suggesting that you'd like to see the person again. "Will I see you tomorrow, then?"

To put this into a writing context, let's consider the idea of an essay-form draft of a writing project about a student fee increase. Suppose that you were arguing against the increase. You would have engaged, indirectly, in a dialogue with those who disagree with you or who don't understand your position by stating your arguments and following up with answers to any questions they might have. How might you end such a draft, supposing that you had moved your summary conclusion to the beginning?

You might close with a curt comment. "Clearly, the administration has no interest in students." Rude, but it does get you out of the conversation.

You might close with a polite suggestion that those who disagree with you do something else. "We know that the administration has many problems to consider in arriving at a sensible budget, but we hope that they will continue to keep in mind that students need to have a voice." While we like this better than the go-to-hell tone of the first ending, it seems a little smarmy and passive-aggressive to us.

You might close with an evaluative comment. "I have experienced frustration again and again in this exchange. I have felt that the administration has evaded me and the real issues." This ending definitely has a combative tone, but bringing the argument back to the personal level at least lends an air of authenticity to the argument, making it clear that the writer has a personal investment. Of course, this sort of ending can easily degenerate into whining.

You might close with an evaluation of what has, rather than what has not, been accomplished. "We've broached the issues at least. We hope that we can continue, perhaps to delay or roll back some part or all of the tuition increase. At worst, we will have established a framework within which to pursue other student ends."

Notice how much more satisfying this ending would be to an audience who disagreed with the writer's position. Only people who were angry with the administration would be satisfied by the earlier, more negative endings. A writer who wanted simply to impress other angry students with his or her moral outrage might retain such an ending.

A writer who wanted to have an impact on the administration would be well advised to end on a positive note. For example, you might close in the hope of seeing the audience in some other context. "I call for a series of meetings between members of the provost's staff and members of student government. If we cannot talk, we certainly cannot moderate the situation." It's hard for a reasonable person to refuse a request to talk. Depending on how well the rest of the arguments were put together, the person who closed in this way might well find himself or herself in a meeting with the administration.

But we've already mentioned that an essay-form writing project works like a dialogue. You should treat the conclusion as a dialogue as well. We'll use the last conclusion as a model. What comments might we expect someone who disagrees with our position to make to the statements of this conclusion? Let's first suppose that a member of the administration might be reading this conclusion. We'll bracket the comment he or she might make.

"I call for a series of meetings between members of the provost's staff and members of student government. [Hmph. They'll probably make a lot of unreasonable demands. They don't have a clue where the money really comes from.] If we cannot talk, we certainly cannot moderate the situation. [Even if we do talk, the budget still remains in the hands of the legislature and the Board of Regents.]"

Having guessed at the reader's possible reaction, we can revise the ending.

"I call for a series of meetings between members of the provost's staff and members of student government. *Of course, our first goal will be to present our point of view in the hope of reducing or eliminating the budget increase, but we recognize that we may not have all the information. We hope to learn more about the budgeting process as well.* If we cannot talk, we certainly cannot moderate the situation. *Perhaps together we can find ways of addressing the legislature to persuade them to take the needs of higher education more seriously.*"

As authors, we close this explanation by reinterpreting the line from "East Coker" with which we began. "In my end is my beginning." We like endings that may serve as the beginning of new conversations. So whenever possible we end on a positive note. However, we know that now and then it feels right to tell someone off. When we write a go-to-hell ending, we try to keep in mind that we're simply transferring bad feeling from our lives into someone else's, and we can probably expect the recipient to transfer the feelings back again with interest.

We can close this whole section by asking you to notice that though we've written seven different conclusions to one piece of writing, we haven't begun to list all the ways stories or conversations end. How do you like to say good-bye?

EXPERIENCE

Examine a draft you're working on and categorize it as either predominantly story form or predominantly essay form.
1. If it looks like a story form to you, describe the central conflict.
   - At what point in the draft is the conflict resolved? Your conclusion begins at that point.
   - What loose ends—issues, people, or actions—brought up prior to the conflict need to be tied up by mentioning them and telling the reader what has become of them?
   - Outline the project beginning at the point at which the conflict is resolved. Your outline should explain briefly the *direct consequences* of resolving the conflict.
2. If your draft looks like an essay form to you, imagine how you'd close out a conversation with a person who disagrees with you or a person who may not understand you.
   - Write a brief conclusion which emphasizes the main points you want the reader to carry away.
   - Then imagine comments the reader might make on each sentence of your conclusion. Rewrite the conclusion to take those comments into account.

Part IV
Revising

Revising happens throughout our writing processes. Research shows that the best writers are flexible from the first word they put on paper until the last galley proof goes off to the printer. Experienced writers also know that attentive readers must review a paper at each of its stages, giving comments for changes in everything from basic arguments to word choice.

Learning to revise means learning to look at your paper with determination to make it better in every way, not only according to your own judgment but also according to the judgments of teachers (editors) and peers (potential readers). Revision often means adding resources to the paper: another trip to the library, more interviews with experts, or some other investigation of sources that will improve what you have written.

Revising also means being willing to take a project apart to see how it works and where it doesn't work. When you ask basic questions about the purpose and audience of a project, you can see the potential for changes in the organization, development, and language of a writing project.

In short, revising implies reexperiencing the total process of writing a paper. You may find that you need to get started, to discover new ideas for your project, to do a significant amount of redrafting, to rearrange or delete from what you have already written, and to pay attention to the most minute details of form. We won't pretend that revision is easy, but we do know that it's worthwhile. We also know that you can do it with help from your teacher and the other writers in your class.

In the chapter entitled Peer Suggestions for Revision, we outline some methods for responding to writing projects to foster revision. The reader simply responds by summarizing the main ideas of the draft, identifying the strongest part, and suggesting some possible additions, deletions, and rearrangements to be made. In this section, we focus again on research, since often revision will require adding support from outside sources as necessary additions to the project.

After you have mastered the basic methods of the peer review process, you can advance to the chapters which follow—Narrative Strategies for Revision, Analytical Strategies for Revision, and Personal Dimensions of Revision. In these chapters, you'll focus more tightly on particular ways of rethinking a draft. Sometimes learning to revise your papers can also mean that you have to change your own attitudes toward writing. One of our friends says that he always thinks that the draft he is working on is the final draft until he sits back to rethink what he has done or until he asks a colleague to read what he has written. Then he realizes, as do we all, that revisions still have to be made. That's what these chapters on revision will show you how to do: think over what you thought was finished.

Chapter 7
Peer Suggestions for Revision

LISTENING TO SUGGESTIONS FOR CHANGE

Some writers like making changes in a writing project. They enjoy the process of considering and reconsidering the ways ideas are ordered and expressed. Others, we hardly need tell you, find revision anything from tiresome to excruciating. Each kind of writer has something to learn from and teach to the other. By the end of this section on responding to suggestions for change, you should have learned some techniques for listening actively to the suggestions of others about your writing.

Written language does not afford you the opportunity of facing all your readers. As a writer, you have to try to lower the probability of misunderstanding by listening to peer readers, teachers, friends, and anyone else who will respond honestly to your work. Each person you listen to can help you to glimpse the infinite number of valid ways people may interpret what you say. Using the information they give you, you can revise to make your work more like the experience from which you drew it. But you have to listen—really listen.

How to Listen to Suggestions for Change

When people argue, they don't listen. They spend their energy thinking of counterarguments rather than trying to listen. They try to win rather than to understand. A psychologist named Carl Rogers has developed a uniquely effective method of listening to help people settle arguments peaceably. A Rogerian counselor may ask people to try to understand each other by an exercise during which each person tries to understand and state the *other's* viewpoint on an area of disagreement. Each person explains his or her viewpoint and then listens to and coaches the other to help him or her get the facts and the words just right. Their goal is to listen and achieve communication, so the counselor interrupts them whenever they begin to argue or to negotiate.

Suppose two roommates, Chris and Billy, are disagreeing about house-keeping. Billy might say, "I want you to want to do some of the house-keeping. I want it to be as important to you that the carpet is vacuumed as it is to me."

And Chris, trying to take Billy's viewpoint, might respond, "Oh, I see. You don't want me to think of the housekeeping as your responsibility. You want us each to take a fair share of the responsibility."

The counselor might interpose a question here. "Is that right, Billy? Are you talking about what's fair?"

"That's close, but I'm really not talking about what's fair. I'm not accusing you of being unfair. I just wish we both had the same attitudes. Right now, I'm always annoyed when I walk into the apartment."

And Chris might respond, "Oh. You mean you wish we both wanted the same level of neatness?"

"Yes, that's right."

Notice that Chris hasn't agreed to feel or behave as Billy suggests. But now at least Billy has some assurance that Chris is beginning to under-stand, and learning Billy's language has helped Chris to experience Billy's viewpoint. Rather than getting emotionally involved in an argument, they focus on listening. As they listen, each begins to understand the other's viewpoint.

Working in this way, the roommates would gradually reduce the com-munication problems between them by building a language that they understood in pretty much the same way. The process would help them to concentrate on the real issues between them. They would understand their relationship more clearly. On the basis of their clearer understanding, they might either strengthen their relationship or decide to dissolve it. Which-ever direction they took, they would be working on the basis of mutual understanding.

If you try this sort of exercise over even a mild disagreement with someone, you'll find yourself surprised twice—first, when you experience the frustration of being misunderstood and having to define and redefine what you have said to explain what you mean, and second, when you real-ize that people do communicate with each other despite all the ambiguity of language.

Rogerian Dialogue with Peer Readers

To take an example from writing, suppose that, in talking with a peer reader, you discover that he or she has interpreted a writing project of yours in a way you hadn't expected. You've written an essay examining the decline of Soviet communism. You're sure that you've presented the facts dispassionately, but when your peer review comes back you find that the summary of your main point reads, "This essay celebrates the downfall of totalitarianism and the beginning of true democracy in the Soviet republics."

You wince. That reading sounds naive and chauvinistic to you. Somehow your reader has found a meaning you didn't intend. Perhaps your reader is "reading between the lines," but you can't be sure. How can you find out where this interpretation came from?

A Rogerian dialogue may help. You might begin by saying, "So let me get this straight. As you read this, you see a writer delighted that the Evil Empire has been vanquished?"

"Well, that's putting it a little strongly. It's more like someone who thought all along that Soviet communism wouldn't work. It's as if you were seeing your theories proven right."

"Do you mean that the discussion is all about the advantages to the Soviet peoples of getting rid of the bureaucracy?"

"Not quite. What I get is a sense that you think the decline was inevitable. You talk about how one form of Soviet communism led to another with each one moving further from the original plan."

"Hmm. I see. So I'm 'celebrating' the prospect of the next step toward a more Western system. Actually, I wanted to sound a little more objective than that. Can you point to where you get that impression most strongly? I'd like to tone it down a little."

Notice that the writer has not argued with the reader's interpretation—not one word. The writer has accepted the interpretation as a valid experience of the words and has focused on understanding how the reader came to the interpretation. Having accepted the interpretation, the writer has empowered the reader to assist in the process of identifying possible areas of change in the writing project.

You won't fully understand suggestions for change until you have put them into your own words and actions. As you look at a suggestion for change to a project, your judgment is affected by two facts. You didn't make the suggestion (you don't have ownership of it) but you are the person who will have to do the work (you do have responsibility for it). So naturally you feel ambivalent. "I can see that might be a good idea, but I'm not sure I want to do it."

Putting the suggestions into your own words helps you to own them so that you can then estimate whether the effort necessary to complete the changes will reward you sufficiently. At this stage, you're not committing yourself to any changes. You're simply imagining how the suggested changes might affect the project. Once you own the suggestions, you'll be better prepared to take responsibility for accepting or rejecting them.

Finally, translating and analyzing criticism drains off negative reactions. If you respond to suggestions for change with anger or depression,

you may find that critical analysis enables you to take the criticism less personally. Readers' suggestions become information, nothing more and nothing less.

EXPERIENCE

Once you have completed this assignment, you should be able to engage a reader in Rogerian dialogue in order to understand your reader's suggestions for change.

➡️WARM-UP

1. For some small domestic or personal disagreement, engage a friend, roommate, or relative in a Rogerian dialogue.
   a. Begin by trying to state your partner's viewpoint in his or her words.
   b. Encourage your partner to keep correcting your ideas and your wording until they are exactly right. Don't argue—not one word.
   c. Then trade positions and ask your partner to state your position in your words.
   d. When you've finished, describe the experience and your reaction to it.
   e. What have you learned about the other person?

➡️FOR YOUR WRITING PROJECT

2. Using the Rogerian dialogue technique, engage a peer who has responded to a piece of your writing in a discussion of what you need to do to revise.
   a. Your peer reader should begin by summarizing your writing project in his or her own words.
   b. Don't argue with your reader's interpretation—not one word. Instead try to understand and state your peer respondent's interpretation *in his or her words.* Encourage your peer reader to correct you until you have stated his or her reading accurately.
   c. After you have stated your peer's point of view, exchange roles and focus on a piece of your peer respondent's writing. Your role is now to coach your peer on your opinions about his or her writing project. Keep coaching until he or she states your opinions exactly right.
   d. Do any aspects of your peer reader's interpretation trouble you? Ask him or her how you can add to, delete from, or rearrange what you've written to bring his or her interpretation closer to the one you originally intended.

CONSTRUCTIVE RESPONSES TO A WRITING PROJECT

Like conversation, writing becomes more interesting as people take turns, each adding something to the discussion. In writing classes, we call these conversations among writers **peer review**. Once you have completed this assignment, you should understand how to give a constructive peer review to a draft.

First drafts of writing projects require constructive peer reviews. A writer needs someone who will try to read a project in the spirit in which it was written, to understand it well enough to value it for what it is or what it is trying to be.

Constructive readings help you as writer to see where a writing project is headed, where its strong points lie. If you are working on a paper about violence in movies, you will do well to find a reader who is interested in violent movies, even if your reader disagrees with your viewpoint. If you can find someone in your writing community who likes the way you write, so much the better.

Someone interested in you and your subject can help you know what you're doing well, and the positive reinforcement from such people helps to get you started on your revision processes. If you've written your first draft to try to discover what you think about a subject, an appreciative reader can often give you some good clues about where you're going. And of course having someone appreciate what you're writing helps motivate you to revise it to make it better.

"Look at this," you say to the person sitting next to you. "Can you follow what I'm saying here?" Asking this kind of question can help you to modify the direction you're taking before you've written pages and pages that you have to rewrite.

"You've written movie reviews before. Is this what it's supposed to sound like?" When you're trying something new, it's often important to secure "permission" from an expert to venture into the new territory.

"I'm not sure this is what you want" is an implied request teachers often hear. Students usually mean, "This is what I'd like to do. Please tell me I'm not going to get into trouble."

Writers usually are not interested in detailed advice about spelling, word choice, punctuation, or sentence structure in a first draft. We just want to know whether the idea seems to have possibilities. For that reason, as readers of first drafts we try to screen out all those details to focus on the overall concept of the project. We need to see the big picture before we can give sensible advice about the small details, especially since we know that a sentence we correct today may disappear from the draft tomorrow.

We can give a project a thorough and formal, but still appreciative, review by a three-step process—summarizing the main point, pointing out the strongest portion or quality of the writing project, and envisioning the final form of the project. Reviewing in this way helps to make sure that readers respond constructively to a project. We use the term **constructive** in two senses.

In its usual sense, **constructive** means "leading to positive change." When the reader summarizes the main idea, identifies the strongest point in a draft, and imagines the final product, the writer often can see more clearly how to change the project to improve it.

A **constructive** process of response should also lead the reader to see the big picture—to construct the meaning of the piece of writing. Summarizing the main point requires the reader to use the material that's on the page to put together (to construct) the main idea. You must construct the main idea of a piece of writing before you can suggest intelligent changes. We'll say that again. *You must construct the main idea of a piece of writing before you can suggest intelligent changes.* A writer can't use uninformed, unintelligent criticism.

Knowing where the strong points lie helps the writer to revise the rest of the project to meet the standard of his or her own best work. Finding the strongest portion or quality of the project also helps to put the writer into a receptive frame of mind, making it easier for the writer to accept later suggestions.

Knowing how a reader expects the project to look in its final form helps the writer to see the next step to take. This is an especially helpful response to give to writers. As you read, use your imagination to try to fill in the gaps in the draft and see how it will look in its final form. Ask yourself where you have seen such writing printed. If you imagine that the final draft might appear in a magazine with photographs or as a chapter in a book illustrated with graphs and charts, tell the writer what your imagination tells you. If you can name a particular publication and tell the writer why his or her writing brings that publication to mind, the writer will know whether he or she is creating the right impression.

As a reader, you can test whether your response is really constructive by noting how completely and specifically you explain to the writer your reasons for concluding that just *this* is the main point, just *that* is the passage you like best, and just *this* magazine is the right forum for the writer's work. Your opinion is worth exactly as much as the care with which you formulate and express it.

Interpreting Responses

Before reviewing someone else's work, you need to warm up by reviewing your own work. Once you have tried to take an objective look at your own writing, you'll also have a context against which to evaluate the quality and quantity of others' suggestions for change in your work.

If the reader's comments agree with your own, you can conclude that you've succeeded in conducting an objective review of your own work. If you find that the reader's review has differed substantially from your own review, you need to ask for yet another review from someone else. A third review will usually confirm one or the other of the previous reviews.

Suppose the writer gave you the following draft of an essay, asking you to tell her what general point you thought she was making, what she did best, and what kind of writing this reminds you of.

DRAFT BY Amy Derrick

Violence in Films

Within the last few years, it seems that movie violence has increased to an all time high. Nearly every film we see depicts some incredibly violent image. What do these things do to a society? Why has this increase occurred? Should we, as a society, be concerned with this increase? Many groups are pointing the finger at films and filmmakers, blaming them for increased violence in society. Hearing accusations like this makes me wonder two things. First, is it fair to blame one person or one thing for the problems of an entire nation? Second, has violence really increased so much in our society, or are we just hearing more about it because of the media?

We live in a violent society. Many people argue that the graphic depiction of some incredibly violent act merely numbs people. Therefore, we are not as affected when we hear about real-life violence. I do not believe that this "numbing" can be blamed on filmmakers alone. It is not uncommon for a television news program to show parts of bodies found in a wreckage or blood on a street after a fight. The difference between a fictional portrayal and actual footage of violent incidents is that the movie audience knows that what they are seeing is not real.

What, then, is the cause of the increase in film violence? The most obvious answer is that technology in the film industry has increased to an all time high. Also, people in today's society mature at a faster rate than people of past societies did. Movie going audiences seem to be less satisfied with having things left to their imaginations. It seems more important to them to see the image rather than have to imagine it. I suppose this could be caused by the amount of information that is readily available through visual media, that is television and movies. People are not reading as much any more.

Movies are a great source of escape for people in today's society. They need to be able to get away from their lives which may be either humdrum or hectic. It is important for people to have a large fantasy element. Movies like *Die Hard* and all of the James Bond movies can give people this kind of escape. It is the films like these that are often criticized for their violent content. It seems pretty funny to me to criticize a movie like this because they are generally so cartoonish that it seems impossible for anyone to take them really seriously. They provide two hours of good, clean, heart-stopping excitement, which is what people need today.

On the other hand, there are films that are so horrifying that people come out of the theater feeling sick to their stomachs. I can, to some extent, understand why people would worry about films like this spurring violence in society. I am afraid that the accusations are a little off base. Most of the people who go to see movies are stable enough to know that what they are seeing is not the way to behave. It does concern me that horror film characters like Freddie Krueger from the *Nightmare on Elm Street* series have become heroes in our society. Krueger was a child-killer in the films, and he is being idolized by people in our country.

We live in a fairly messed up society. I think that we need to examine our own lives before we start pointing the finger at others and blaming them for every problem. Americans are looking for the escape that movies provide. So called "violent films" would not be financed by the studio unless they made a lot of money.

One of Amy's readers wrote the following review.

REVIEW

Main Idea

This draft argues that movies glamorize violence but that the consumer is ultimately to blame for the violence. The writer observes that movie technology makes all the violence possible. She divides violent movies into two categories—cartoon and sick-to-your-stomach.

Strongest Writing

I liked the distinction between the two kinds of violent movies. I enjoy "action" pictures but I don't like the slasher movies at all. It makes sense to me to think that a movie which shows people being cut up with a knife that's available to anyone has a greater potential to do damage than one that shows someone stopping a terrorist attack.

Expectations

This draft makes me think of the essays you see in magazines in the doctor's office. The magazines usually have a kind of family focus and take a concerned viewpoint about the effects of media on children. It might be in *Parents* magazine or perhaps the *Reader's Digest.*

Given this review, Amy can begin to think about which direction her next draft will take her. Since the summary agreed with her own summary of the draft, she can assume that she is conveying her general point effectively. The positive response to her two categories of violent films suggested to her that she ought to expand that discussion, perhaps by adding examples. The Expectations response surprised her. She had envisioned an audience of college-aged people. Another reader confirmed the opinion that this discussion sounded more like a project for *Parents* magazine than for *Rolling Stone.*

Still interested in reaching the younger audience, she developed the following list of movies she might discuss.

FROM THE JOURNAL OF Amy Derrick
Modern films containing graphic violence
- *Total Recall*
- *The Godfather*
   (Sonny ambush scene)
   (Horse's head scene)
- *The Accused*
   (Rape scene)
- *Friday the 13th*
- *Bonnie and Clyde*
   (First film to show graphic violence)
- *Wild at Heart*
- *Silence of the Lambs*
- *The Lost Boys*
- *Faces of Death*
- *The Terminator*
- *Nightmare on Elm Street*
- Brian DePalma's *Scarface*
   (vs. Howard Hawks's *Scarface*)
- *Eating Raoul*
- *The Cook, the Thief, his Wife, and her Lover*

By discussing some of the graphic scenes in these movies, she planned to elaborate on her distinction between cartoon and sick-to-the-stomach violence. She hoped the modern examples would interest a college-aged audience who saw such movies and who would appreciate her distinction.

Another perspective often helps a writer to see more clearly the possibilities in his or her own work. None of us can know for certain what will interest a reader until we actually find a reader and ask for an honest reaction.

The reader's constructive response affects us like an interested listener who says, "Hmm. Interesting. Tell me more."

EXPERIENCE

➡WARM-UP

1. Using the list of movies Amy Derrick has provided (and adding or substituting any you think of), work with your peer group to revise Amy's essay in response to the comments of her reviewer. Compare your revisions with those other groups produce.

➡FOR YOUR WRITING PROJECT

You'll need a finished draft of a paper and a partner with a finished draft to or you may choose to revise a paper you completed at some point in the past. When you have completed this assignment, you should have at least two responses to a draft of one of your projects, and you should have completed at least one review of someone else's project.

2. Before class, read carefully through your paper and summarize it in a paragraph which contains the major points of the paper. Then identify the most successful section of the paper and explain what you think is good about it. Finally, describe the kind of writing you had in mind when you composed this draft. Make your comments on a separate sheet which you keep to yourself.

3. In class, trade papers with someone and repeat the procedure of summarizing the major points, identifying the most successful section of the paper, and describing the kind of writing this draft brings to mind. Once again explain your comments.

4. Return the essay and the review to the essay's author and discuss the review with the author. Resist the temptation to suggest changes at this point.

    If you have time, repeat the procedure with a different partner.

5. Compare the review you wrote of your own work with those you have gotten from others.
    *   How do their comments compare with your own?
    *   If they differ from your own perspective, do their viewpoints seem reasonable?
    *   How can you use their comments?

SUGGESTIONS FOR CHANGE IN A WRITING PROJECT

Once you have finished a draft or two of your project, you are prepared to get suggestions for change in your work. At this point you find someone to give you critical comments on your work. You need to be prepared to return the favor, to respond honestly, carefully, and supportively. By the time you have finished this section, you should understand how to offer helpful, tactful suggestions for change.

Can you, as a writer and critic, suggest change in a way that helps people to understand your point of view without losing their good humor? Of course.

Earning the Right to Suggest Changes

When you write critical comments, you should make sure to follow the Golden Rule of Criticism. You've never heard of it? It is "Appreciate before you criticize."

Practically speaking, the Golden Rule means that you should read all the way through any piece of writing before you write one word of criticism. Nothing makes us, as writers, angrier than for critics to take a piece of our work, sit down with a red pencil and begin making comments and suggestions for change before they have a clue about our main idea, audience, or intentions. We've invested effort in our writing, and we prefer that people who suggest changes at least invest the effort of reading what we've written to try to understand it before they start tinkering with it.

Once you've properly appreciated a piece of writing, you've bought the right to offer criticism, that is, to make evaluative comments. Your first criticism should be positive. You should tell the person which part of the piece seemed strongest to you and why. Having taken the two preliminary steps of reading all the way through the piece of writing and making a positive criticism (the techniques are detailed in the Experience under Constructive Responses above), you have then earned the right to suggest some options for revision.

Three Kinds of Suggestion for Change

While the process of revision is quite complex, we can somewhat simplify the task by recognizing that all changes in a piece of writing may be reduced to three basic operations—**addition, deletion,** and **rearrangement.** We can further focus the process by distinguishing **revision** from **editing.** During revision you rewrite to create substantive changes in the meaning of a text. During editing you rewrite to create minor changes to preserve or clarify the meaning of a text.

We'll define *revision* as "the process of adding, deleting, or rearranging significant pieces of text." In practice, "significant" usually means at least one sentence in length. In our experience, most writers are likelier to add significantly to a piece of writing than they are to delete significantly from it. We also find that writers need to be encouraged to consider rearranging a text. Rearrangement requires holding the whole text in your mind and making subtle and complex decisions about logic and effectiveness, so it's no small task to significantly rearrange a project, especially a lengthy one.

As you read someone else's writing project, you may find yourself feeling uncertain of your authority to suggest change. That's probably a sign that you're trying to pretend to be a teacher. Since the class already has a teacher, that's really not necessary. Or you may be trying to pretend to be the writer of the project. Since the project already has a writer, that's really not necessary either. Your role is simply to respond as the person you are.

If you are a little uncomfortable or uncertain about making suggestions for change, try prefacing your remarks with a hypothetical disclaimer: "If I were doing this project, I'd _____." Fill in the blank with whatever you'd do. The writer can accept or reject your suggestions.

Identifying Potential Additions, Deletions, and Rearrangements

Before you can suggest changes, you have to review your appreciative response to the project in order to bring to mind the project's main idea, its greatest strengths, and your vision of its final form.

In order to find places where the author might **add** to the project, simply note where you become interested, wishing there were more said about a certain point. Tell the writer what else you'd like to know.

Or note where you disagree or think that a potential reader would disagree. Frame your disagreement as a question: "Have you considered the idea that . . . ?" The writer can then incorporate commentary on your question.

Or note where you simply have a feeling something is missing. Your instincts as a reader are useful to writers. Be as specific as possible about what's missing.

Or note where you've read some other discussion that supports or rebuts a point the writer is making. Mention where the writer can pick up what you've read. Giving the writer suggestions for further reading is probably the most valuable kind of suggested addition. You already know that using sources helps to build a writer's credibility by demonstrating that he or she knows the subject matter and that published writers agree with him or her. More importantly, writers need to become aware of the conversations people are having about their subject in print. If a writer is going to contribute something worthwhile to the conversation, he or she needs to know what's out there. Since none of us can keep up with all the reading we need to do, we have to rely on our friends and colleagues to help us do our research.

Don't limit your suggestions to library research. If you think a questionnaire, an interview, ethnographic research, or an experiment might add something useful, by all means mention it. The classes you are taking may well provide inspiration for such suggestions.

In order to find places where the writer may need to **delete or rearrange** an idea, note where you think the writer has become repetitive or gotten off the track. It may be that the repetitive or illogically ordered part needs to be moved elsewhere in the piece. If you try imagining it elsewhere in the essay but can't find a comfortable place for it, the appropriate place may be in the trash can.

Personally, we find deletion to be our least favorite form of revision. Writing on a computer, we enjoy the luxury of easily rearranging the parts of a text, so if we can't find a place for a piece of text, we move it to the end of the document and leave it there until the very last draft, hoping that we'll turn up a use for it. If we still can't find a use for it, we heave a deep sigh and cut it out. Instead of grousing about how long it took to do all the work, we tell ourselves that we would have no regrets if we had spent the same amount of time watching a movie.

In Chapter 1 we presented a journal entry by Jon Neuleib in which he recalled his earliest writing experience, trying to compose a poem about lakes. He followed that entry with an entry in Chapter 3 expanding on that childhood experience. In the draft you are about to read, Jon takes up a larger body of water and a larger issue—the need to preserve the world's ocean resources. Jon worked on this project in the context of his preparation as a member of his college debate team.

You'll notice, as you read, that although Jon knows a good deal about the subject matter and has a good command of the language, his draft wanders. He has read and absorbed material on the issue in the process of preparing for debates. With subjects we know well, we may pack whole paragraphs of meaning into a single sentence. Typically, second drafts require a good deal of "unpacking" of thought—explaining in detail what seems obvious to the writer. As you read, make some notes about where you would suggest that Jon unpack his thought. Also note possible deletions and rearrangements.

DRAFT BY Jon Neuleib

Ocean Resources

1. Ocean resources are not only the fish in the water and the oil beneath the seabed, although those are important resources. "Resources" also includes a place for ships to sail, a potential energy source, and a source of aesthetic pleasure. This is the heart of the issue and the main reason why the ocean is an issue of pressing concern for humanity.

The major threat to these resources and our ability to manage them is pollution. The polluted waters are unable to support life both on land and at sea. The aspects of clean-up that have been mandated for the ocean have not come even close to addressing the true magnitude of the operation. The areas of the earth that are closest to the ocean are becoming more and more heavily populated and this in itself is putting more and more strain upon the ocean.

2. The first reason that this pollution is so important to those of us that live on land is that we draw a significant amount of food from the oceans. The possible food and pharmaceutical uses of the ocean are being squandered as we kill off habitats we know nothing about. The uses that we have for other aspects of the ocean are as equally important as this one but this area is of special concern to the global community. The ocean has often been seen as a panacea to the world's food problem. The problem that arises between the two areas is that we cannot feed people from an unsafe and dwindling supply of marine resources.

3. The second area in which the ocean is vital to those of us that live on land is the mysterious interplay of the land and the sea. The coastal estuaries of the United States have received some attention under programs such as Superfund but the problem is outrunning methods to solve it. The role that the ocean plays is far from being understood and just as we do not know if it can absorb large amounts of toxic pollution, we are uncertain of its ability to contain thermal pollution.

4. The newest group of resources that we can draw from the oceans are the minerals that lie beneath the ocean's floor. Although we already draw a large amount of hydrocarbons in the form of gas and oil, minerals such as manganese, gold, and titanium are also to be found in the seabed. Our ability to draw upon these resources is increasing technologically at the same time that the environmental costs are causing some groups to consider denying our ability to utilize them. The recent war in Iraq, and its threat to our steady supply of foreign oil, brought into question where domestic off-shore development could take place and if we should open up new areas to exploitation. This is not to suggest that governments have not put extensive resources into developing their own experimental programs in this area. This is the area that is mentioned in most of the periodicals on the ocean as one in which a great deal of growth is possible in the future. The role that the U.S. plays or does not play in the exploitation of this resource is the only real question.

5. The last resource that the ocean provides us with is the oldest one besides a source of food. The ocean has always served us as a major

thoroughfare. Shipping is the only cost-effective way to transport many goods and the only way, at all, to move some goods. Although air travel has increased while ocean travel has dropped, air transport is too expensive and ocean transport has shown steady gains in recent years. Shipbuilding is showing gains from its near collapse in the mid-80s due to low oil prices after the cut-off in the early 80s. Oil tankers are a vital part of the world's fleet as they transport one of the items that could not be realistically transported by air. The tanker fleet is also the prime example of how this use of the ocean threatens the environment. Few incidents have had as much impact upon the coastal environment as the Exxon Valdez spill. More and more these ships are becoming the heart of our maritime policy. Any policy that is addressed towards the industry or towards pollution in general would have to deal with the tankers. To an even larger extent, if we think of the place that off-shore drilling has in our policy, it is easy to see how important this sector is to ocean issues in general.

6. One third of the strategic defense of this country is based on our superiority underneath the waves. Even as events in Iraq demonstrate that we must rely increasingly on our conventional forces to meet Third World threats, our Navy still considers Soviet submarine forces as the major threat to our nation. This is the area in which government has traditionally seen the need to support the technological resources of the private sector. The military aspect of maritime policy has always reflected this but in a time of leaner financial times, it has become hard to support the previous policy.

7. Even as politicians have decided that the cold war is over, some Third World navies have made advances that suggest that we need to address this aspect as well. In this arena we do not need to deter a strategic strike but to return to a defense of our shipping resources as we defended them in World War II.

8. We must obviously prepare our Navy for the variety of threats that it may face in the future. We must also decide how to utilize those forces in the event of a conflict. How we determine who owns the sea will decide a large portion of how we deal with those forces, but this is an issue for the third portion of the paper.

9. The size and nature of maritime transport sector also has important impacts on our strategic position. The reason that sealift is so important is that it allows us to avoid confronting an opponent with nuclear weapons. Our ability to "put troops on the ground" is essential to deter threats from smaller powers who believe that we would not resort to nuclear weapons to confront them.

10. There are, of course, experts who contend our naval abilities have in fact caused us to become involved in situations rather than avoiding them. This is what makes the area of interest and makes it important to policymakers. The only clear position is that it is an area where decisions need to be made and where those decisions will have large impacts upon the globe.

11. One of the things that makes this topic area so interesting is the way that the various facets reflect upon each other. In the area of national defense, how we conduct civilian research, pollution control measures, and ownership all have long reaching effects on our military program. In the area of pollution, making our navy comply with international treaties has been an expensive part of our limited defense funds.

12. The link that exists between the commercial fleet and the military one has already been established. The industry should be seen as a single entity with various different aspects. One important part of the U.S. Navy is its research in oceanography. Just as acoustical technology is essential to our ability to maintain our underwater capability, weather and geographic knowledge are essential to our Navy as a whole.

13. All our technological advances are dependent on advanced weapons systems that need a great deal of information provided to them for them to work. It seems that we have made our systems more fragile as we have made them more lethal. The same improvements that may help us map the ocean floor may help our destroyers track foreign subs. Even the "pure research" that would be gained from the exploration of the ocean floor would have military applications as defense planners map attack routes for our SSNs to follow. This is not to suggest that the military is somehow behind all civilian developments or that it co-opts all relevant information, but it is important to remember that all policies have a ripple effect across both the military and civilian sectors of the maritime world.

14. Who owns the sea and the resources in it is arguably the first question that needs to be addressed when we consider an ocean policy, but it is usually the last one addressed by policy makers. We need to take action more wide-reaching than arresting a few obvious polluters and washing a few seals. There are three basic designations under which the ocean can fall. The first is the continental shelf which was determined under international law to be part of the country that owns the shore adjacent to it. This has been supported by the international community for a number of years with the United States declaring sovereignty over its shelf in the 1960s. The second and third categories are getting harder to define as the inter-

national community squabbles over the proper limits of national claims. The designation of the Exclusive Economic Zone, or EEZ, was first introduced in 1945 but has taken over thirty years to gain steam. For almost a decade after this formal introduction of the concept of the EEZ, the large maritime powers, such as Japan, the Soviet Union, and the U.S., opposed what they saw as an infringement of the idea of the freedom of the high seas. Once the issue was brought to the U.N. and given a formal framework, the United States capitulated to what it saw as mounting international opinion and declared its own 200 mile EEZ in 1983.

15. The United States agreed to this because of the conditions that were established for use of the high seas by third states [i.e., nations that pass over waters whose ownership is contested by two neighboring coastal nations]. One of the obvious areas of conflict is how the ocean is to be divided up by neighboring coastal nations whose borders do not meet the sea at a crisp ninety degree angle or nations that are less than two hundred miles across a body of water from each other. Currently, in the South China Sea, which would intuitively belong to the People's Republic of China, the PRC will not claim an EEZ because of the counter-claims that exist with Taiwan and Vietnam. In the U.S. the proclamation of the EEZ has brought many benefits for our coastal economies but it also mandates that the coastal nations be responsible for the environment of their EEZ. It is a white elephant of sorts if one remembers the amount of pollution that exists along our coasts and in the adjacent sea. Whether it is more advantageous to have the profits from those catches going to the U.S. or foreign fisheries is an issue that is for policy to dictate. The idea of the EEZ meshes in this way with the idea of the high seas. While the U.N. proclamation allows third countries to pass over the territorial waters of the coastal state it is not clear who is responsible for the pollution those shippers may cause. If the Exxon Valdez had been under foreign ownership, the resulting legal mess would probably never be figured out. It is also important to question the legitimacy of a third country's interdiction of an EEZ with military vessels. It is considered a right for the coastal state to police its EEZ with reasonable force and this could lead to military confrontations in the future. In the disputed South China Sea area, Vietnamese patrol boats have fired on third country fishing boats that were considered within their unofficial EEZ. In this way, it is obvious to see that although this may be the first issue that policy makers must address, having decided how to do it fairly does not solve all the problems involved in the maritime world. The interconnectivity of the various

issues are all seen in the ownership of the sea but none of them will be settled by merely focusing on who owns the sea. It is important to seek policies that would deal with a variety of issues while not causing new ones to crop up.

One of Jon's reviewers offered the following comments on his draft.

REVIEW

Summary

This draft argues that we must safeguard the sea as a resource. The ocean provides three major kinds of support to the human race: food, transportation, and aesthetic pleasure. Pollution threatens the ocean as a food source. The draft doesn't say much about aesthetics or food but goes into a lot of detail about the transportation angle. Who controls the sea seems to be the most important question here. The draft explains the Exclusive Economic Zone which is the distance offshore that countries claim belongs to them.

Most effective passage

I'm most interested in the discussion of the international transportation angle. I've read about the issue of how pollutants affect the food supply and ruin coastlines. I don't know as much about the transportation angle. You've already written more on that angle than on the other ones, so you've got a good start. It seems that you have more information on that part.

Expectations

This looks like something I might read in *Time* magazine. It's informative but it takes a stand on the issue, which is something I like. I'd rather read a draft I disagreed with that took a stand than one that just presents information. This might be a cover story article toward the middle of the magazine under a heading like "The Environment." It would probably have a box with statistics of some kind and another with background information about some important study on the issue.

Additions

I can see a lot of possible additions from research. You make arguments that seem to be based on sources, so I would say the first thing is to put in the sources. I also have some suggestions about cutting and changing order so it's hard for me to say what else to add until I'm sure about the order. See below.

Deletions or rearrangements

If I were doing this project, I'd cut paragraphs 2, 3, and 4. I might cut more but I'd start with those. I like the transportation discussion best and I think that it's the newest information, so I would work with that. I understand that the other material is probably necessary for your debate, but for this paper, I don't think it works as well. I'd also rearrange the paragraphs as follows: 1, 5, 14, 15, 6–13. Your statement (paragraph 14) that who owns the ocean was most important told me that the paragraph about that idea should be near the front. Then you could go on to talk about how transportation depends on who owns what.

Unpacking Your Thought

Jon must now begin to unpack his thought—to explore the implications and details of his ideas. In response to the review, Jon produced a number of changes, among them the following additions (the new material is printed in italics).

Who owns the sea and the resources in it is arguably the first question that needs to be addressed when we consider an ocean policy, but it is usually the last one addressed by policy makers. There are three basic designations under which the ocean can fall. The first is the continental shelf which was determined under international law to be part of the country that owns the shore adjacent to it. This has been supported by the international community for a number of years with the United States declaring sovereignty over its shelf in the 1960s. The second and third categories are getting harder to define as the international community squabbles over the proper limits of national claims. *The designation of the Exclusive Economic Zone, or EEZ, was first introduced in 1945 but has taken over thirty years to gain steam as Yann-Huei Billy Song explains in 1989:*

"The idea of the EEZ, like the continental shelf, was influenced greatly by the Truman Proclamation in 1945. Following it some Latin American countries—Chile, Ecuador, and Peru—asserted exclusive jurisdiction over all resources up to 200 miles offshore and therefore set the conceptual framework of what is now known as the EEZ. . . . In 1972, the idea was brought before the United Nations Seabed Committee and when the third U.N. conference on the Law of the Sea (UNCLOS III) met in Caracas in 1974 the idea was discussed widely."

For almost a decade after this formal introduction of the concept of the EEZ, the large maritime powers, such as Japan, the Soviet Union, and the U.S., opposed what they saw as an infringement of the idea of the freedom of the high seas. Once the issue was brought to the U.N. and given a formal framework, the United States capitulated to what it saw as mounting international opinion and declared its own 200 mile EEZ in 1983. *The law as it stands at this point is explained by Song in 1989:*

"Under the 1982 U.N. Convention, an EEZ is the marine area (including the water column and the subjacent seabed and subsoil) beyond that adjacent to the territorial sea, extending up to 200 nautical miles . . . . Within the EEZ, the coastal state has sovereign rights over the living and non-living resources of both the water column, particularly fish stocks, and the seabed and subsoil, including oil deposits, manganese modules, and other minerals. . . . Third states, however, enjoy freedom of the high seas in the coastal state's EEZ, including freedom of navigation and overflight and the freedom to lay pipelines and submarine cables."

Jon has unpacked his thought substantially by bringing his research knowledge into the picture. In fact, he has gone a little too far in the direction of unpacking. We rejoice whenever we see a student using outside sources, but the effectiveness of those sources depends on whether the writer integrates them into the argument. So in the next phase of revision, Jon must paraphrase most of the direct quotation, rearrange the draft in a more logical order, and do substantial cutting (you can see the results in Chapter 9). As writers work with a subject, they must often elaborate on a point before they can see that the point needs to be condensed, rearranged, or even eliminated. The creative process strongly resembles sculpting, carving, or hand-building with clay. The artifact must exhibit a form both useful and interesting. The process of writing forces us to shape our ideas, and in the process of shaping our ideas, we often modify or abandon them.

EXPERIENCE

➡ WARM-UP

1. Using the review comments we have provided (and adding or substituting any you think of), work with your class or peer group to rewrite paragraph 5 so that it smoothly follows paragraph 1. Then paraphrase the long quotations Jon has added to paragraph 14.

➡ FOR YOUR WRITING PROJECT

You'll need a draft and a partner with a draft to do this assignment. Trade papers with someone whose judgment you trust to write a review of your essay using the following format.

Before class

2. Read through your essay and note the following points. Make your notations on a separate sheet which you keep to yourself.
   a. Identify points at which you might *add* information.
   b. Identify points at which you might *delete or rearrange* information.
   c. Describe the forum in which you imagine your final draft might be printed. Describe any changes you think you'll have to make to meet the requirements of the forum.

In class

3. Trade papers with someone, and repeat the procedure you performed on your own essay.

   If you have not yet given this draft a constructive reading, refer to the section immediately preceding this one for directions and complete the constructive reading before continuing.
   a. Identify points in the essay at which the author might add information to further explain an idea. Explain why you think the additions would strengthen the essay.
      You must suggest some possible additions. Your job is to think of *possible* changes. They don't have to be major changes, and they don't have to be absolutely necessary. But it won't do to say, "This looks fine to me." Instead say, "If I were writing this paper, I might . . . ."
   b. Then suggest possible rearrangements or deletions in the same way. *Again, you must suggest some possible deletions or rearrangements.* Explain your suggestions to the author.
   c. Describe the forum in which you imagine the final draft might be printed. Describe any changes you think the writer will have to make to meet the requirements of the forum.

4. If time permits, trade with someone else and redo steps one and two.

5. Compare the review you wrote of your own work with those you have gotten from others.
   • How do their comments compare with your own?
   • If they differ with your own perspective, do their viewpoints seem reasonable?
   • How can you use their comments?

6. Read the review(s) you have received so far and translate them into your own words. Try to treat each review as information, not as personal commentary. Now put the review away.

7. Look at your summary of the review you've just been given.
   a. List the suggestions for change both you and the reader(s) offered.
   b. Add the suggestions only you offered.
   c. Add reader suggestions you liked but didn't think of.
   d. Now develop a plan to carry out the suggested revisions. At this point, you're not going to carry out the plan. Just imagine what you would have to do to get the revisions accomplished, and list the steps in a logical order.
8. Now look at notations you neither made nor agreed with.

   The reader may be wrong about the suggestion for change, but you have to at least consider the possibility that he or she is right.
   a. If the notation simply makes no sense to you, return to the reader to ask for further explanation.
   b If you still prefer not to follow the reader's suggestions, write a paragraph which begins, "I don't want to make these changes because . . . ."
9. Make any final changes you think necessary after completing step 8 above.

Chapter 8
Narrative Strategies for Revision

The methods outlined in Chapter 7, Peer Suggestions for Revision, are a general way of responding to an essay. For more focused work, we turn to some techniques from **rhetoric**. Rhetoric, the study of the communicative process, has produced a great many perspectives on communication. As you learn to become a more effective writer and peer reader, you can begin to employ some of these perspectives to help writers to resee a piece of writing. When you take a new perspective on a draft, you can see more clearly what needs to be done to make a rough draft into a disciplined piece of writing.

REVISING TO SUIT AUDIENCE AND PURPOSE

A narrative presents the events of an experience in the order in which they happened. Narratives serve many purposes. We read and write stories for entertainment—novels, plays, movies, gossip, anecdotes, and jokes. We also read and write stories for a more serious purpose—to reason about our experience. In fact, story form crops up wherever it's important for people to share an experience of the way a process works. Story form governs sets of instructions as simple as recipes and as complex as this textbook. It can also govern letters, reports, statements of opinion, speeches, jokes, and virtually every other kind of writing you could imagine. When you have finished this section, you should understand how to identify a narrative that is important to an idea you want to write about. You should be able to use that narrative to motivate yourself to revise and to influence your audience's opinion about an issue.

Writers can process a single experience into various kinds of writing, or genres (Bakhtin, 1986), all of which have a narrative base. Suppose a terrible storm strikes a city. The newspapers will tell us the news in story form, focusing on people and their actions. Police reports of accidents during the storm will follow story form as will the insurance reports that follow the police reports and the testimony in court that follows the police reports and the insurance reports. These stories will focus on identifying cause-effect relationships between the storm and damage or crime. Counselors may assist people in dealing with the consequences of the storm by asking them to retell the story of their experience. A screenplay writer may get an idea for a movie. Comedians will tell jokes about the storm.

Other commentators may subordinate the storm narrative, use it to explain or argue some point. Teachers, politicians, editorial writers, and ministers may use the story of a storm to make a point about preparedness, city services, or the instability of life. A resident of the city may write a letter to a distant parent telling the story of the storm, intending to give the parent a view of her life. The parent may write back, telling children how tough it was in the old days when you had to walk ten miles to school through blizzards uphill (both ways).

As people process and reprocess the experience of the storm, it gradually fades into the background. Eventually, only the lessons learned from the storm remain, but whenever those who experienced the storm want to refresh their sense of the importance of the lessons, they have only to recall the experience.

Personal Narrative as the Source of Motivation to Write

A narrative of personal experience lies at the core of any personally significant writing project you attempt. Whenever you write and whatever form your ideas take, the story of your experience lies behind your writing. In that experience, you find the source of your interest in your work. In our storm example, the writers turned their experience directly into writing projects. But the relationship between experience and writing can be far more subtle and complex.

The personal experience behind your work might not necessarily be a direct experience of the subject of your writing. As a male, for example, you might develop an interest in feminist issues. You obviously could not share the experience of being female in the culture, but you might participate experientially in some other way. Perhaps you grew up in a politically conscious family that made you aware of traditional roles and the problems with them. Perhaps you can identify with the feelings of oppression feminists talk about because you belong to a minority group. Perhaps you disagree with the feminists on all or part of the issue of gender in culture.

As a female you might develop an interest in the effects of political power in American culture. Because of the patriarchal structure of our society, you might have no direct experience of running a government, a company, or a school. But you might have observed the unwholesome effects of unequal power distributions in a family. Or you might have encountered ideas since you got to college that have led you to re-interpret your experience in a school or a job. Or you might have found that you have an ambition to wield power.

The ideas you learn from teachers are rooted in their personal experiences as well. This book, for example, sprang from our own experiences as students and teachers of writing. In writing courses, we have sometimes found ourselves frustrated with the separation between school assignments and the rest of our lives. At other times, we have been delighted to find writing and experience closely allied. We wanted our students to write about what mattered to them rather than to complete assignments in which they had no personal investment.

Perhaps the sociologist who wrote the article you read recently studies families because he was discontented with the family in which he was reared. Perhaps the mathematician whose course you are taking now was a physics major until he met an excellent math teacher. It could be that the person who teaches your English literature class learned to love reading because she was read to by a grandparent.

Whether the writer is a scientist, an artist, a teacher, or anything else, the writer writes about personal experience of the practice of his or her profession. The scientist writes narratives in the lab, the artist in the studio, and the teacher in the classroom.

Narrative Reasoning

Many of your responses to the Experience assignments have probably taken narrative form. Often when you use narrative form for that sort of assignment, you intend simply *to express yourself*—to put your experience into words so that you can reconsider it and decide what it means. The basic question about such narratives is whether they are honest. If the writer directly confronts experience, he or she stands a good chance of learning something.

Except for the arts, few college curricula will afford you many opportunities to write purely for expressive purposes. More often, the narrative provides an audience with a pattern of reasoning about experience. Rather than passively recording an experience as if you were a videocamera, you select and arrange events in some reasonable order.

Even in "artistic" courses like playwriting, the expressive purpose usually loses out in the long run to aesthetic purpose, the experience of enjoyment. When a writer intends a narrative *to entertain the reader*, he or she has to attract the reader's interest with a conflict of some kind. The basic question readers

ask about a fictional, artistic narrative is "What happens next?" We are interested in what happens next because two characters—usually a hero and a vil-
lain—are warring against one another in some way. Our interest rises as the
conflict increases, peaks at the climax of the conflict, and wanes as the rest of
the details of the plot work themselves out.

When a writer intends a narrative *to inform the reader*, he or she has to
be sure that the actions described are repeatable—capable of being repeat-
ed successfully by a person who has read the narrative. Practical, technical,
and scientific courses often require informative writing. If you write a set
of instructions for assembling a stereo, you can test your instructions only
by asking someone to use them to assemble a stereo. If a scientist writes a
research study, the study must include a description of the procedures.
The description must be detailed enough to allow other scientists to repli-
cate the procedure and achieve the same results. If we have done our job
properly, you'll be able to follow our instructions in this book and finish
some significant pieces of writing.

How Audience Changes Narrative

So far we've seen that narrative represents experience and that people
can process that experience into a great variety of different forms. But what
causes people to use narrative in different ways? The most important influence on the narrative we write is the audience we address. A family story
will illustrate that point.

Suppose you overheard the first author of this book telling his two
cousins a family story about an antelope hunting trip with Uncle Mel.
Since the storyteller was speaking to his cousins and you were only eaves-
dropping, the storyteller wouldn't have to fill in the details about Uncle
Mel. Cousins Chris and Ricky would already know that Uncle Mel lived in
Montana and worked on wheat ranches. The storyteller wouldn't have to
tell the cousins about Montana's terrain or climate. He could assume that
they knew about hunting trips and about Uncle Mel's tendency to have the
occasional drink while hunting.

The storyteller could assume that his cousins knew that a .308 was a
rifle, not an airplane or an address, and that they knew that if you were
hunting antelope, you were on the plains, not in the mountains. When he
told about how Uncle Mel shot an antelope from the hip, Chris and Ricky
would know that he meant it literally, not metaphorically, and that hitting
anything at all was a great feat of marksmanship for a sober person and a
very lucky chance for a drunk one. Experienced hunters themselves, Chris
and Ricky would not be surprised to learn that Uncle Mel had only
wounded the animal; they would be able to appreciate the black comedy

that ensued when the wounded antelope attacked Uncle Mel and then escaped.

You might miss a lot of the meaning of the story. In a way, the knowledge the storyteller shares with his cousins is a **code**: a code that is restricted to him and to people like his cousins who share his experiences. When writers feel readers share their assumptions, they use a **restricted code**. When they feel readers do not share their assumptions, they use an **elaborated code** (Bernstein, 1975).

To use a restricted code is to assume the reader shares the writer's experiences and values. The writer knows the readers will be interested in hearing another story about Uncle Mel, and that they won't be offended by descriptions of hunting. So the writer assumes the readers will cooperate by using their imaginations to supply a lot of the details or by tolerating repetition of details they've heard before. One of the main purposes of family stories is to express the values common to family members.

You probably haven't been antelope hunting or met Uncle Mel, so you are aware as you read this of what it feels like to be on the outside of a restricted code. You need a lot more information to make the story work for you. The assumptions of the family story genre don't work for you since you aren't the appropriate audience. The story doesn't express the values you grew up with.

Let's suppose that you cleared your throat loudly enough that the storyteller noticed you and invited you to hear the story. Let's also suppose you were reared in Montana, like the storyteller's cousins. You would have no way of knowing about Uncle Mel unless someone had told you. Since the storyteller couldn't assume that you shared his interest in Uncle Mel, he'd have to determine whether you had any interest in hunting.

Once he had established that you indeed enjoyed such stories, he might continue, but some of the details about Uncle Mel would have to be filled in, **elaborated** for you. Once he had filled in Uncle Mel's character a bit, including explanations of how Uncle likes to hunt and tends to drink, the storyteller might go on and tell the story. He would have to establish his point of view by explaining why he as a child had been taken on a hunting trip and left with his tipsy uncle while the others went off to stalk a herd of antelope. The storyteller might approach you through the genre of hunting story or tall tale. He might even embroider the truth a bit for the entertainment of his audience.

The information he gave you about Uncle Mel would form an **elaborated code**—elaborated because it was based not only on similar experiences, but also on elaborations in language of experiences you did not share. The less a writer shares experiences and values with his or her audience, the more he or she must elaborate to make the story work.

Shifts in Audience and Purpose

Note that the purpose of the genre shifts slightly to respond to a different audience. Specifically, the story began with purposes of expressing knowledge common to family members and entertaining the family members at the same time. As the audience has widened, the story has now begun to acquire an informative purpose. It's begun to take on some of the qualities we associate with a genre we call the **informative essay.**

Let's suppose that a person reared in New York City joins the storyteller's audience, which now comprises relatives, friends with similar backgrounds, and friends with dissimilar backgrounds. How would the storyteller decide which elaborations to put in and which to leave out? Perhaps he would decide that instead of a hunting story, he was involved in a travelogue, the sort of narrative essay you see on TV nature programs.

People from an urban eastern environment are not as likely as are westerners to have had much experience with hunting stories or tall tales, so the storyteller would have to do a lot of elaborating about the characters and situations, especially about hunting. He might begin worrying that the western friends and relatives would be bored by the information they know already. Actually, that's not very likely. While it is possible for readers to fill in details from their imaginations and experience, most readers appreciate the writer's doing it for them. A reader who knows more about the subject gets more out of the details.

For example, the storyteller might describe how he heard the rest of the hunting party firing and then immediately saw a herd of antelope come over the crest of a hill running in his direction. As he described the running herd and the hunter levering a round of ammunition into his rifle, firing, levering another round into his rifle and firing again, a listener who already knew about hunting would have memories of such experiences which would help her in imagining the scene he described. She could recall the sharp crack of the rifle and the smell of the gunpowder, and perhaps even feel the prairie wind.

Misfiring

But let's suppose a person who is not from either Montana or New York City joins the audience. Let's suppose this person is not from the storyteller's family, opposes hunting of all kinds, and opposes drinking on religious grounds. The storyteller would obviously have a lot of elaborating to do to keep this person in the audience.

So the storyteller would be faced with a choice.

He might decide to fill in all the information and in addition try to present Uncle Mel in a light that would not offend the rest of his audience. At this point, he really would begin to run the risk of losing the portion of his audience who were more experienced with hunting. The language event would probably **misfire**—that is, someone in the audience would be left out, bored, or alienated because of inappropriate language behavior on the speaker's part (Austin, 1962).

The storyteller had begun with the intention of telling an entertaining story, and he was able to hold on to a modified form of that intention through the first three cycles of elaboration—to the cousins, the person from Montana, and the person from New York. Given an anti-hunting audience, it would be appropriate for him to try to persuade the audience of the value of antelope hunting. He might enlist the assistance of the rest of his audience. But he probably could not hope to entertain a person who finds hunting morally offensive. Neither would it make sense for him to speak persuasively about the value of hunting to people who already shared his values. He'd have to decide to focus on one part or the other of his potential audience. A fuzzy focus on both parts of his audience would probably lose both parts.

Faced with a person who differs radically in values from the rest of the audience, the storyteller must recognize that the nature of the language event has changed. When he begins to lose his original audience, he knows that he has changed the basic nature of the language event. He has entered yet another genre, in this case, the **persuasive essay**. The essay might turn out to be an editorial with some storylike qualities. The family story about Uncle Mel might appear, without mention of alcohol, as a brief example illustrating the value of hunting. Or the story might fade entirely into the background as the source of the value the editorial writer invested in hunting.

Using Narrative to Persuade

When a writer intends a narrative to persuade the reader, he or she employs a certain kind of logic very different from the rational logic we often associate with persuasion. According to Walter Fisher, we are reasoning about experience when we tell a story: "[S]ymbols are created and communicated ultimately as stories meant to give order to human experience and to induce others to dwell in them to establish ways of living in common, in intellectual and spiritual communities in which there is confirmation for the story that constitutes one's life" (63).

Fisher is arguing that we tell stories to influence each other. Stories build worlds for us to share, to live in, to attack, and to defend. Listening to someone's story enables us to have that person's experience, which is like visiting that person's world. Once we are in the world of the story, we can begin to understand and accept events which would otherwise seem unbelievable or incomprehensible. The experience gives us some common ground with the storyteller.

As an example of **narrative reasoning,** consider the beast fable.

You're probably familiar with the expression "sour grapes." The phrase derives from a fable you may also know, having to do with a fox who couldn't jump high enough to reach some grapes he wanted. At the end of the fable, he stamps off muttering to himself that the grapes were probably sour anyway. The fable, nominally about a beast, actually criticizes the human tendency to downgrade that which we can't achieve. "Why would anyone want to be president of the class? People like that are so egotistical."

The sour grapes idea is true enough to have gotten into other stories critical of human nature. In Aldous Huxley's *Brave New World,* a utopian novel, the government uses genetic engineering to give people one of three grades of intelligence—alpha, beta, and gamma. Not content to segregate people biologically, the government subliminally conditions them to desire what they have and despise what they don't have. At night, recordings play "sour grapes" messages into the ears of each group. Alphas listen to a tape encouraging them to feel superior to the betas and to abhor the lowly gammas. Betas learn to be happy with their middle position, spared both the burdensome responsibilities of the alphas and the ignominious labor of the gammas. The gammas take comfort in drugs and their resentment of their superiors.

Now our description of the stories is not nearly as persuasive as the stories themselves. Nor can we influence people very effectively by presenting the argument of the stories in a series of neat, essay-form statements.

"People devalue that which they cannot have. We know that because the sort of rationalizations people engage in after failure usually focus on the advantages of not having achieved the goal."

Anyone looking at the statements we have just made would immediately criticize our reasoning. "That doesn't necessarily follow. What about the person who becomes depressed, even suicidal, after a failure? Or the person who can't let go of someone who no longer loves him or her? I'd like to see some statistics, some case studies, and a lot more explanation of your reasoning."

The beast fable and the utopian novel persuade a reader at a level that essay-form logic can't reach. We follow the stories and accept their conclusions, saying to ourselves, "I can see how that could have happened. Yes, life is like that sometimes."

Narrative provides a potent persuasive tool, as you can see. Because we are used to the idea that a story is a monologue, as readers of narrative we experience a strong impulse to read on, to focus on what happens next, and to suspend our disbelief. We are accustomed from childhood to accepting the most outlandish premises about animals that talk and stories that all end happily. Rather than questioning, criticizing, and finding fault, we take in the story, or perhaps the story takes us in. In either case, we find it easy to accept the arguments implied in the story.

The Power of Narrative Argument

People whose job it is to inspire belief—people in politics and religion, for example—know and use narrative technique. You have probably had the experience of engaging someone in a discussion of politics or religion. Such discussions often end in shouting matches because political and religious beliefs usually have a narrative base, and narrative arguments can be rebutted (argued against) but not refuted (proven wrong).

We can rebut a narrative argument with all the usual tactics—contrary examples, contradictory statistics, or criticism of the logic that underlies the narrative. But the story remains.

When someone says, for example, "I have experienced sexual harassment in this school," you can argue that it's unlikely, that no one else has reported harassment, that it's not clear that the behavior was intended as harassment. But you cannot refute the person's story. You cannot say, "No, you didn't." You can't know what the other person experienced. You can only rebut the statement. "I haven't experienced that sort of oppression."

We can use narrative offensively as well, to attack more logical forms of argument. For example, suppose that a rich, well-educated person enters politics proclaiming an intention to serve the poor and oppressed. Such a person would have learned all the facts, figures, and arguments appropriate to the intention to serve the people. But we might well ask questions about the aspiring politician's motives. "What experience have you had of poverty or oppression? What makes you interested in the people? How are you going to profit personally from this interest?" A politician who cannot provide credible personal narratives in response to such questions deserves our suspicion, even our scorn.

Evaluating the Truth of Narratives

In Walter Fisher's opinion, people respond intuitively to two qualities which help us determine whether we believe a person's story—**narrative probability** and **narrative fidelity.**

Narrative probability is a quality of coherence. If a story has *narrative probability*, the events in the story seem to the audience to hang together in a cause-effect sequence that would happen to the sort of people in the story. If the fable writer can present you with a believable talking fox or a plausible future society, then you may believe that the events that occur in that framework represent a reality relevant to your own. It will seem to make sense that if a wily character like a fox could want some grapes, then he could deceive himself about his feelings when he failed to get them.

Narrative fidelity is a quality of lifelikeness in a story that causes the point of the story to "ring true" to the audience. To a person who accepted that certain tendencies in modern society, particularly the reverence we hold for science and technolology, might lead toward a decay of values, it would seem reasonable to accept that the future might hold situations in which science entirely triumphs over a value like individual freedom.

In its most enduring forms, narrative becomes mythology, the sort of story that embodies a culture's most basic truths and values. When we read stories from a mythology we believe in, we respond intuitively to the truth they hold for us. The truth may be the value of hard work, family, intelligence, true love, or luck. It may be a statement like "The course of true love never did run smooth," or "Power corrupts," or "Only the strong survive."

Of course a culture's basic truths and values often look like clichés to us. Hucksters of all kinds trade in our beliefs to sell us everything from beer to TV religion, so we develop a resistance to the value of our own values. The members of a generation may become cynical, unable to believe in values that have been used for dishonest or venal ends. Therefore each new generation has to tell its own stories about its beliefs. Believing in stories about values prepares people to take the next step, of believing and acting on belief.

If you have worked through Planning Form in Part III, Drafting, you may remember a journal entry by Martha Buchanan. She had become interested in writing about a man who was subjected to shoddy treatment in a nursing home. Her work on this project began with a journal entry which simply sketched the deeply distressing series of events. Martha's teacher urged her to elaborate on the entry, suggesting that it could become a persuasive argument for the rights of institutionalized persons or a profound criticism of the ways governmental agencies depersonalize the old. As you read her draft based on that entry, consider what parts of the narrative affect you most. Suppose that Martha is aiming for the audience that reads the magazine section of a Sunday newspaper. What parts of this draft would you advise Martha to expand to make it more suitable for that audience and forum?

FROM THE JOURNAL OF Martha Buchanan

Richard Kelley was victimized because he was old, poor, and proud.

If he had had financial resources, he never would have been in a nursing home. Moreover, if he had needed long-term care at some point, he would have been respected by the staff (private pay), and would have had his own bathroom. If he had been a sacred cow, the staff never would have done more than whisper about his sexuality. "Is he or isn't he?" If he had had his own bathroom in his room, he never would have been in Nick's room in the first place.

If he had been a younger man, he would have had the resources (physical and emotional) to live alone. If he had been a younger man, he would have still had value. Public aid recipients in nursing homes are basically throw aways. They receive $30 a month to pay for all their personal needs. How much does a pair of shoes cost?

If he had been less prideful, the staff would not have resented him so much. His pride was a barrier that refused easy access to his thoughts. He was degraded by being in a nursing home, but he wasn't totally destroyed. He rarely shrugged his shoulders in resignation at a situation that he felt was unfair. He made straight for the administrator's office. He was known as one that got you in trouble by the lower staff. If no one was answering call lights, he'd ask why not? If the food was burnt, underportioned, he'd ask for more and better for Helen [his sister].

He made enemies. Many enemies. Yet, he never did anything out of malice. His concern was for Helen. If something happened, he didn't name names. He asked that it not happen again. Unfortunately, part of my job as management was to find out why it had happened in the first place. It is impossible to assure that a situation will never come up again. The most you can do is assure that the event has been investigated and that necessary measures have been put into place to do better. The staff knew that if Richard was unhappy with the food one night and one week later a new procedure was begun, that Richard was the only one who had the self-esteem and the knowledge to have said something.

Martha began with the journal entry which recorded her motivating experience with her friend in the nursing home. In the next two drafts, she steadily elaborated the story with details that supported her arguments. She produced the essay that follows. As you read it, ask yourself whether it demonstrates narrative probability and fidelity. Do the events follow in a probable chain of cause and effect? Do you believe that life is like that?

DRAFT BY Martha Buchanan

Helping Chuck Die

THE BEQUEST
Saturday, August 10 at eight A.M. I was lounging in bed drinking coffee. The phone rang. It was a woman named Virginia. She identified herself as a nurse from a local nursing home.

"Richard Kelley had a bad night," she said. "He probably won't make it through the day."

Without thinking of how callous I sounded, I replied, "Why did you call me?" She told me that my name was on his chart as the person he wanted notified if something happened to him.

ASCENDING THE MOUNTAIN

Richard Kelley, "Chuck" to those close to him, was one of the most noble men I have ever known. I first met him at a different nursing home where I worked as the director of admissions.

He was different from the others, and he knew it. He was reserved. He carried a dictionary and a thesaurus in his inside jacket pocket along with a note pad and a pen. He was always impeccably dressed. He wore a jacket with elbow patches and never went outside without his hat. He knew a lot, but preferred to keep it to himself.

His manners were flawless, and he used them as armor. The one chink in his almost impenetrable armor was Helen. Helen was the reason he was in a nursing home. Sister and brother, the two of them spent most of their lives together. When he was nine and Helen eleven, their father had died in an industrial accident. His death was the catalyst for the bond between the two of them.

In 1925 when he was fifteen, his mother sent him to Joliet to work in an uncle's clothing store. He went to school at night and visited home whenever he could.

He graduated from night school and moved to Chicago, where he took dancing lessons and performed. He was Helen's pride and the rest of his family's shame.

He was drafted in World War II. After the war, he returned to live with Helen and his mother. He was 35 and a bit old to dance. He found employment in a men's clothing store. Helen worked for the phone company.

Neighbors said that the Kelleys kept to themselves. Their world excluded outsiders. When Mrs. Kelley became ill, Helen quit her job and cared for her for seven years. After she died, Helen and Chuck began to have health problems of their own.

They made an apartment out of the first floor of their home and rented it out. Soon they were unable to care for the house. Helen had become ill, was hospitalized. They lost their home to medical bills.

They moved into a public housing facility for the elderly. They weren't allowed to live together. A man and a woman cannot live in the same apartment in public housing unless they are married.

REACHING THE SUMMIT

Then Helen fell and broke her hip. Because Chuck could not live with her to care for her, she was placed in a nursing home.

For several months he visited her every day. Finally, sick of long bus rides and loneliness, he decided to move to the nursing home to be close to her.

They had been there two years when I met Mr. Kelley. He was extremely polite with me—overly polite. His reticence forced me off center. I couldn't brightly walk down the hall, take his hand and say, "How are you, Mr. Kelley?" Instinctively I knew that such superficiality, such concern was unwelcome.

After several months, I had earned the friendship and respect of the other residents. But Mr. Kelley and I remained polite acquaintances.

Saturdays were eventful days in our relationship. One Saturday, very early in the morning, I received a call from a nurse who was on duty at the home. A retired musician who was in the home because of a brain tumor had punched Helen on the jaw and decked her.

Helen is a very sweet, unassuming woman. At the time I thought she was sweet and docile because there wasn't much left for her to work with. I was outraged that someone who had aged without rancor and bitterness, who was always pleasant regardless of the situation had been hurt. I flew to the nursing home.

Helen was crying uncontrollably. Mr. Kelley was furious. The musician was docile. The administrator of the home came to remove the musician from the facility. While his outbreaks were not his fault, the safety of the residents was endangered by his presence.

I took Helen to the hospital. Because she was so upset, and because Mr. Kelley was so upset, I asked him to come with us. Mr. Kelley became Chuck that day. We became friends.

He felt helpless to help Helen. She couldn't stop crying. He was glad to have me there taking care of the situation. Helen hadn't broken anything in the fall, but her jaw required several stitches.

On the way back to the nursing home, we stopped at Wendy's. I had not imagined, could not imagine what it would be like to be denied such a simple pleasure as a trip to a fast food restaurant. Helen was childishly excited about a milkshake. Chuck was more contented than I had ever seen him because he had a "good" hamburger.

This glimpse of life from the other side was uncomfortable, and made me feel guilty. I resolved to try to do more for the residents and to not think too deeply about the prison that the nursing home really was.

From that point on, I became Helen's protector, Chuck's good friend. I was invited to sit with them every morning. I discovered that Helen was deceiving us all. She was as sharp and quick as Chuck. She chose to play the part of a little old lady who sees nothing, knows nothing, in order to feel less deeply the pain and loss in her life.

Chuck and Helen had a special language, much like that which twins develop. It was impossible to understand their conversation unless they chose for you to understand. The tenderness between the two of them was reflected in their ease with each other and concern for each other. All Chuck had left was Helen. All Helen had left was Chuck.

Nursing homes are run by big businesses. Big businesses are in the business of mergers and acquisitions. The nursing home was bought by an east coast company. Changes were to be made. One of the changes was the elimination of all present management positions. I was fired.

As I was packing my office, several residents came to my door and cried. I hugged them and spoke brightly. But then Chuck came to the door. He was shaking. Tears rolled down his cheeks. I hugged him. I told him that I had spoken with a few of the nurses and that they had promised me that they would watch Helen for us. I told him that everything would be fine with the new management, that this is the way it is in business.

Before I left, I gave him my home phone number. I told him to call if he or Helen ever needed anything. We had traveled a long way from the time when he was Mr. Kelley and I was Ms. Buchanan.

Exposing Chuck on the Summit

Two and a half months later I picked up the phone. "Have you read the paper? They've arrested Richard Kelley for aggravated sexual assault. He's in jail."

Richard Kelley, 79-year-old gentle man, in jail for aggravated sexual assault? He was accused by two male kitchen workers (both with criminal records) of sodomizing a man who was in the advanced stages of Alzheimer's disease.

It was common knowledge, the sort of *common* which the dictionary defines as "vulgar, unrefined or coarse," that Richard was an old gay man. He had never married, was "unnaturally" devoted to his sister, and put on airs.

Nursing home food can leave a lot to be desired. Attitudes toward the elderly literally slop onto the serving trays. Food is frequently cold, under or over cooked, or inedible for any of a variety of other reasons. Helen had great difficulty keeping her appetite and her weight up. Chuck would take her tray and ask for a new one if something was seriously wrong.

The kitchen workers never liked Mr. Kelley. The kitchen staff saw him as an enemy. He never did anything out of malice. His concern was for Helen. If his polite requests could not remedy a situation, he rarely shrugged his shoulders in resignation. He was known as the one that got you in trouble.

As shocked as I was, I knew that Chuck was being repaid for his pride. I called a social service contact who gave me the name of the inmate advocate. Chuck had been in jail for two days and wasn't doing well. She couldn't believe that the nursing facility had insisted upon his arrest. She had tried to find placement for him at another facility, but he was a public aid recipient, had received quite a bit of negative publicity; no one wanted him. I asked her if they would release him to me, if he was willing to come. She gave me the name of the public defender and suggested that I call him. She arranged for me to see Chuck immediately.

I was shaking when I walked up the stairs to the visitors' room at the jail. What if he resented my interference? Richard never let anyone forget that first and foremost he was a human being. His poverty and his age were incidental to his essential humanity.

When I was led to the actual visiting room, I was shocked. They were not going to let me touch him. We were to be separated by glass and were to communicate over a phone system. They led Richard in. He looked terrible. The man who never was out of his room without his jacket, who always managed to look dapper (somehow dapper is the most appropriate description of his looks) was in a bright orange jumpsuit. His hair was sticking up; he was unshaven.

He greeted me with great surprise. "Martha Buchanan! Whatever are you doing in this place?" I responded with, "I was going to ask the same thing of you." I asked him to come live with me and my girls until we could work something out. He didn't want to agree, a part of him rejected the obvious fact that he needed help.

He questioned me over and over. "Are you sure? Why would you want to do that?" I didn't ask him if he was guilty. Inwardly I acknowledged the fact that sometimes people do things that you would never suspect them capable of doing. Regardless, I wanted him out of there. After testing me and reassuring himself that I was sincere and old enough and wise enough to know what I was getting myself into, he agreed. After one more day of judicial nonsense, his bond was reduced to a personal recognizance bond, and he was released to me.

REACHING FOR CHUCK'S HAND

The first day Chuck stayed with us he talked more to me than he ever had before. I asked him why he hadn't called me. He hadn't called anyone. He didn't feel that there was anyone to call. I continued my policy of not asking him about what happened. Finally, late that first night, he asked me why I would invite an accused rapist into my home, to live with me and my children. I answered simply, "I trust you." He then told me what happened.

Mr. Kelley had a prostate problem. He could not "hold his urine." He had had surgery seven years before, but it hadn't corrected the problem. His room had no bathroom. Public aid rooms usually don't. He shared a bathroom with ten other men. When he went down to use the bathroom, it was occupied. Nick's room was next door to the bathroom. Nick was beyond caring, or even noticing if someone used his bathroom. He had no idea why he was accused of sodomizing Nick.

Very ashamedly, he told me that his prostrate surgery had left him impotent. He wasn't capable of getting an erection. Later we read the initial police report which stated that the two men saw him coming out of Nick's room and tucking in his shirt.

By the time of the next police interview, the men said they saw him standing on a chair over Nick's bed with his pants down and his penis in Nick's mouth. Chuck couldn't climb up on a chair if his life depended on it. Evidently no one had tried to picture the circumstances described in the report. How could he be standing on a chair with his penis in the mouth of an almost comatose man who was lying prone in bed?

By the time I met Richard Kelley, he didn't have much left. He had no money, no property, no valuable personal possessions. He had had Helen, his pride and his name. All three were summarily ripped away from him. Banned from the nursing home where he and Helen once lived together, he was not allowed to visit her at all. His pride and his name were shattered.

In the middle of the night, when all else was quiet, I would hear him crying in the night. "Oh God! Oh, why? I don't understand." I worried that he would choose not to live anymore.

But I wasn't giving him enough credit. The administrator that I had worked with was administering another facility. She couldn't admit Chuck, because of the publicity, even though she knew his medical history, believed in his innocence. However, she could admit Helen, and Chuck could visit her there.

Slowly, step by step, Chuck began to try to regain his name. He called his physician and his surgeon. They verified his impotency. He called his cousin. The cousin went to see him. He went to see Helen. The staff and residents of the new facility treated him like a pariah. He held his head up, and amidst the whispers and contemptuous looks, he managed to keep his dignity.

An attorney was found to represent him. Chuck took a lie detector test. But the attorney was working *pro bono*. His concern was first to have the charges dropped, but failing that, to drag the process out so that Chuck would die before being brought to trial.

Chuck and I both thought that once the medical evidence was presented, the charges would be dropped. Then, once the lie detector results were available, the charges would be dropped. It didn't happen. The prosecution was willing to let the case go away quietly, but was unwilling to publicly announce that they had arrested a 79-year-old man, thrown him in jail, and destroyed what health he had on the word of two young men who themselves had criminal histories. Of course, Chuck had never been arrested before. He'd never been in trouble of any kind, except for a close one with alcohol and the military police in Hawaii during World War II.

LOSING MY GRIP

I learned from having Chuck stay with me. His delight in the freedom of choosing for himself when he would awaken in the morning, where he would go, a slow walk through the park. He wanted to visit the barber shop where he had gone for years to get his hair cut. He was so pleased to walk in and sit in the chair.

Coffee. He couldn't get enough coffee. He said it had been years since he had a cup of coffee that wasn't putrid. And food. I was embarrassed by the simple food that I had to offer. He relished it. His favorite meal became chicken and noodles over buttered biscuits.

Chuck was a decent man. He had no way of knowing the financial strain he would be to us. When he knew me at the nursing home, I was making enough money to meet all of our basic needs and some of our wants. That fall that Chuck came to live with us I had returned to school. The girls and I were eating very inexpensively and eating only one meal a day. Of course I had ramen and peanut butter for them, but we all understood that the pickings were going to be slim for a while.

But Chuck needed three meals a day. He was elderly and under stress. At first when I'd give him his breakfast and his lunch, he'd say, "Well, aren't you hungry?" I'd explain to him that I didn't eat breakfast or lunch, that I'd gained quite a bit of weight and didn't need it.

But soon, he refused to eat unless all of us ate together. He was losing weight. He couldn't eat ramen and peanut butter toast throughout the day. I felt guiltier and guiltier. I also became angry. I was buying him food that he refused to eat.

One meal a day was not enough. When I was gone, I'd ask my older daughter to heat his dinner. But he wouldn't eat it. His face lost all its color. I was beginning to panic and have nightmares about him dying in the house.

My old friend the administrator stuck her neck on the chopping block. She admitted Chuck. Staff, residents and families were in an uproar. She whispered his medical history to the telegraph operators in the facility. Some believed in his innocence; some believed he was a threat to themselves, or to the residents.

I drove Chuck to the nursing home. I felt so defeated. He had harbored dreams of being able to live in housing for the elderly when he first felt the flush of freedom. Three months later, he was resigned to returning to the nursing home.

Soon after that day, Chuck and I lost contact. I was totally involved with school. His world again became the world of the nursing home.

HELPING CHUCK DIE

Two years later I received the phone call from Virginia. I asked her about his cousin, had she notified him? Part of me wanted to escape, run away from the guilt, the pain, the intensity of being there while Chuck died.

"No, you're the only name he gave us." I called a friend who had known Chuck from the other nursing home, told her he was dying and hoped that she would care. She did. She went with me to the nursing home. She helped me as I helped Chuck die.

He was a dear man who taught me much. I thanked him. I stroked his head, held his hand and helped him die. He didn't die easily. He hung on and hung on. He could only be holding on for Helen.

I told him repeatedly that she would be all right, that it was time for him to go. He had been in a respiratory pattern called Cheyne-Stokes respiration. It is the signal that death is unavoidable, imminent. It is characterized by long periods of apnea, followed by a few shallow respirations. The periods of apnea become longer, until finally breath is gone.

Chuck's will was strong. He didn't want to go. He had told me that he didn't want to go before Helen, that Helen would be lost without him. I held his hand, stroked his head.

His body was becoming colder and colder, but Chuck kept breathing. Each time he gasped for air, I cringed. I wanted him to go peacefully; he deserved to go peacefully.

For hours, he seemed to feel nothing. His face was expressionless; he laid motionless. At one point, I thought he had gone. He hadn't taken a breath for quite a while. Then he gasped for air again.

But he was losing. I was repeating over and over again, "It's all right Chuck. Helen will be fine. You can go now." Every fiber of my being was concentrated on helping Chuck die.

Finally he took a breath, and his expressionless face contorted into a grimace. His face became expressive—first irritation, and then an expression which shocked me. I had never seen it on his face before, but it was unmistakable. If he could have talked, he would have said, "God damn it to hell."

THROW-AWAYS

Richard Kelley was helped to die because he was old, poor and proud.
If he had been a younger man, he would have had the physical and
emotional resources to live alone. He would still have had value. But
public aid recipients in nursing homes are throw-aways. Reflective of the
lack of respect and value is their income. In Illinois they are allowed
only $30 a month to provide for all their needs. How much does a pair
of shoes cost? Or a pair of slacks?

If he hadn't been poor, he never would have found himself in a
nursing home. He could have made one of many other choices when
illness and age produced problems for him. If he had needed long-term
care, he would have been respected by staff. He would have had his
own private bathroom. If the staff had wondered about his sexuality, they
would have whispered. If the staff had accused him of molesting another
resident, the administrator of the facility would have checked
thoroughly. She would have been heavily vested in retaining him in the
facility, instead of relieved that an opportunity to get rid of a public aid
resident had arisen.

If he had been less prideful, the staff would not have resented him so
much. His pride was a barrier that refused easy access to his thoughts.
He was degraded by being in a nursing home, but not destroyed.

Richard Kelley, 81-year-old gentle man, is dead. He died hidden
from our view, safely away from our collective responsibility and guilt.

HELPING HELEN DIE

They are helping Helen die now. Not so dramatically, nor are their
intentions so overtly callous. But they are helping her die all the same.
She, too, is old and poor and alone. When I go visit her her eyes are
bright—too bright. Her pupils are fully dilated; it's impossible to tell the
color of her irises.

I ask, "Why is Helen sedated?" The bustling, busy nurse who knows
best answers, "Honey, we have to. Helen just cries all the time; she gets
herself too upset. It's for her own good."

I ask, "Why is Helen tied in a wheelchair?" Nurse says, "Well, she's
too unsteady on her feet. This new medication makes her even more
unsteady. We don't want her to fall."

Helen wears a diaper. She either can't or won't ask someone to help
her to the bathroom. I suspect that she's learned that it doesn't matter. If
she asks, they won't come in time.

Helen is alone now. No one but Chuck and I knew that she was
competent and capable. She so convincingly portrayed the feeble-

minded sweet old lady who really doesn't know or understand what is happening around her that the illusion has become the reality. No one is around now who can appreciate her magician's transformation. She cried. Because she cried, they decided she needed to be sedated.

When I go visit Helen, she plays her game with me for a while. If I stay and insist upon talking to her, insist upon making sense out of her seemingly nonsensical utterances, she will drop the facade and talk with me. She waits to die. We are helping her, too.

EXPERIENCE

➡WARM-UP

1. In collaboration with your peer group, describe the primary purpose of Martha Buchanan's draft, "Helping Chuck Die" (to entertain, inform, or persuade the audience).
   a. Describe the basic conflict.
      • Why is it natural for the characters to experience conflict with each other over this issue?
      • At what point does the conflict begin?
      • At what point can you say that conflict has been begun to wind down?
      • What can you do to increase tension and interest between the beginning and the winding down of the conflict?
   b. Describe what the reader should know or be able to do after having read Martha's narrative.
   c. Use Fisher's tests of narrative probability and fidelity to evaluate the story's effectiveness. In a paragraph, explain why the draft does or does not hang together in a reasonable cause-effect sequence. In another paragraph, explain why the draft does or does not seem reasonable given what you believe about the world.
   d. List the events in the narrative and explain how each event leads to the next one.
   e. Then complete the following sentence: "This story shows that
   _____."

➡FOR YOUR WRITING PROJECT

2. For a writing project you are presently working on, describe an experience that is motivationally relevant to the project.
   a. Look back over the journal entries you have already completed for this course to see if any of them contains the seed of the present project. The experience may involve a feeling, an idea, a goal, or a person—virtually anything in your life.

     b. To get started, try answering the question, "What are we really talking about here?"

     c. Explain what the experience meant to you and how it led to your interest in the writing project.

     d. Or you might try completing the following sentence. "I first remember being interested in [the subject of your project] when . . ." Then discuss what was going on in your life at that time.

3. Reread the draft of your project with revision in mind.

     a. Think about how you can use the experience in your draft.

- Can you use the motivating experience directly as an example or an introduction to some idea?
- Can you use it indirectly to clarify your focus on the main idea of the project?
- Does your experience imply some additions, deletions, or rearrangements in the draft?

     b. Describe the primary purpose of your project (to entertain, inform, or persuade your audience).

- If you intend to entertain, describe the basic conflict. Why is it natural for the characters to experience conflict with each other over this issue? At what point does the conflict begin? At what point can you say that conflict has been begun to wind down? What can you do to increase tension and interest between the beginning and the winding down of the conflict?
- If you intend to inform the audience, describe what they should know or be able to do after having read your narrative. If you have written a set of instructions, find a volunteer who can test the effectiveness of your explanation. Ask the volunteer to attempt the process you have described and to suggest changes which will assist him or her in using the instructions.
- If you intend to persuade the audience, use Fisher's tests of narrative probability and fidelity to evaluate your draft's effectiveness. In a paragraph, explain why the draft does or does not hang together in a reasonable cause-effect sequence. In another paragraph, explain why the draft does or does not seem reasonable given what you believe about the world.

          List the events in your narrative and explain how each event leads to the next one.

          Then complete the following sentence: "This story shows that _____."

     c. Trade papers with a peer and repeat steps a and b.

Identify possible additions, deletions, or rearrangements that might strengthen the probability or fidelity of the narrative.

4. Clarify your audience and purpose.

   a. Look at the following list and think about these groups as potential readers of a writing project you are currently working on. Rank them in terms of how much elaboration you'd have to supply in order to make the project work for them. Note the point(s) in your list at which the different readers would necessitate changes in genre.

      • High school classmates
      • College friends
      • College professors you know
      • People you work(ed) with at your present (or most recent) job
      • People who read your favorite magazine

      Once you've ranked the potential audiences, list some of the elaborations you might supply in order to make the project work for the most appropriate audience.

      Describe your purpose, the change you would like to achieve in your audience.

      Identify the elaborations which would be most important to the audience's appreciation of the project.

   b. Repeat step a using a peer's project. Discuss your analysis and suggest possible additions, deletions, and rearrangements in the project based on your analysis.

   c. Using your own and your peer's analysis of your project, plan revisions that will clarify the purpose and audience of your project. Specify the additions, deletions, and rearrangements that will improve the project.

FINDING A NEW PERSPECTIVE

"I think I can change his mind about it." Have you thought or said such a thing? How about, "I used to believe that but I've changed my mind"? We talk about changing minds as if we had godlike power to see through people's eyes into their thoughts and feelings and then to make them think a different thought or feel a different feeling. If you think about how difficult it is to influence yourself to do your homework when you don't feel like it, keep your mouth shut when you know your temper will get you into trouble, stay on your diet and exercise plan, or admit that you're wrong when someone points out a mistake you've made, you can begin to grasp the complexity of changing someone else's mind.

This section focuses on the process of changing your own mind—of discovering a new point of view on events you're writing about and then using that new point of view to revise a draft of a writing project. Trying to look at a writing problem from a different point of view requires some flexible thinking. It's the mental equivalent of packing up and moving to attend a new school or take a new job. You have to break out of some old habits, and in exchange you receive some new insights. We can think of the process as a transaction: you spend something to get something.

Transactional Writing

How much perfume would a company sell with an ad campaign that showed pictures of their profit and loss statements? Pictures of the families of their employees looking hungry and ill-fed? How about sermons about our civic duty to smell good—the sort of campaign you find on public television stations? Though the novelty of such a campaign might sell a bit at first, you could depend on a rapid decline in consumer interest.

No, advertisers know that their own reasons for making and selling their product don't weigh as heavily in purchase decisions as do consumers' personal reasons for buying. People buy and wear perfume to increase their personal attractiveness. Partly people buy an interesting fragrance, and partly they buy the image the company gives to the fragrance, which consumers believe will become part of their own image. Thus, when advertisers want to communicate a message to a consumer, they must put themselves in a position to understand the consumer's motivations.

Someone who advertises perfumes may try to influence potential customers by creating a romantic fantasy in which potential buyers can imagine themselves playing a part. When the customers buy the perfume, they are buying not only a scent but also an image of themselves entwined with someone fascinating behind the gauzy curtains of a canopy bed, galloping a horse across a flowered meadow, or scampering impetuously from one lover to the next.

Money, which is a measure of value, is exchanged for a product with an appealing image. Since the image is partly created with language, language itself becomes a valuable commodity. People who write the ads try to use just the right words and pictures to create the image that people want to buy.

Like advertisers, you use language **transactionally,** to exchange value with people around you, all the time. When you thank someone, when you praise someone, or when you express affection to someone, you are using language to create good feelings in exchange for something the other person has given you. When you want something from someone you know, you use language to give the person good reasons for the exchange.

"I'll make dinner if you'll clean up afterward." "I promise I won't do it again." "Pleasure to meet you." "Let me tell you how I want this done." "I'll be very careful with your book, and I'll get it back to you in a week."

In all these cases, you analyze the other person, often instinctively, to decide what value you should offer to make the transaction. If the person is unwilling to enter into the transaction with you, you use language to continue to negotiate the terms of your agreement.   "Okay, I can get the book back in a couple of days instead of a week." "Well, then I guess I won't make supper."

You may seek to change a friend's opinion on a matter that seems relatively trivial to you, such as where to have dinner this evening, and suddenly find yourself in the midst of a heated quarrel because you have reminded your friend of experiences with a dictatorial sibling or parent who ignored your friend's opinions. You may find that your interaction has changed your friend only slightly but has changed your attitudes about your friend substantially. In such a case, the transaction has developed out of your control.

Decentering to Negotiate Effectively

Like an advertiser, you need to put yourself in the other person's position, to understand the other person's needs, if you are to succeed in meeting your own needs. Writing teachers sometimes use the term **decentering** to refer to this process of moving out of your own perspective. **Recentering** might be an equally appropriate term, for your goal is to move to a position in which your own interests and those of your audience line up.

The more strongly you believe your views on a subject, the more difficult it becomes to recenter yourself at a position from which you can see the other's views. Your beliefs are likely to be strongest on subjects concerning which you have personal experience. In the case we cited above, the friend's preferences about where to eat were tied up with some disagreeable experiences of family.

Paradoxically, many people who can become quite vehement on where to eat dinner or which team is likely to win the conference lack strong opinions on what we might consider important issues such as capital punishment or abortion. Unless you have some direct experience of these life-and-death issues, you have no reason to feel profound convictions.

While it is the responsibility of every thinking person to be aware of such issues and to be familiar with the arguments about them, passionate conviction will not necessarily follow from second-hand awareness or information. Where people lack experience on an issue they sometimes develop strong convictions by relating the issue to other values that are based on experience.

For example, religious people may relate capital punishment and abortion to their experience of their church's teachings about the value of life. Feminists may see the same issues in the context of their experience in a culture run by males whom they see as violence-prone and insensitive to a woman's right to control her body. African-Americans may base their attitudes on their experience of a white-dominated culture that uses capital punishment more frequently on minority than majority citizens and that makes abortion available only to those who have the means to pay for it.

If you oppose abortion, you may find it easy to assume that people who favor abortion are heartless or atheistic. If you favor abortion, you may find it equally easy to assume that people who oppose abortion are religious fanatics or male chauvinists. Such beliefs make you feel good about yourself and save you the trouble of learning about people's actual motives.

But people rarely behave according to the simple motives stereotypes would indicate, and it makes people angry to be stereotyped. It goes without saying that angry people aren't likely to change their minds. However, if you take the trouble to find out what your audience knows and believes, you are in a position to convey to them that you understand them. People are much more willing to trust and listen to reason if they feel that they are understood.

Showing Respect for Your Audience's Views

Effective communication relies on good information about the person with whom you're communicating. You'll have trouble negotiating who will cook supper with someone if you don't know whether the person is hungry or what the person is hungry for. We call the process of obtaining information about a reader's experience and values **audience analysis,** and the basis of audience analysis is respect. To respect readers is to assume that, like you, readers are people who have good reasons for their beliefs and behavior, and that it is worthwhile to understand those reasons (Young, Becker, and Pike, 1970).

Where do reasons come from? We believe that people's strongest reasons come from direct experience. When you do audience analysis, you try to experience the other person's perspective in order to learn how that context changes the information you want to communicate. You can improve the likelihood of a successful transaction by asking yourself some questions about what your audience wants and about what motivates their beliefs.

Rather than trying to get something for nothing—changing your audience's mind without changing your own mind—you can exchange minds. You can trade an inaccurate, ineffective, incomplete mindset for a better informed, more useful one which includes your audience. In transactional communication, each of you changes in some way to accommodate the other.

In effect, then, you have to change your own mind before you try to change someone else's. You have to take in their reasons. You also have to take in their values, their feelings, and their experience if you can. The same process—living with people—that enables you to speak and be understood in your family enables you to write and be understood outside your family. The difference of course is that you have to work harder at getting to know people you don't live with every day. You have to imagine what you can't experience directly.

Changing Your Mind with the Pentad

"Oh. That's lots of help. Be imaginative, huh?" Before you panic or start free-associating, consider how we define imagination. *Imagination* simply involves seeing something in a new context. You don't have to change who you are. Rather you change where you start from. You ask yourself, "What would make me change my mind if I were in the audience's position?"

Writers can frame that question in simple ways, perhaps the simplest being to ask the other person directly, "What do I need to do to persuade you to change your mind?" At the other end of the scale, we can conduct the elaborate market research that precedes the introduction of a new product. Whatever method we choose, the goal is to find common interests, ways in which our own needs intersect with our audience's needs.

A method of shifting perspective often taught in college writing courses is the **pentad.** To use this method invented by Kenneth Burke, you pretend the audience's world is a sort of drama in which the actors work out their parts in a certain scene. We focus on five elements of the drama, hence the term **pentad.**

As an example consider the place we call "home." There is no logical reason that a certain place and a certain small group of people should mean more to us than all the other places and people in the world. But we all have or want such a place and such people. Whether home implies relatives, friends, or even coworkers, we know that home is a place where we can "be ourselves"—understand and make ourselves understood through speaking a language we have taken trouble to establish and clarify between us.

The place we call home is a **scene** where significant early experiences have occurred. Within that early scene, each of us learns to **act** with a **purpose.** We find **means** to accomplish our purposes, and eventually each of us comes to a sense of himself or herself as an independent **actor.** Each of these terms of the pentad names a significant aspect of the situation in which we communicate. In addition, we can visualize each term in connection with the others to help us understand the dynamic connections between them. We can consider how scene influences act, for example.

Think of the people you regard as close family. Your mental picture of them constitutes an important **scene** in which you act, even when you aren't home. From those people, places, and experiences, family members develop beliefs and ways of living. For example, people who were reared in small towns may learn to value the friendliness, the easy pace, and the stability of small town life. Of course, some people reared in small towns may be annoyed by those same phenomena and may value the excitement and fast pace of an urban scene.

Shared values and experiences constitute reality—they build a world— for family members. The shared world provides a **means** of communication: common grounds, the basis of communication between people. Because of their common grounds, family members can communicate in a kind of code that is clear to family members but sometimes difficult for non-family members to appreciate. When you talk about the city where your parents live, the schools you attended, the summers you spent together, and all the other experiences you share with family members, your conversation means a great deal more to you than to people who have not shared those experiences. When someone joins your family, learning your history is an important part of building the new relationship.

If we are truly to communicate with a person who enters our family, or if we are truly to join a family, we must begin from a standpoint of shared experiences. It's often necessary to find an Oz of some kind—a world in which our home values and experiences don't help us—to appreciate the depth with which we can make ourselves understood to people from our own world.

You can see into people's **purposes** by listening to the stories they like to tell. The authors will use our own families as examples. Our parents and grandparents date their stories by the Great Depression and the Second World War. They talk about hardship and privation, living off the land, ranch life in Colorado and Wyoming, and coal mining in Illinois. Their themes are of battling against circumstances. Our parents see themselves as pioneers fighting to wrest a living from a rugged environment. As children listening to those stories, we learned the names and personalities of our relatives, and we learned the value of physical strength, of skill with tools and weapons, and of persistence and courage in difficult situations. We also learned respect for animals and the physical environment.

If you know something about people's early experiences in family, you can understand them as **actors** more clearly. To continue with our personal example, our lives are different from our parents' lives, so the values we learned from our parents appear in ways that reflect our own experiences. We have purposes different from our parents, and we use different means to accomplish those purposes.

We exercise physical strength and skill in athletic games rather than in making our living on a ranch. Courage and persistence are qualities we see as important to our intellectual lives; we try to say and write what we believe without thinking too much about the consequences. Our respect for the land and animals is acted out through participation in environmental groups and through making our personal lives as environmentally conscious as we can. Although our experiences are different from those of our parents, we can still appreciate one another's stories because we believe in many of the same values.

Having common grounds doesn't automatically ensure like-mindedness of course. Common grounds can turn into battle grounds. As people **act**, they simply will encounter conflicts. Many people find that the scene in which they grew up created problems because their parents imposed rules based on their own values, and those values derived from experiences the children didn't share with their parents.

"Please turn off the light when you leave the room" means one thing to someone who was reared during the Depression and quite another to someone who has only read about the Depression. "Turn off the water" means one thing to someone who grew up having to conserve well water and another to someone who has always just turned a faucet. Parents and children can see different scenes in the same environment.

Family gives people a starting point, a place we can think of as the scene in which our earliest actions take place. Whenever we think we are acting entirely logically, we have but to think of the phrase "going home." What sort of picture does that conjure? What does the house look like? Where is the house located? Who lives in the house? What feelings arise when you think of that picture?

Using the Pentad to Think About a Writing Project

The pentad, as you can see, enables us to think more deeply about a subject. Like any worker's tool, this analytical system increases the problem-solving power of the person who knows how to use it. Journalists increase their ability to write a good story by using a simple list of questions (called the Five Ws) which resembles the pentad. Remembering to ask Who, What, When, Where, and Why produces surprisingly better information than simply taking down whatever happens to occur to you.

You might use the pentad to get started on a writing project, but at that point it offers no great advantages over the Five Ws. Later on, when the project becomes more fully realized and complicated, the pentad may help you to see relationships you haven't seen before.

In explaining how to use the pentad, Burke uses works of literature, which are completed pieces of writing, not germs of an idea. He analyzes the literature by asking questions about the relationships between two of the terms in the pentad, rather than simply using the five terms as a sort of shopping list as people usually use the Five Ws.

We can illustrate the discovery of these relationships by asking, for example, what relationship exists between scene and act. Suppose, for example, we were revising an essay on how families influence career choices. In the first draft, suppose we had argued that pressure from parents may play anything from a determining role to a negligible role in the decision. Before beginning the second draft, we might ask, "How does the *family scene* affect the *act of career choice?*"

That might provoke us to define the influence of family more broadly. Perhaps indirect pressures play a part in career choices. We may need to consider the house a person grows up in and its contents. Are there books? Tools? Music? Art? Is it in the city? In the country? How often do people reared in the city in a house without books decide to become teachers? We may need to consider the experiences the scene provides. Does the scene include people of other races, religions, economic strata, or political persuasions? Is the climate harsh or hospitable? What cumulative effects might a combination of factors have on a person's ability to find out about or appreciate different choices of career?

Relationships between the scene and the act may lead us to hypothesize complex and subtle relationships between parents' choices and children's abilities to make choices. These discoveries and others the pentad may generate allow conceptual breakthroughs that lead to reconsidering the large issues of a writing project—to changing form, clarifying audience or purpose, or even to changing one's own mind about the issues.

In Chapter 6 we worked with a draft of a motorcycling essay by Scott McCullough. You may want to skim that draft now to get it in mind before reading Scott's analysis using the pentad. After showing you Scott's analysis using the pentad, we'll ask you to play the part of his peer reader—advising him what part of the new material he turns up you would be interested in seeing incorporated into the draft.

DRAFT BY S. Scott McCullough

Look at me! La-de-doody-do!

My first bike was a Kawasaki H1 with a bald rear tire, worn swingarm bushings, and no title or registration. It was a wickedly fast machine, but it handled like a cement truck and wobbled drunkenly at speeds over 50 mph. My friend Larry and I would take it out on the country roads after work, gleefully taking turns blasting off towards the horizon. Of course it was foolish and illegal, but although the police never caught us, the riding bug did. In a moment of idiocy, I traded that first bike for a console stereo that didn't work and have regretted it always.

Being a biker in the conservative Corn Belt is tantamount to waving a flag over my head and screaming, "Look at me! La-de-doody-do! I'm a freak!" When I pull up to a stop sign in a car, I'm anonymous; but when I ride up to the same stop sign on my bike, most straight citizens studiously ignore me. They stare straight ahead at the horizon to avoid making eye contact, surreptitiously locking their doors when they think I'm not looking. Children, lacking that ingrained fear and misunderstanding, smile and wave, displaying the same innocent fascination I remember from my own childhood. Perhaps that joyous interaction and fascination is part of what makes riding such a splendidly satisfying experience.

My second bike was another Kawasaki, this time a less-violent KZ 650. It was good looking, moderately fast, and cornered like a jet fighter. My friend Scott Bunton, who was separated from his wife at the time, had a Honda CBX, and we would ride at criminal velocities for hours at a time. Although I lacked any formal rider education, several near-disasters taught me how to steer and brake at speed. By the time I sold that bike, I had become a smooth, proficient rider.

I then bought two identical 1971 BMWs, one worn-out but still running, the other much better maintained but in need of engine repairs. I rode the worn-out bike for two troublefree years before selling it dirt-cheap to a friend. I then proceeded to go way overboard on the second bike, spending colossal sums of money for high-performance engine parts and machine shop services. You can probably guess what happened next: 3000 miles later, the high-dollar motor went south. Now I'm borrowing the worn-out engine from the first bike, preparing to dump yet more money into my second. The whole engine fiasco has been as painful a lesson as falling down, and I vow never to fall prey to the temptation again (although I probably will anyway).

Even as a very young child, I was fascinated by motorcycles and craved the experience of riding one. That craving became acute at the age of eight, when my father took me to see *Easy Rider*. At about the same time, I began to notice the people riding motorcycles as much as the bikes themselves. Suddenly, I realized that motorcycling was not merely a physical activity, but that it was also highly social, bringing together people with highly divergent interests and backgrounds who shared the love of riding. Bikers always seemed to enjoy life more fully and expansively than any people I had ever met before. I knew that someday I wanted to be one of them, forever travelling to wonderful and mysterious destinations.

Many people are cowed into believing that such a joyous life is somehow evil, or illegal, or a waste of time. What a sad and beleaguered attitude! I believe that life is to be lived as fully and completely as possible without harming others. Those who fear death the most often seem to live the least, while those who love life the most are often most willing to risk it. Bikers are perceived to be so threatening largely because they challenge risks instead of fleeing them, and because they often refuse to succumb to social pressures to conform. Most people spit out "biker" like a shameful label, reserved only for the lowest and most pitiful dregs of society. I have known many bikers, have lived among them, loved them, have ridden and partied and laughed and cried with them, and declare with pride (rather than admit with shame) that *I am one of them!* I could use the innocuous title of "motorcyclist" instead, but it seems to imply a sense of reservation and equivocation that I do not mean to convey.

Riding a motorcycle and being a biker are two separate activities. Mere motorcycle riders tend to be novices, dabbling in riding the way they might dabble in woodworking or needlepoint, hesitant to ride in inclement weather or to cross the county line. They feel a vague sense of shame and humiliation when their respectable friends see them riding. "I didn't know you rode one of those things," their friends might say. "Don't you know how dangerous they are?"

"Oh, I just wanted to see what it was all about," they sheepishly reply. "I don't really ride much, not really."

"Well you're just lucky you haven't killed yourself already. Those things are *so* dangerous. Anyway, only dirty scuzzbags ride motorcycles. Didn't you see that movie on TV the other day about a gang of vicious bikers who killed women and raped children and smoked LSD and snorted marijuana and . . . ."

After such an embarrassing exchange, the casual motorcyclist usually slinks back home, parks the bike in the garage, and calls the paper to place a classified ad. Their social fears and inhibitions prevent them from ever discovering what riding is all about. They have condemned themselves to a life of passive travel inside a climate-controlled box, isolated from the infinite variety of sensory inputs all around them, doomed to experience the world vicariously.

Real bikers, on the other hand, thrive on the constant variety of sensations, exposure to the elements, potential risk, and logistical hardships which motorcycling provides, and preach the joys of motorcycling with the zeal of a Jehovah's Witness on speed. "You've never ridden? Gee, I never knew. Let's go for a ride next Saturday! I know a fantastic road up by Ottawa, you'll just love it. Oh yeah, and while we're up there we could ride through this great state park, then there's a place about 30 miles west of there that has the best barbecue in the world, and then. . . ." Their lusty quest for the ultimate ride on the ultimate road and their exuberant desire to share their excitement with others sometimes makes them seem dangerously unbalanced to timid souls.

Because they share so many wonderful rides and adventures, bikers come to feel that they are a family, and to address each other as brother or sister. I have gained many brothers and sisters during my years of riding, people riding bikes as diverse as BMWs, Nortons, Harleys, Moto Guzzis, Indians, Ducatis, Triumphs, Hondas, Yamahas, and Suzukis (and some on marks whose names I cannot even recall). Being a biker is nothing at all like what the movies portray; indeed, much of the rest of society seems mean and savage in comparison. The biker society is based upon trust, self-discipline, and respect, coupled with a shared love of riding. The longer I ride, the more impressed I am with the utter honesty with which most bikers address one another. They dispense with the duplicity and evasiveness so pervasive throughout our culture, replacing it with a refreshing truth and directness. The few truly bad people who happen to ride motorcycles are no more representative of that family (also known simply as the brotherhood) than the few truly bad people who drive cars are representative of all car drivers.

Riding is like a good clean acid trip or good sex: when the roads are smooth and twisty, the scenery and weather are right (not necessarily beautiful, but harmonious), and I'm completely melded with the bike, I sometimes realize that I've transcended mortal existence. That sense of spiritual connection with absolute reality is so incredibly urgent and blissful, and time passes so deliciously slowly, that any other sensations or experiences seem shallow and insignificant in comparison. Although I enjoy riding alone, sharing such exquisite rides with a passenger or with other bikers is a unique and tremendously satisfying experience. That supreme spiritual satisfaction, combined with the camaraderie and sense of family between bikers, makes motorcycling one of the most fulfilling (legal) activities I have ever experienced.

The spirit of adolescent rebellion that animates this draft would not be damaged, would in fact be heightened, by an attempt to take the subject a

little more seriously. We found the draft entertaining but a little self-indulgent. Scott's teacher asked him to work with the pentad to discipline his
thought processes in the hope of discovering another level of significance
in the essay.

FROM THE JOURNAL OF S. Scott McCullough

1. **Actors:**
   Me as a young child, me now, bikers I saw as a child, bikers I know
   now, "straight citizens" (non-riders), "dabblers" (wannabe bikers), their
   disapproving friends, Scott Bunton, my father, and of course, the
   motorcycles and the open road. I want to emphasize the machine and
   the road as vital players in this project. Although they are inanimate,
   they are more than merely sets and props.

2. **Actions:**
   Human Characters: Riding, cornering, experiencing, proselytizing,
   sneering, disapproving, pretending, defending, believing, living.
   Inanimate Characters: Snarling, accelerating, winding, appealing,
   beckoning, idling, breaking, flowing.

3. **Scenes:**
   On the road, in smoky roadhouses, in greasy garages, in cars. The
   American two-lane blacktop highway is my intended arena, winding
   through cornfields and cresting the tops of mountains, passing over great
   rivers and through deserts, snaking through major cities and skirting
   hamlets.

4. **Purposes and Attitudes:**
   Riders: To ride free, regardless of the elements; to live as they see fit,
   regardless of public opinion; to share their excitement with others; to
   eternally seek the perfect ride on the perfect road.
   Non-riders: To discourage risk-taking; to misunderstand and
   misinterpret; to cluck and worry; to quiver in self-righteous indignation;
   to subscribe to false stereotypes.

5. **Means:**
   Riders: Superficially, by purchasing a bike and riding it. More
   specifically, their purpose is so intertwined with social (and antisocial)
   behaviors that they must make a conscious decision to become riders.
   Few people deliberately become car drivers; driving a car is considered
   the norm in our time. Riding a motorcycle, however, requires much
   more deliberation and brings a tremendous stigma.
   Non-riders: Superficially, by refusing to accept the challenge of
   riding. That's no issue. The real issue arises when they attempt to stop

other people from riding, either by physical, emotional, or political means.

Ratios (Relationships) between Terms of the Pentad:

1. I see a strong relation between the actors (specifically the riders) and all the other terms. The strongest seems to exist between the riders and their primary purpose, riding. If they did not feel a strong desire to get out and ride, they would pursue some other action.

The other relationships, ranked in descending order, are:

2. *Actor-Act:* Since the rider is so closely identified by and with the act of riding, the actor and act become nearly integral. If a person does not ride, that person is not a rider.
3. *Actor-Means:* Since they must deliberately assume the activity and the identity, the riders constantly interact with the means by which they accomplish their purpose.
4. *Actor-Actor:* A strong relation exists between the riders and other actors, including fellow riders, disapproving non-riders, and the inanimate characters (the bikes and the road). Since riding is such an introspective activity, I also see a strong internal relation within the riders themselves.
5. *Actor-Scene:* Ranking this relationship last seems contradictory, since riding would be difficult (if not impossible) without a road. However, the road is ubiquitous, in a Pirsig Zen-and-the-Art-of-Motorcycle-Maintenance sense. The road goes ever on, and if one road ends, another begins somewhere else. What road I ride on and where it leads to seems less important than how much pleasure I derive from riding it on some occasion.

A writer needs the opinions of teachers and peers to determine what to do with the new ideas generated in a session with the pentad. Suppose that Scott wanted to place this project in a periodical like *Rolling Stone*. His reader would likely be someone between the ages of eighteen and thirty who lives in an urban environment and who is interested in entertainment media such as music videos, movies, and television, as well as in the people who work in those industries. To the *Rolling Stone* reader, nonconformity to middle-class norms is an assumption, old news. In a transaction with a text, these readers would expect a writer to do something more unexpected and original with this familiar theme. Which of Scott's ideas would you suppose such a reader would be interested in reading more about?

Scott's teacher suggested that he expand on the actions and scenes to start with. A project about the experience of riding motorcycles should more vividly evoke the experience. He also suggested that Scott follow up on his reference to Robert Pirsig's book, *Zen and the Art of Motorcycle Maintenance*. His suggestion that motorcycling is an introspective activity might lead him to deepen a draft which at present stays pretty near the surface.

Perhaps nothing about writing is more challenging or, finally, more rewarding than taking a new perspective on a project, breaking out of old assumptions to find new ideas. A method like the pentad can help a writer to gain intellectual leverage on a problem. Then, in consultation with others, the writer can make the changes which give the project dimension, depth, and originality.

EXPERIENCE

➡WARM-UP

1. Describe a time when you negotiated with someone.

   The person may have been a phone caller from a magazine subscription service, someone knocking on doors to enlist your participation in a religion or political cause, a classmate who wanted notes or some other form of assistance from you, a friend who wanted to buy you lunch, an admirer who wanted your company, or any other person who offered you something of value in exchange for something else of value.
   - Was the person successful? Can you say why?
   - How did you feel during the interaction? Afterward?
   - What might the person have done to be more effective in negotiating with you? Did you make your preferences clear to the person?

➡FOR YOUR WRITING PROJECT

2. Analyze the draft of a writing project you are working on in the following way.
   - List the characters.
   - Outline their actions.
   - Describe the scene in which they act.
   - Explain their purposes and attitudes.
   - Describe the means by which they accomplish their purposes.
   a. Which of the elements of the pentad seem most closely related in the project you have analyzed? Scene and act? Actor and action? Means and purpose? In cooperation with your teacher or peer group, try using the table below to help yourself visualize the most important relationships.

Stay flexible with this exercise. That is, try several ratios before deciding you've had enough; new perspectives take some work. But don't turn it into busywork filling in little boxes. When you've found an interesting new angle to write about, stop and write about it.

Ratios (Relationships) between Terms of the Pentad

	Actor	Act	Scene	Means	Purpose
Actor					
Act					
Scene					
Means					
Purpose					

b. Has new information occurred to you about your subject, your audience, or about some other aspect of your writing project? What additions, deletions, or rearrangements might this imply in your draft? Make a list of the steps you'd need to take to make the changes.

Chapter 9
Analytical Strategies for Revision

_____

_____

_____

In this chapter you will learn how to take a new, more focused perspective on the logical arguments in a draft. Taking an argument apart helps you to see how to put it back together more strongly so that it resists attacks from those who argue against you. You will also focus in this chapter on the background assumptions and expectations readers bring to the scene (or **forum**) of an argument. Building your arguments on common assumptions will further strengthen your case.

ANALYZING ARGUMENTS

In the academic world, we usually focus on analyzing and debating our perspectives on the ideas that interest us. We argue in order to think more clearly. Revising writing in college very often involves strengthening arguments. Learning about the intellectual arguments in an academic environment also helps you to understand the rules and learn how to get along, as learning a family's stories help you to feel at home in the family. When you have finished reading this section, you should understand some basic techniques of logical argument well enough to analyze an argument to attack it or improve it.

By the term **argument,** we do not mean the boorish shouting matches or the cordial exchanges of sarcasm that occur when two people are angry and eager to hurt each other. Those are merely quarrels. _Argument_ is a verbal contest with customs, rules of fair play, a playing field, an audience, judges, and trained contestants. Interscholastic debate programs, meetings of governmental bodies, political debates, and legal proceedings are environments—textual worlds—in which argument takes place.

If you have written research papers, you have already begun to experience the intellectual world of argument concerning theory or research in an academic subject such as English, history, biology, mathematics, music, psychology, and so on. Research papers are usually impersonal in both their form and content.

It won't do, for example, simply to assert that recordings containing explicit sexual references are protected by the First Amendment to the Constitution unless you can provide reasoning and legal precedent to support your assertion. Your opinions aren't sufficient by themselves to people who disagree with you. Your readers need to be able to trace the path of your reasoning, so you have to show them the evidence.

In a way you are telling a story, the story of your thought processes. You can be sure that people who disagree with you will criticize your thought processes, so you have to be careful to use evidence and reasoning to form a tight chain. "I am opposed to censorship because it violates the First Amendment" won't do.

You have to state the First Amendment, explain the rationale behind it, state the case you particularly have in mind, explain why the First Amendment applies to it, cite similar cases that were decided in the way you favor, and dismiss similar cases that were not decided in your favor. In all this discussion you have to pay strict attention to a code of ethics that requires accurate statement of the law and relevant cases. And there is much more than we have mentioned.

Each academic discipline has its own attitudes about what counts as evidence and logical argument. In a literature course, you might use the text of a poem, essay, story, or novel to analyze a character. In a psychology course, you might use a set of numbers on which you'd perform tests of significance like chi square and ANOVA to discuss the differences between two sets of responses people made to a questionnaire. In a history course, you might use old documents such as newspapers, diaries, and government records to prove your case, while in an archaeology course, you might find that comparisons of one bone structure with another would help you to prove a case. Each of these viewpoints defines the logical world in a text written for a particular discipline, and learning the logic of an academic discipline helps you to see the world as members of the discipline see it.

The Legal Origin of Argument

You can understand some basic principles of most forms of academic argument if you consider how legal argument works. In court, lawyers use a combination of fact, law, and precedent (decisions rendered in similar cases) to argue for their client's best interests—in other words, to tell the story of the events from the client's point of view. A third party, a judge or jury, listens to both lawyers, weighs the evidence they present, and decides what course of action should be taken.

The person who acts as judge or juror must try to set aside prejudices and preconceptions in order to listen dispassionately to the evidence. Human relationships between lawyer and judge or juror then recede into the background as the audience of legal argument strives to focus on finding the facts in the matter. In order to set a standard of judgment for judge and jury, the people who framed the law have hypothesized something called the **reasonable person**. In any situation, a judge or juror must weigh evidence in the context of law and precedent and try to think as a reasonable person would think.

Take divorce, for example. The people who are getting divorced usually think the facts are clear, but their viewpoints are influenced by their emotions and by the same misunderstandings and differences that caused the relationship to fail. Both people are often angry, hurt, and motivated by the desire for revenge. As people sitting in judgment of their situation, we may conclude that their desire for revenge is understandable, but we will probably not find them reasonable. That is an important distinction in the law. We understand that each side in the divorce may want to do the maximum harm to the other, but we must help people to behave reasonably even in such trying circumstances. In such times, people need help in trying to formally dissolve the legal part of their relationship and to create an orderly division of property, so they go to court.

Of course legal proceedings produce error along with truth and injustice as well as justice. Where human motives are concerned, it's hard to define truth and justice in a way that everyone will agree with. It may even come down to which side has more skill in defending its own case and attacking the weak points in the other side's case. It is therefore the duty of both sides to argue with skill.

The British philosopher Stephen Toulmin (1958) studied many legal cases to discover how people reasoned through a case. From his studies, he developed a **layout**, an outline of argument, as follows. Arguments begin with a three-part structure comprising the facts of the case (called the **data**), the point of the argument we're making (the **claim**), and the logical connection between the data and the claim (the **warrant**).

So if you're **claiming** that your client should have custody of the six-year-old daughter and $1000 a month in child support, you need to offer some data which support the claim. The **data** might include your client's history as a parent, your client's employment and residence, or anything else that suggested your client's qualifications as a parent. The **warrant**— the logical premise that connected data with claim—would be that a person who in the past had been the more qualified parent would continue in the future to be the more qualified parent.

The Toulmin layout—data, warrant, and claim—resembles a story line which leads the judge through a series of events. Our arguments must conform to the story line or the case falls apart. People who oppose our viewpoint will try to tell an equally credible story, arguing that their client has always done everything possible for the child. If successful, our opponents will persuade the judge to stop believing in the validity of our argument. Then, like a dream, our story will dissolve into fragmentary images.

Ways of Attacking an Argument

When the opposition attacks our claim, they will invent a **rebuttal** (Toulmin, 1958), which may be anything from using our own data and warrant to support a different claim to attacking every detail of our argument. We'll have to be very careful to begin with data which we can support with records or the data will not count. If we say that our client has been a faithful parent, we have to be prepared to provide records of time and money spent on the child.

We can also assume that the opposition will attack the warrant, the logical premise from which we have reasoned, so we must be prepared with **backing,** a reason behind our reason. If we have reasoned that our client's record as a parent establishes that he or she is the better choice for custody, the opposition will try to suggest that the past guarantees nothing about the future. Our defense against that argument may be to suggest that past conditions haven't changed, that the other parent was never much help so his or her absence will not matter, and so on.

As a last-ditch effort, the opposition will at least try to make us allow a **qualification** of our claims. If we argue for sole custody, the opposition will rebut with an argument for joint custody on the premise that all children need two parents and that no two parents are equally qualified to rear a child.

Using Toulmin's Layout to Analyze an Argument

If you have worked through the section in Chapter 7 entitled Suggestions for Change in a Writing Project, you may remember the following draft. Written by Jon Neuleib, this draft advances an argument that we must preserve ocean resources since we rely on them utterly for much of our sustenance. Jon had written the draft to prepare for his work as a member of the college debate team, so he had focused on creating effective arguments.

Jon's reviewer had suggested that he would need to "unpack" his thought on this issue, to cite some research and focus his discussion. We can use Toulmin's model of argument to analyze and either defend or dispose of some of Jon's arguments. We will number the paragraphs for reference and italicize some of the arguments Jon still needs to unpack.

DRAFT BY Jon Neuleib

Ocean Resources

1. Who owns the ocean and its resources? We need to answer this question not only to divide the wealth but to assign responsibility for keeping the ocean clean. This economic question is the heart of the environmental issue and the main reason why the ocean is an issue of pressing concern for humanity. Two major threats loom if these issues are not resolved: world-wide pollution and international conflict over ocean resources. *Time* describes the vastness of the problems by noting that "the blight is global, from the murky red tides that periodically affect Japan's Inland Sea to the untreated sewage that befouls the fabled Mediterranean. Pollution threatens the rich teeming life of the ocean and renders the waters off once famed beaches about as safe to bathe in as an unflushed toilet" (44).

2. The polluted waters are unable to support life both on land and at sea. *We read about efforts to stop dumping in the ocean, but the issue cannot be solved by arresting a few obvious polluters and washing a few seals.* Clean-up projects that have been mandated for the ocean have not addressed the true magnitude of the problem. The areas of the earth that are closest to the ocean are becoming more and more heavily populated, putting more and more strain upon the ocean.

3. We do not know how badly we may be harming the oceans. Ocean waters can regenerate as was proved after the 1979 oil spill in the Gulf of Mexico, a disaster which observers thought would destroy the shrimp industry. Evidently, "the ocean has a greater capacity to break down hydrocarbons than scientists thought. But there may be a limit to how much damage a sector of ocean can take. Under assault by heavy concentrations of sludge, for example, the self cleansing system can be overwhelmed" (Toufexis, 44).

4. We have managed to live with the oceans in their current state, but we may be risking some larger breakdown. Marine scientist Herbert Windom explains our uncertainty: "We see things that we don't really understand. And we don't really have the ability yet to identify natural and unnatural phenomena. We know more about space than the deep ocean" (Toufexis, 44).

5. *The ownership of the sea and the resources in it is arguably the first question that needs to be addressed when we consider an ocean policy, but it is usually the last one addressed by policy makers, an oversight that may lead to future conflict.* There are two important designations under which the ocean can fall.

6. The first is the continental shelf, which was determined under international law to be part of the country that owns the shore adjacent to it. This agreement has been supported by the international community for a number of years with the United States declaring sovereignty over its shelf in the 1960s. The second—the Exclusive Economic Zone, or EEZ—was first introduced in 1945 but has taken over thirty years to gain steam (Song). An EEZ is the marine area extending up to 200 nautical miles off a coastal state. The state has sovereign rights over the resources in the area, but other states enjoy freedom of the high seas in the coastal state's EEZ, including freedom of navigation and overflight and the freedom to lay pipelines and submarine cables (Cruickshank).

7. For almost a decade after this formal introduction of the concept of the EEZ, the large maritime powers, such as Japan, the Soviet Union, and the U.S., opposed this apparent infringement of freedom on the high seas. Once the issue was brought to the U.N. and given a formal framework, the United States capitulated to mounting international opinion and declared its own 200 mile EEZ in 1983. The law as it stands at this point is explained by Song.

8. The United States accepted this agreement because of the conditions that were established for use of the high seas by third states [i.e., nations that pass over waters whose ownership is contested by two neighboring coastal nations]. Obvious areas of conflict occur when neighboring coastal nations' borders do not meet the sea at a crisp ninety degree angle or when nations lie less than two hundred miles across a body of water from each other. Currently, in the South China Sea, which would intuitively belong to the People's Republic of China, the PRC will not claim an EEZ because of the counter-claims that exist with Taiwan and Vietnam. The situation is not nearly as tidy as the U.N. text would make it seem. In the U.S. the proclamation of the EEZ has brought many benefits for our coastal economies, but it also mandates that the coastal nations be responsible for the environment of their EEZ. It is a white elephant of sorts if one remembers the amount of pollution that exists along our coasts and in the adjacent sea. The EEZs also change the use of the resources, as Covey in *Sea Technology* reported when noting a 47 percent decline in joint venture catches since 1988: "Fishing in the U.S. EEZ has steadily declined, with the virtual elimination of the once huge Pacific foreign fishery. East Coast EEZ foreign fisheries were reduced to 37.22 metric tons, mostly mackerel. Fish once caught in the EEZ by foreigners are now caught by U.S. fishermen" (10).

9. Whether it is more advantageous to have the profits from those catches going to the U.S. or foreign fisheries is an issue that is for policy to dictate. The idea of the EEZ meshes in this way with the idea of the high seas. While the U.N. proclamation allows Third World countries to pass over the territorial waters of the coastal state, it is not clear who is responsible for the pollution those shippers may cause. If the Exxon Valdez had been under foreign ownership, the resulting legal mess would probably never be figured out. It is also important to question the legitimacy of a third country's interdiction of an EEZ with military vessels. It is considered a right for the coastal state to police its EEZ with reasonable force and this could lead to military confrontations in the future. In the disputed South China Sea area, Vietnamese patrol boats have fired on third country fishing boats that were considered within their unofficial EEZ.

10. Although this may be the first issue that policy makers must address, having decided how to do it fairly does not solve all the problems involved in the maritime world. The interconnectivity of the various issues is seen in the ownership of the sea, but none of the issues will be settled by merely focusing on who owns the sea. *It is important to seek policies that would deal with a variety of issues while not causing new ones to crop up.*

11. One of the things that makes this topic area so interesting is the way that the various facets reflect upon each other. In the area of national defense, how we conduct civilian research, pollution control measures, and ownership all have long reaching effects on our military program. *The United States must be able to protect its self-interest if it is to participate enthusiastically in pollution control and clean-up.* In the area of pollution, making our navy comply with international treaties has been an expensive part of our defense program. The Navy has canceled a contract for 11 million plastic bags but has then had to develop other methods of dealing with waste such as trash compactors or melting plastics into bricks. Such projects cost the Navy at least $1 million per ship (*Time*, 1988).

12. While expenses such as these are often cited in opposition to environmental programs, some environmental research activities actually help defense efforts. One important project of the U.S. Navy is its research in oceanography. Just as acoustical technology is essential to our ability to maintain our underwater capability, weather and geographic knowledge are essential to our Navy as a whole. Our ability to use our forces and to achieve victory is supported by our oceanographic ability as Gross in *Sea Technology* reports: "We have progressed to a complexity and sophistication wherein the

determining factor between victory and defeat may well be exploit-
ing our knowledge of the environment" (45).

13. All our technological advances are dependent on advanced weapons
    systems that need a great deal of information provided to them for
    them to work. It seems that we have made our systems more fragile
    as we have made them more lethal. The effectiveness of our technol-
    ogy depends on the work of the Oceanographic Department of the
    Navy. Admiral Miller in *Sea Technology* explains that "increased
    technological complexity and sophistication of Navy weapons and
    sensor systems require an increased understanding of the
    environment in which they operate. Accurate and up to date knowl-
    edge of ocean and atmosphere dynamics is critical to the successful
    employment and deployment of Navy weapons systems" (21).

14. The same improvements that may help us map the ocean floor may
    help our destroyers track foreign subs. Even the "pure research" that
    would be gained from the exploration of the ocean floor would
    have military applications as defense planners map attack routes for
    our SSNs to follow. This is not to suggest that the military is
    somehow behind all civilian developments or that it co-opts all rel-
    evant information, but it is important to remember that all policies
    have a ripple effect across both the military and civilian sectors of
    the maritime world. We must obviously prepare our Navy for the
    variety of threats that it may face in the future. We must also decide
    how to utilize those forces in the event of a conflict. How we deter-
    mine who owns the sea will decide a large portion of how we deal
    with those forces.

15. Even a partial list of the problems in protecting the ocean makes
    clear that international cooperation on a unheard-of level will be
    required to clean up the ocean. The task of cleaning up pollution
    demands that we use scarce resources. Opposing policy makers
    will want to know why we should risk stirring up more pollutants
    and whether the ocean can solve pollution problems for itself. As
    we increase our technological abilities to explore the ocean depths,
    we must bear in mind the effects that increasing our undersea mili-
    tary capabilities would have on the global situation. We must deal
    with problems with international law, maritime economics, and
    policing a huge EEZ. Although we can begin by monitoring our per-
    sonal behavior, we must end by bringing every seafaring nation in
    the world into agreement.

Works Cited

Chesbrough, RAdm. G. L. "Naval Oceanography: 'Wind and Waves are Always
    on the Side of the Ablest Navigators.'" *Sea Technology*. Jan. 1991: 19.

Covey, Charles W. "Ocean Resources: An Economic Overview." *Sea Technology*. Sept. 1990: 10.
Cruickshank, Dr. Michael J. "Ocean Mining: For the Future, A Good Omen." *Sea Technology*. Jan. 1991: 38.
Graham, David M. and Richard J. Arnold. "Science, Ocean Programs Big Winners in FY 91 Budget." *Sea Technology*. Mar. 1990: 17.
Gross, Dr. M. Grant. "NSF: Ocean Sciences, Arctic & Global Climate Change Research." *Sea Technology*. Jan. 1991: 45.
Miller, RAdm. W. C. "Ocean Sciences at ONR: The Challenging Future." *Sea Technology*. Jan. 1991: 21.
Song, Yann-huei Billy. "China's Ocean Policy: EEZ and Marine Fisheries." *Asian Survey*. Oct. 1989: 983.
Toufexis, Anastasia. "The Dirty Seas." *Time*. 1 Aug. 1988: 44.
Wiseman, Charles. "ASW Budget Remains Strong." *Sea Technology*. Nov. 1990: 21.

We will analyze one of Jon's arguments and then invite you to try your hand at the analysis.

We read about efforts to stop dumping in the ocean, but the question is whether we can solve the problem by arresting a few obvious polluters and washing a few seals.

Jon has enough skill with language and rhetoric to know that he probably couldn't get away with asserting what he has implied with his "question." The question form disguises a **claim** we'll state explicitly in order to attack it: "It's a waste of time to focus on individual problems when we should be looking at the big picture, which is economic."

We would first want to see the **data** from which this claim proceeds. Like some other claims in Jon's draft, this one offers neither factual backing nor reasoning. Jon implies that he knows of cases in which the government has wasted time on small-scale clean-up. As his peer readers, we might ask him to cite a few instances. One of the commonest faults of academic writing is the tendency to intellectualize—to refuse to confront concrete problems in the here-and-now, to retreat to theory and the "big picture." We would like some reassurance that Jon is not advocating cessation of environmentalists' efforts to clean up beaches and rescue sea life.

If we found that Jon could cite data for his claim, our next step would be to question his **warrant,** the method of logical reasoning behind the claim. Supposing that he could cite instances in which we have recklessly ignored the most effective approach to the problem, we would want to know whether his instances were isolated or whether they represented a pattern broad enough for us to believe that bad judgment rather than a reasonable division of our efforts to various parts of the environmental problem was involved. In short, we would ask whether a reasonable person would support the claim he made from the data he presented.

We would also want to understand the **backing** behind his warrant. If he argues that his evidence represents a trend of sentimentality on the environmental question, we would assume that he backs his choice of evidence with his own credibility. We might question why we should believe his report of the evidence. For his part, if he could establish that he paid more than lip service to the environment, we might take his objections more seriously. If, for example, he could present evidence that he had ever worked to clean up a beach, we might begin to believe him.

Jon would need to anticipate and be prepared to counter **rebuttal.** An obvious line of rebuttal would begin with the assertion that international politics has little to do with ethics or individual needs. Governments are much likelier to protect their industrial base than the environments in which they operate. Nations have and defend borders precisely because they expect other nations to ignore their interests. In the real world, we might argue, saving one beach means more than a dozen international resolutions to cooperate in researching the problem.

Finally, we might expect a reasonable **qualification** of this claim. Instead of the blanket assertion that environmental activism wastes time, we might feel more disposed to consider an assertion that naive activism attacks the symptoms rather than the causes of the problem.

As you can see, quite a lot of reasoning lies behind a simple generalization when you begin to unpack it. Supporting a single assertion may require an elaborate framework of argument. It therefore behooves writers to reason cautiously, especially in writing for academic audiences who expect reasonableness above all.

EXPERIENCE

➡ WARM-UP

1. Have you ever been involved in a dispute as an intermediary representing one person to another? Perhaps you talked to one friend for another, to one family member for another, or to a colleague at work for another colleague.
   - What tactics did you use to try to assist the combatants to resolve the dispute?
   - Did your involvement change your relationship with your friends?
   - Did you succeed?
   - How did you feel about your involvement?
2. Have you ever been involved in a situation in which someone else acted the lawyer's part on your behalf?
   - How did you feel about your "lawyer"?

- Did having counsel change your feelings about the person you were disagreeing with?
- Did you get what you wanted?

3. In cooperation with your class or peer group, use Toulmin's layout to analyze one or more of the italicized assertions in Jon's draft.

4. For two courses you're taking now, or have taken in the past, describe the basic methods of reasoning about experience.
   - What counts as evidence? As good reasons?
   - How do you evaluate evidence and reasoning?

➡**FOR YOUR WRITING PROJECT**

5. Trade drafts with a peer. Using Toulmin's layout, analyze the three most important assertions in a draft of a peer's writing project.

   - **Claim.** Describe the central point of the writing project.
   - **Data.** List the most important pieces of information which support the claim.
   - **Warrant.** Describe the reasoning process by which the claim flows from the data.
   - **Backing.** Try to attack the warrant. In what ways might an opponent claim the reasoning process is faulty?
   - **Rebuttal.** Try to attack the claim. What other claims seem reasonable based on the data presented?
   - **Qualification.** Try to attack the strength of the claim. In what ways might you say the writer has overstated his or her case?

   a. For each point you attack, suggest additions, deletions, or rearrangements in the information which would strengthen the argument against attack.
   b. Rank your suggested changes from most to least important.

ANALYZING FORUMS

A forum, you may recall from Chapter 4, is a place of publication. When writers envision a writing project, they also envision a forum which they know well to give them a sense of reader's expectations. You may recall from Chapter 5 that the forum continues to figure in a writer's more detailed planning for audience. A writer can examine publications to develop a sense of the "rules" about subject matter, length, and so forth in writing for that publication. As the writer works through the drafting and revision processes, a project often takes unexpected directions, so that the original plan and the actual draft begin to diverge. If you are the writer you may think, "Well, that's okay. It'll still work for the audience I had in mind." Or maybe you think, "Oh no, this will never work. I'll have to change everything." When you reach this point in a project, you need some information from people who actually read the sort of project you are writing. You need to find out how much of your vision is illusion.

Projection

You know that in communicating with someone who knows you well, you can usually be yourself. But at some point, you find that the people in your world don't want you to be yourself. You come home with a new look, a new friend, a new political idea, or, worst of all, a new belief, and you find familiar people seeming distant and strange. They say, "That just isn't you," by which they mean wearing your hair differently, dating someone from a very different background, or joining a different political or religious movement wouldn't suit the person they think you are based on their experience with you.

Suddenly both of you are *disillusioned*. You thought he was reasonable. He thought you were sensible. You both see how wrong you were.

Where do the illusions come from in the first place? Psychologists explain some of the mistakes we make about other people as the result of **projection**. We look at another person and project our hopes, fears, wishes, or beliefs onto the person as if he or she were a movie screen.

We believe that family members ought to accept each other as they are, so we project that belief onto parents. "Of course they want me to be happy. They're my parents, aren't they? And being a _____ [you can fill in the blank with whatever label applies to you] makes me happy, so it must make them happy too."

If we are angry with someone but haven't admitted it to ourselves, we may project that anger onto the other person. "I really hate dealing with someone who's so angry all the time! My boss and I will never get along because we're such completely different people!"

Uh-huh. Right.

Whenever we think that someone is "just like me" or "nothing like me," whenever a person seems very familiar or utterly foreign, we need to beware of projection. That familiar person we see may be our own reflection in the mirror of someone else's eyes. That strange person we see may be our own unacknowledged darker side.

In writing, we are often projecting when we write for the "general audience" or "people who are interested in _____." (You can fill in the blank with the subject of the writing project you're working on right now.) We write an essay and instead of making a point of finding out what sort of information the intended reader needs, we say, "This is good for the general audience," "for people my age," or " for everyone interested in the care of iguanas." The general audience is really you.

It's easiest just to assume that readers think and speak like you and easily understand and agree with what you say. But that easy assumption blinds you to the real differences between people. If we weren't different, we wouldn't need to communicate. If people could read our minds, they'd share our experiences, and we wouldn't need words. But we do differ from each other, and most of us can't read minds.

Suppose you wrote an essay on conflict in families. Working from your own experience of family, you talked about the causes of sibling rivalry, the effects of overprotective or overlenient parents, the ways that children act out the conflicts between parents, or the pressures children feel to conform to their parents' hopes and expectations. Who would be the most competent reader of this essay?

You would, of course, since the experiences and the family are your own. You know the people and the events, so you have no difficulty accepting your own conclusions about them. You can simply tell the story of what a louse your older sister was, of how she drove your parents crazy and caused them to be more restrictive with you than they needed to be, and then you can draw the obvious inference. Youngest children have the toughest situation: unnecessary restrictions, fewer privileges, perpetual second-class citizenship. Your general audience would include you and all younger children with your experience. But why bother to state a truth obvious to the audience?

What if you were trying to explain the point to parents? It wouldn't be fair to parents to assume that they shared their children's attitudes, nor would it be fair to assume that they could never understand because they're old.

You could guess that parents wouldn't like to be told that they made second-class citizens of younger children. You might also guess that parents would disagree with someone who asserted that they had imposed unnecessary restrictions or that younger children endured any more hardships than older children.

Presence and Points of Departure

But somewhere in your chain of reasoning, you could probably find a fact, a conclusion, a value, or a method of argument parents could buy. You can increase your effectiveness and lessen the influence of projection if you try to discover and begin with points of agreement between you and your audience as points of departure for your arguments.

"The fact is that she got her own car in her sophomore year, and I didn't. Since she got a car when she was sixteen and promptly wrecked it and went on academic probation, and I wasn't allowed a car when I hadn't yet driven and my grades were high, it seems safe to conclude that they were using their experience with her to make rules for me."

"Of course, everyone agrees it's important to be fair. Isn't it more important to respond to people as individuals than to make up one rule and apply it to everyone as if they were the same person?"

Points of agreement represent the common ground between you and your audience. If you begin your argument with a point your audience accepts or understands, you can try build on that acceptance or understanding to affect their interpretation of something they don't yet believe as strongly as you do. It's a slow process, but if you can give your viewpoint the same **presence**—that is, the same importance and clarity in the mind—as your audience's original viewpoint, you can hope to affect their beliefs.

Finding Common Points of Departure with the Reader

In a book called *The New Rhetoric* (1958), Chaim Perelman identifies six **points of departure** that may help you to be more persuasive (or informative) to your audience. You can tell from the metaphor, "points of departure," that he is thinking in spatial terms. You know that in order to persuade someone with oral language, you literally have to be present in the same space in order to have the common points of departure for your conversation. We call that common space a **forum**. Literally, the Latin word means a fenced-off place. In written versions of argument, the fenced-off space exists at an abstract, figurative level in the expectations of readers. We'll illustrate the idea of points of departure in both oral and written forums. To begin with, we'll ask you to consider a familiar situation—the classroom. We'll use a math classroom.

We all like to think that our reasoning processes work with the self-evident clarity of a mathematical equation: given a and b, then c is true. In your math classes, when the instructor solves problems on the board, the instructor will give you some **facts.** "The value of r is 11." "The value of x is 20." You may then use those facts to arrive at **truths,** statements that describe the relationships between facts. "Solving the equation then we see that the value of y is 15."

But if you don't have the same facts, you don't arrive at the same truth. Everyone needs to start out believing that r is 11 and x is 20 if y is to equal 15. As you well know, having the same facts in common and using the same reasoning methods doesn't guarantee that you'll all come out with the same answer. How much easier must it be for people to draw different conclusions based on the uncertain information of language! Such is the importance of common points of departure.

In solving a math problem on the board, the instructor will work with the **presumption** that you know the formulas in order to be able to follow the explanation. Even if your answer differs from the instructor's, you can follow what he or she is saying much more clearly if you begin with the same set of information. We all know that the presumption that people know the formulas is not always well-founded, but we agree that the presumption is necessary to the efficient conduct of a class. What similar presumptions do you make about readers as a writer? That the person who reads your work has had your experience? That he or she has interpreted it the same way?

In math class, people who haven't done the homework are making a point about **values.** Perhaps they feel that the effort to complete the homework is too high a price to pay for the benefit they get. People who do complete the homework obviously don't agree. Perhaps those who complete the homework have a different **hierarchy** of values. They believe that math skill is important to their future careers. Connecting the homework to a value like career, which is near the top of most people's hierarchies, can do a lot for personal motivation. Readers too want to be given reasons to value the information you present. They all have other ways they could spend their time.

The math instructor motivates everyone to do the homework with a familiar method of reasoning (or **locus,** the singular form of **loci**). "The homework counts as 20% of your grade." We accept the reasoning that work assigned for a course should count toward the grade. You can see how commonsensical that line of reasoning is by considering how you would react to a teacher's announcement that none of the homework would count toward the grade. "All that work for no credit? Ouch!"

That line of reasoning is an example of a more general line of reasoning about cause and effect. We believe that effects have causes, and it doesn't seem reasonable to us that an effect can be achieved without a cause. Like anyone else, a reader of your writing works with assumptions about how people reason.

You can probably begin to see how points of departure work. The more points of departure you have in common with your reader, the likelier your reader is to understand and accept your work. To review, we'll list the six points of departure once again.

- **Facts:** pieces of information that both parties accept. Note that by this definition "1 and 1 equals 2" ceases to be a fact if one party to the disagreement questions it.
- **Truths:** generalizations that both parties accept and that interpret or order a set of facts. Note that by this definition it is true that the

Tooth Fairy trades money for teeth if both parties believe that's why they find quarters under their pillows in the morning.

- **Presumptions:** working hypotheses that both parties accept. An example is the presumption of innocence in a court of law. There is a difference between a presumption of innocence and the fact of innocence. The presumption simply puts the burden of proof on the prosecution (or plaintiff in civil cases).

- **Values:** objects, people, or beliefs that people prize in some way. Money is a concrete value to most people. A reputation for honesty with money is an abstraction most people value.

- **Hierarchies:** systems in which values are rank-ordered. Shakespeare was setting a hierarchy that rank-ordered a good reputation and money when he wrote, "Who steals my purse steals trash; 'tis something, nothing; / 'Twas mine, 'tis his, and has been slave to thousands; / But he that filches from me my good name / Robs me of that which not enriches him / And makes me poor indeed." *Othello*, III, iii, 157–61.

- **Loci:** commonsensical ways of reasoning people will accept unless there is good reason not to. For example, we tend to prefer larger quantities to smaller where education, intelligence, money, clothes, and fame are concerned. We might take exception to a commonsensical line of reasoning based on quantity if we believed that quality suffered, so that we might prefer fewer classes to which we paid better attention, a less capable employee who always showed up for work to a more capable one we couldn't depend on, or a lower salary for work we loved to a higher salary for work we hated.

Moderate Difference as a Motivation to Communicate

You can see how necessary common starting points are for fostering understanding and cooperation between participants in communication. You can evaluate your communicative task by enumerating the number of points of departure you have in common with your audience.

If you have exactly the same facts, truths, presumptions, values, hierarchies, and loci as your audience, you ought to be able to communicate with perfect clarity. That person would be your General Audience or your "person interested in _____." But you probably wouldn't need to communicate with such a person. He or she would already have most of your knowledge and beliefs.

If you have nothing in common with your audience, you will find communication virtually impossible. Someone who argued every fact, generalization, assumption, value, hierarchy of values, and method of reasoning with you would drive you mad. A conflict with such a person would probably produce violence. Of course, you probably wouldn't communicate with this person either. You wouldn't have any place to begin.

But most instances of communication fall in the gray area of partly shared points of departure. Most of the time, you'll be able to find some common starting points with your audience. Indeed, if you think you have either everything or nothing in common with the audience, you probably aren't seeing the audience clearly, which brings us back to our original point about projection and disillusionment.

When you write a draft, your understanding of your reader will control the information you produce. You'll tend to notice information that confirms your preconception and ignore information that rebuts your preconception. So it's important to work to adjust your perception of the reader so that it reflects as accurately as possible the differences that make communication necessary and the similarities that make it possible.

As an example, we'll consider a draft by Linda Hindahl. She had proposed (in the section of Chapter 4 on Teachers as Writing Partners) writing an essay on small town life for a regional publication she read called *Midwest Living*. The essay centered on an experience at a basketball game which had helped her to feel at home in the small town to which she had moved. In her first draft, an extension of a journal entry, she had simply told the story of moving to the town; of feeling that she was outside, on the margins of the town's life; and of finally feeling welcomed as a result of her son's participation in a basketball game. Her reader had suggested that the extended description of the basketball game dragged a little. In order to remedy that problem, Linda's teacher had suggested dividing the narrative of the basketball game into segments and interpolating her comments on small town life between the segments. A standard method of increasing interest in a narrative is breaking up the events by inserting a subplot. This revision involved a "sub-essay." In short, this draft has undergone considerable crafting.

Now in the latter stages of the project, Linda needs to ascertain whether the reader of *Midwest Living* would expect such a project. As you read it, imagine you are a "thirty-something" resident of a midwestern town. You are married with children. Your favorite magazine prints articles on midwestern life with an emphasis on traditional values. Its most recent issue contains articles on midwest vacation resorts, traveling through Amish country, bicycle touring, and remodeling a farmhouse from the 1850s. In the regular monthly departments you find recipes, restaurant reviews, and gardening tips.

DRAFT BY Linda Hindahl

A Place in the Country

There was magic in the air. Of course, it was only something you saw in retrospect. As my husband, Bob, and I walked into the gym that evening, it seemed just like any other basketball game.

Actually, Bob and I were getting rather tired of the basketball season. Our oldest son, Jeremy, whose game we were there to see, was playing on the high school junior varsity team. (Well, maybe "playing" is too strong a word. He spent most of the season on the bench, hoping the team would get far enough behind that the coach would put him in for the last two minutes.) Our younger son, Colin, had joined Biddy Basketball that season, also. Between games and practices for both boys, most of our spare time had been spent learning to yell such phrases as "Put it up!" and "Sink one!" and "Way to go, (insert player's name here)!" and "Come on, Defense!" and my personal favorite, "What kind of a call is that?"

The gym was fairly empty when we got there because junior varsity games were not exactly a big draw. Bob and I chose seats on the top bleacher which provided a wall to support our backs as well as a prime position for one of our favorite activities—people watching. We had always been people watchers and Delavan home games provided us with especially nice experiences because so many of the faces were familiar. Exchanging greetings with friends and acquaintances, I experienced a wave of warmth as the realization struck me that I had finally become part of this small town.

In truth, it was only by chance that we had come to live in this tiny town. Delavan only has about 2,000 people, almost a third of which live outside the city limits on farms or in small country subdivisions. Bob and I were born and raised around Peoria, the third largest city in Illinois, but had always known that we wanted to live in the country. Our opportunity came when someone Bob worked with got a divorce. He and his wife had started building a house on a lake near Delavan but had only barely framed it in before they decided they did not want to live there—or anywhere else—together. As part of the divorce settlement, Bob's co-worker was awarded the lot and house (if four walls on a foundation could be called that) on the lake. He decided that he didn't want to finish it and sold it to us. Trying not to be too gleeful at what we felt to be our good fortune at the expense of someone else's bad fortune, we sold our house and moved to the country.

The teams ran out of the locker rooms and took three quick laps around the court. As they passed in front of our bleacher, it occurred to me that I knew every one of the boys on the team—Jason, Mike, Josh, Andy, Terry . . . . Over the years they had all been in Jeremy's class at one time or another and, as a room mother, I had met them all. Tonight was Mike's first time as a starter and I had to laugh as the other "first-string" boys picked him up halfway through the third lap around the gym and carried him back to the bench in a bit of an initiation. I couldn't help remembering my own initiation into small town life.

We had moved into our home in August and there had been a Presidential election that November. When election time came, I had naively asked my neighbor where we voted.

"Oh," she replied. "We vote at the Dillon Township Hall."

"O.K." I had responded, impressed that we actually had a special township hall for voting. In East Peoria, we had only used the high school. "Could you tell me where it is?"

"Oh, sure. Go back out to Springfield Road and turn north. Go down the hill to the first road to the west and turn onto it. Follow it around a curve and down a hill and it will be right there on the west side of the road."

Oh, great! I had thought. Now I have to know my north! (Country people never give directions in terms of "left," "right," or "straight ahead;" it's always "north," "south," "east," or "west.") But I hadn't been too worried; my husband would know which way is north. Well . . .

After looking over a local map (which provided us with the lovely letters N, S, E, and W), we had finally decided we knew how to get there. Springfield Road was easy to find since we were still using it all the time to get back to East Peoria. We had gone down the hill and turned left onto the first road. After about a quarter of a mile, the chipped gravel surface of the road had given way to just plain gravel and taken a hard left turn up a small hill. As we had come down the other side, I had expected to see the Township Hall immediately. However, as the road became more and more closed in by trees and undergrowth, we had begun to wonder to each other if we had taken the wrong road.

"Hold it!" I had eventually yelled, causing Bob to hit the brakes and skid on the gravel. "I think I saw something back there."

He had slowly backed up the road to a small break in the trees where two tracks the width of a car led into a small clearing. At the far edge of the clearing sat a tiny white building with a sign over the door proclaiming "DILLON TOWNSHIP HALL." Totally amazed, my husband had turned the car into the clearing and parked next to two other cars which were there. Upon entering the building, we had been hit by a blast of hot air from three or four portable heaters; the building apparently had no central heating system. Several wasps, which the heat

*had rudely awakened from the nests dangling over our heads, were
buzzing each new arrival while their companions were contesting
property rights with the voting judges over their donuts. We had each
been handed a ballot and pointed toward the voting booth, which were
the only things that resembled any other election we had ever voted in.*

*It seems that in the 1850s, when Dillon Township was organized,
the members of the Board had chosen the exact middle of the township
to build the hall so that it was accessible to the whole township. The fact
that the exact middle fell in a gully in the wilderness had affected their
decision not a whit. None of the successive elected officials had ever
considered a new hall in a more likely location to be a necessity.
Actually, I had been amused and charmed by the whole experience and
was somewhat dismayed when, several years later, my husband was
instrumental in getting a newer building built in a more populated area.*

The team we were playing that night was supposed to be a fairly
even match for ours. Jeremy had told us that we didn't have to bother
coming because he was sure that he would not get to play. He sounded
so downhearted when he said it that we had hurried to say, without any
real conviction, "No, we'll be there. This may be your night." He was
usually right, though, so we figured that we would just be there for him.

The game got under way, and the boys were not doing particularly
well. At times, I began to wonder if the coach was teaching the boys
comedy routines at practice rather than strategic plays. They seemed to
gain possession of the ball only to trip over a teammate's foot and lose it
again. It occurred to me that somehow the games always sounded more
exciting and favorable to our players when I read about them in the
paper than when I attended. Considering my first experience with Ruth
Larimore, editor of the local "news" paper, that shouldn't have been
surprising.

*I had joined the local Newcomer's Club right after we moved to
Delavan and had volunteered to be the Publicity Chairman. The duties
of that office had entailed getting announcements of upcoming meetings
and information about each meeting in the local paper. I had been quite
excited about my responsibility and spent hours on drafting and revising
my first article. I eagerly set off to submit my first published work.*

*Bounded on one end by a grocery store and on the other by the
bank, the business district of Delavan occupies two blocks down the
center of town and contains the aforementioned grocery store and bank
plus one other grocery store, a dime store, two restaurants, a flower
shop, a tavern, the doctor's office, and the newspaper office. The
newspaper is housed in a narrow 1880s building right in the middle of
the block. It is basically a one-person operation, being run by the*

daughter of the previous editor. As I had stepped into the doorway
alcove and reached for the ornate doorknob, a large white sign caught
my eye:

Office Hours

Open: Most days at 9:00 or 10:00
Some days as early as 7:00
or as late as Noon or 1:00

Close: About 5:00 or 6:00
Some days as early as 3:00
or as late as 9:00

I'm usually here all day unless I'm not,
in which case I'm usually somewhere else.

This last statement had proven to be the case when the knob would
not turn under my hand. I had reluctantly left my text in the open box
hung by the doorway marked "News Items," and gone on home.

The Delavan Times *comes out once a week on Wednesday. I did not*
have a subscription, so I had eagerly gone into town to purchase a copy
the following Wednesday so that I could view my first published words.
When I had asked the cashier at the grocery store where the local paper
was, she reached under the counter and brought out a four page
publication smaller than The Enquirer *or* The Globe. *I had paid my fifty*
cents and rushed out to the car to read my article. My expectations had
been rewarded—I had produced a front page story! Yep! There it was
(sans a byline, though!) right between a story about a worker at the local
grain elevator who had smashed his thumb in a truck door and required
stitches and a story about three local cows that had broken down their
fence and wandered into town. Actually, my account of events at the
latest Newcomer's Club meeting seemed a little tame—then I had
realized that half of what I had considered to be my eloquent prose had
been eliminated to provide a "facts only" article. I learned over time that
if Ruth (the Editor-in-Chief) had originated the article, prolific detail and
personal commentary were perfectly acceptable. If not—well, let's just
say that the word count got significantly reduced!

Ruth was definitely there that evening, and I smiled as I watched her
take notes.

But the game was heating up. Our guys had actually made a basket
and were running down the court to set up their offense. As I glanced at
the scoreboard, however, I saw ten points go up for the other side. A
general groan went up and a lone voice shouted, "Hey, wake up, Jake." I
glanced across the floor to where the scorekeeper was agitatedly trying
to correct his mistake—and thought again about small town priorities.

The gym we were sitting in was called the Jake Poppenga Gym. I had assumed that Jake was a fairly wealthy man who had donated money to build the gym—and I could not have been more wrong. Jake, now in his 80s, had grown up in Delavan. When he had graduated from Delavan High School, he had gone to work for the school as a janitor. Over the following decades, he had continued to work at the school in various capacities—maintenance, bus driving, timekeeping and scorekeeping for various sports. In recognition of his service to the school, the gym had been named for him, not some wealthy benefactor. In recent years, he has suffered two heart attacks and a stroke, which cause him to sometimes foul up the scores at home games. But most of the fans are patient and only an occasional "Come on Jake!" is heard.

The guys seemed to be getting it together to make the game a bit more of a competition, but in the third quarter they seemed to lose everything—they fell behind by 25 points. The fourth quarter started out just as badly; with five and a half minutes left in the last quarter, they trailed by 30 points. We watched as our son and his best friend, another Jeremy who had played even less than our Jeremy, checked in with the officials.

I felt my stomach tighten as it did each time my son was put in. I knew how much it meant to him to not necessarily be spectacular, just not be bad. He had barely taken the court when the ball was passed to him. I saw him glance at the basket, then pull the ball up to shoot for what I thought was an impossible shot, and I gave out a small groan. The ball arched perfectly and passed through the hoop without touching it while giving the net a beautiful little flip! Without much cool or aplomb, I found myself jumping up and down screaming, "Okay, Jeremy!" My much more reserved husband simply patted my hand and asked me calmly to sit down—then distanced himself a bit farther down the bench from me.

The other team took the ball out and dribbled it down the court while our team took up their defensive positions. They had barely made it to their end of the court when *my* son intercepted a pass and threw the ball to our forward, who took it back down court. When they were again positioned at our end of the court, the ball was once more passed to Jeremy. To my dismay, he glanced at the basket and attempted another shot—and made it! He then faded back after the shot, Jordan-style, as if it was something that he did every day. I was aware, between screaming "All right!" and "Way to go, Jeremy!", that all around me were going up the same personalized cheers. In response, my usually reserved husband exclaimed, "That's my boy!"—and resumed his seat at my side.

As I listened to the voices around me cheer for my son, I remembered how some of my friends in the Newcomer's Club had warned me that the town was cliquish. That did, in fact, turn out to be true. Now, granted, Delavan is not exactly Boston, but we have our "Nob Hill," nonetheless. We just call it "Third Street." Along this street are many grand old houses built back in the 1870s and 1880s by the prominent citizens of the time; and while some of them have been sold outside the original family, many are still owned by descendants of those early settlers. In fact, one such family has forebears dating to the Mayflower. Upstart newcomers, like us, would never be able to infiltrate the circles of these "old guard" families.

Understanding this attitude had taken a bit of time and insight. During the 1970s and 1980s, numerous city dwellers decided that they wanted to get out and away from the city, much like my husband and me. Up until that time, the population of small towns like Delavan had stayed pretty static. In fact, in the early 1900s, as America was becoming more and more urbanized, many young people left the area for big city life. Those who stayed behind had developed a proprietary attitude. In fact, many even had ancestors who were part of the original colony which settled Delavan in the 1830s. The older members of these families have retained great pride in their background and had taken umbrage at the throng of "outsiders," like us, who moved into the area in the '70s and '80s, changing the face of the city and the way it was run.

There was, however, one community focus that had allowed us access to a place in the community—school. Our oldest son was one year old when we moved to Delavan, and five years after him came our younger son, Colin. Through the Mother's Club, room mother activity, and sports activities, we had been able to infiltrate the ranks of the younger generation of these old families and become part of and quite attached to this community, the spirit of which was very much in evidence on the night of this basketball game.

The other Jeremy was fouled soon after that and given two free throws, both of which he made. That brought his total points for the year to two! Before the game ended, our Jeremy had been fouled and given two free throws and made both of them as well as another field goal! Oh, the team still lost, but both our Jeremy and his friend considered the evening a personal triumph.

The intermission between games was spent accepting compliments and congratulations from friends and neighbors who were as sincerely happy for Jeremy as we were. I again felt the specialness of being part of that town.

But that was only the beginning of the magic evening. The varsity game was the main attraction.

We were fortunate that year because, for a small school, we had a number of rather good players. Of course, the good ones *knew* they were good and were constantly trying to put on "one-man" shows (which explains why we did not win more games). However, they managed to pull it together for the first three quarters of this game and had a rather large lead by the beginning of the fourth quarter.

Like every other school in every other town in America, there were boys on the team who kept going out for basketball each year even though they hardly ever played. On the varsity team there was one particular boy who was perhaps 30 pounds overweight, wore horn rimmed glasses, and hardly ever saw court time. Jim was a senior and had gone out for basketball every year since the sixth grade. I personally had never seen him play and had felt vaguely sorry for him when I saw him sitting on the bench. Tonight, however, he left the bench and checked in with the officials shortly after the beginning of the fourth quarter.

At this point, we had on the floor our two "hot dog" players (Brent and Mike), two other players who played a little more than Jim (Brad and Greg), and Jim. As Jim ran back and forth following the ball up and down the court, I noticed that each time he had the ball, the fans were more vocal than usual. "Go for it, Jim!" "Hey, Jim!" "Come on, Jim!" "Yay, Jim!" I felt once again just how close-knit our town was and how much enthusiasm the parents in the stand could generate for the children who had grown up with their own. I was reflecting on this and enjoying the cordial atmosphere when I noticed something else happening on the court.

Brad had just passed the ball to Brent and he was wide open for the shot, one he had made a hundred times. I had seen both Brent and Mike attempt much less sure shots in an effort to flaunt their talents. However, as Brent lifted the ball to shoot, he glanced around at his teammates and lofted it to Jim. Jim shot and missed.

The other team rebounded the shot and the boys moved down the court. Greg stole the ball and the action shifted back to the home basket. The ball was passed to Mike, he faded back for the shot—and passed the ball to Jim! Jim shot and missed.

I was stunned! I had never seen Mike pass up even the remotest chance at scoring a basket. I had seen him attempt (and sometimes make) shots from half court! I watched closely as the game continued, and each time the ball was at the "home" end of the court, it was passed to Jim for the shot. He always shot and missed, but the next time around, the ball still found its way to him.

Throughout all of this, the enthusiasm of the fans was building to a fever pitch. "Hey, Jim!" "Go, Jim!" "Come on, Jim!" "Put it up, Jim!" I'm sure that I even heard a few of the cheers come from the other team's side of the room!

Jim continued to take the shots and miss them. With about 45 seconds to go, the ball was passed to Jim and a whistle blew. He had been fouled and would be given two shots. The crowd started screaming wildly for him. I started to feel a little sorry for him, thinking that all of this attention must be making him nervous. He stepped up to the line, bounced the ball a couple of times, then lofted it toward the basket. It hit the backboard, bounced on the rim, and went through the net! Everyone started yelling and clapping. I glanced at the bench where his teammates were sitting, and they were jumping up and down and hugging each other. The referee passed the ball back to Jim and he tossed it again. With seeming ease, the ball arched through the air, hit the rim, rolled around a couple of times, and went through! Everyone in the stands was on their feet, clapping, yelling, laughing.

I am not really sure what happened during the rest of the game and I don't think that anyone else knows, either. We did win the game but I have no idea what the score was. When it was over, we found our two boys, took them to the local restaurant for an ice cream sundae to celebrate Jeremy's personal victory, and went home.

Later that night, just as I was drifting off to sleep, a warm flush ran through me as I reflected on the evening—the kinship, the laughter, the love that was present in that small gymnasium in the middle of that small town in the middle of all those cornfields in the middle of the prairie.

What do you think? Would Linda's project meet the expectations of the *Midwest Living* reader? You can make some guesses and give some good advice, but since you probably don't read the magazine, Linda will need to supplement your opinion with the opinion of a regular reader of the magazine. At this point, Linda herself, though she reads the magazine regularly, finds it difficult to know whether her project suits the forum. Her personal involvement impairs her judgment. In order to answer the question, Linda asked an actual reader of the magazine. The reader answered six questions based on Perelman's six points of departure.

1. Does the project present the specific **facts** of small-town life as you would expect to find them presented in *Midwest Living*?
2. Does the project seem to you to tell the sort of **truth** in general about small-town life you would expect to find in *Midwest Living*?
3. Does the project make any **presumptions** about small-town life that you disagree with as a reader of *Midwest Living*?

4. Does the project deal with subject matter you **value** enough to want to read about in *Midwest Living?*
5. If you compared this article with the eight feature articles in the most recent issue of *Midwest Living,* where would you place it in the **hierarchy** (first to ninth place)?
6. In general, does it make sense to you that a project like this should appear in *Midwest Living?*

The *Midwest Living* reader responded positively to the project but suggested changes (as readers always do). She was convinced that Linda had presented the facts accurately and had told a truth—that small towns were a little cliquish and slow to warm—with which she agreed as a reader of *Midwest Living.* The reader noted that the articles for the magazine often included photographs, and that she would expect the verbal facts to be supplemented with graphic "facts." She found the positive attitude about the Midwest to be a close match with the usual presumption presented in *Midwest Living.* She thought the subject matter important enough to appear in the magazine and placed it in the top three saying, "I wouldn't mind at all if there were fewer articles about cooking and more about real *living."* However, she did note, in response to the sixth question, that the magazine did not often present articles exactly like this one. She suggested that Linda add some history of the town to make the project seem more like the "practical, informative things I'm used to seeing."

As a writer in college, you will often find that teachers who assign writing will be willing to review drafts of your work and give you an opinion before the final draft is due. Like magazine readers, teachers usually—you know this—have expectations they may not articulate until you ask. Since teachers give assignments with specific learning purposes in mind, it's worth your while to be sure that you're doing work that will help you meet those purposes. You can ask your teacher Perelman's questions, beginning with "Have I got my facts straight?" and following through to "Does this project make sense to you as a way of fulfilling the course requirement?"

EXPERIENCE

➥WARM-UP

1. Recall an instance in when you identified with someone—a friend or lover—and the projection began to fade. Describe the likenesses you thought were there and the differences you discovered as time went on.

➡️FOR YOUR WRITING PROJECT

2. In cooperation with your teacher or your peer group, analyze the forum for a draft of a writing project using the following set of six terms.

   In earlier work, you should have identified an audience and a forum for your writing. If you have not yet settled on an audience and forum, do so now. Refer to Chapter 4, the section on Teachers as Writing Partners, for explanations and an experience which will help you to complete this work.

   a. Find at least one (and preferably more than one) actual reader of the forum you have envisioned for your project. Ask your reader(s) to answer six questions with reference to that forum.

      • Does the project present the specific **facts** of [your subject matter] as you would expect to find them presented in *[your forum]*?

      • Does the project seem to you to tell the sort of **truth** in general about [your subject matter] you would expect to find in *[your forum]*?

      • Does the project make any **presumptions** about [your subject matter] that you disagree with as a reader of *[your forum]*?

      • Does the project deal with subject matter you **value** enough to want to read about in *[your forum]*?

      • If you compared this article with the [number of] feature articles in the most recent issue of *[your forum]*, where would you place it in the **hierarchy**?

      • In general, does it make sense to you that a project like this should appear in *[your forum]*?

   b. Imagine that you have gathered your readers in a room and that they are talking about your subject matter. Then ask yourself one or more of the following questions with reference to your writing project.

      • What facts—pieces of information—do the readers already possess? What facts must I supply?

      • What truths—generalizations that interpret or order a set of facts—do the readers already accept? What truths must I point out?

      • What presumptions—working hypotheses—can I assume the readers will grant for the moment? What presumptions will the readers debate?

- • What values—prized objects, values, or beliefs—will my ideas serve for the readers? What values will my ideas offend?
- • What hierarchies—systems in which values are rank-ordered—in the readers' belief systems support the value of my ideas? What hierarchies undermine the value of my ideas?
- • What modes of argument—commonsensical ways of reasoning—I have used will seem clear and logical to my readers? What modes of argument will my readers object to?

b. Plan additions, deletions, or rearrangements in your draft to bring common points of departure near the beginning of the draft.

Chapter 10
Personal Dimensions of Revision

What's your **image**? Like your name, your image is something very personal about you that, in a way, belongs as much to other people as it does to you. You know that, rightly or wrongly, people draw conclusions about you from choices you make—the places you frequent, the clothes you wear, the car you drive, and the friends you make. People conclude that you are trustworthy if your words and behavior match, so if you want to be believed, you have to try to let people see an accurate image of you. When you have finished reading this section, you should understand the concept of personal voice and be prepared to evaluate a draft of your writing to determine whether it presents the image you want.

FINDING YOUR VOICE

Voice and Reader Expectation

We use the term **voice** to designate that part of your image that shows through in your writing. Of course, we're using "voice" metaphorically to designate *an impression readers gain about you from the way you use language.* At the simplest level, we can distinguish two basic voices: formal and informal. You know that generally people expect you to "sound formal" when you write for school and to loosen up when you write for personal reasons. You would expect criticism for writing an informal term paper. The teacher, you might think, would interpret your informality as disrespect or inability to write formal English. The formal voice you learned to use in writing for school is intended to give readers the impression that you think and speak carefully—that is, to help readers trust you.

You know that the formal school voice won't do for every occasion. Sometimes it gets in the way of communication. If you used a formal, term-paper voice in a letter to someone close to you, your correspondent might get the impression you were angry. Your correspondent would sense that you were holding back and wonder what you were concealing. Readers miss those little personal touches that remind them of your personal qualities.

Many writers learn so well to suppress personal qualities for the formal school voice that their school writing acquires a robotic quality. Their school writing sounds computer-generated, like a time-and-temperature recording, a supermarket cash register, or an airport or subway warning. Computer-generated voices sound odd because they are so even— because they are perfectly regular, all the little individual inflections polished off them. Readers find it hard to trust such voices because they get the impression the writer is just going through the motions.

The Authentic Voice

As teachers of writing and judges of various kinds of writing competitions, we've read thousands of essays written in the robot's voice by writers who were playing it safe. We've also read essays, many fewer of them, by writers who decided to work against expectations by using an informal, but equally inappropriate "insider" voice. Such writers, writing comically, flippantly, sarcastically, or confidentially, always seem to be nudging you in the ribs saying, "We're such clever rogues, aren't we? Nobody but us really understands." Like the robots, the insiders usually leave us wondering whether they really know anything at all.

More advanced and flexible writers we've read can combine and discipline the two voices, shifting from formal to informal. These writers use discreet humor or personal commentary to let us know there's a person behind the school or professional writing, to keep it from becoming stale intellectual commentary. These same writers—some of our friends write this way—are willing to risk bits of intellectual commentary to elevate personal correspondence. Talking with such friends about ideas is one of the best pleasures of friendship.

The rarest of all creatures is the writer whose voice speaks directly, ironically, honestly, playfully, intimately, intellectually, but most of all personally to you as a reader. Such writers' *authentic* "personal" voices result from the discipline of scrupulous honesty with themselves and their readers developed through processes of self-examination, peer criticism, and revision.

The authentic sound of the personal voice comes from the authenticity of the writer's desire to reveal a significant part of who he or she is and to enter into an honest relationship with the reader. Writers with the most easy, personal, and unaffected voices are usually those who have spent the most time laboring to discipline themselves to write without affectation.

Authenticity and Academic Writing

Note that we use the term **discipline** in a positive sense, as doing something you believe in. While we know that discipline often involves sacrifice, we think true discipline in writing comes from following one's interests. For example, as a college student when you find a major that suits you, you willingly subject yourself to its disciplines of thought and expression. You internalize the voice of your discipline, because when you write, you want people to gain the impression that they are reading the work of a scientist, an historian, a literary critic, a philosopher, or a professional in whatever field you choose.

Another way of looking at voice in writing is to compare it with voice in music. In music, it isn't enough to have talent. You have to experience discipline in order to sing well. As a voice student, you find someone to help you learn discipline. So you study music with someone whose voice is like yours, a tenor if you're a tenor, a mezzo-soprano if you're a mezzo-soprano. Becoming a disciple of the right singer is so important that a person with moderate talent and good training will often sing better than a person with more talent but no training.

Your college's curriculum is intended to give you the opportunity to test your voice, to find out what you are best at. As a writer in college, you have the opportunity of taking "voice" lessons from many different teachers in a host of different disciplines. Here we use the term **discipline** to refer to academic specialties. English is a discipline. So is anthropology. So is chemistry. So is art history. Each department on your campus represents at least one discipline, and each of them teaches you a way of shaping and controlling your expression to produce a kind of voice.

You can learn to write like a scientist, a humanist, an artist, an educator, a businessperson, or a lawyer, among many other voices. Probably you'll find that one particular discipline gives you some especially comfortable ways of thinking and writing, and you'll become a disciple of that discipline. It will be your major. Another comfortable discipline may become your minor, and the rest may fade into the background, perhaps becoming reading interests.

You can find writers with a personal voice anywhere, in intellectual, practical, and literary writing—in business and math classes, in sociology articles, in philosophy books, in how-to-books, in advice columns, in technical reports, in science essays, as well as in more "artistic" forms of writing such as novels and poetry. Actually, the more artistic forms of writing (such as poems and private journals) often produce some of the least honest writing. Much of this "creative" writing is singing in the shower, wallowing in a pleasant fog of one's own experience and emotions.

Your academic voice, the visible evidence of your training in an academic field, gives you the image of your profession and helps your readers to trust that you know what you're writing about. As you gain confidence and a sense of yourself as a member of your profession, you begin to know when you can relax and be yourself without impairing your professional image.

EXPERIENCE

➥WARM-UP

1. Describe your favorite (or, if you prefer, least unfavorite) image of yourself. It might be a picture, a painting, a drawing, or some other representation.
   - Who created the image?
   - Why do you find that image satisfying?

➥FOR YOUR WRITING PROJECT

2. Learn from your favorite writers.
   a. List several people whose writing you read on your own, without assignments or other impersonal motivations. From that list, choose the writer whose work most closely resembles the writing project you are working on currently.
   b. Find and read through some of your favorite writer's work. Imagine you are the student of that writer. What sort of advice would the writer give you about writing well?
   c. Read through the draft of your own writing project applying the advice your favorite writer would give you in order to make revisions.
   d. Exchange drafts with a peer. Find out what audience the peer is writing for. Read through the draft imagining you are a member of that audience.
      - Can you hear the writer's voice? Note passages where the personal voice comes through effectively and appropriately.
      - Does the writer maintain a level of formality appropriate to the audience? If you find trouble spots where the writer veers into the "insider" or "robot" voice, note them for revision.

CODE SWITCHING

When was the last time you caught a code?

Ahem. Sorry. When was the last time you imitated somebody else's accent?

A midwesterner visiting Texas may find herself developing a bit of a drawl. Someone from Tennessee who has moved to Chicago may find that his vowels develop a slightly nasal quality (sort of a "code id the dose"). A Californian who returns to the Boston family where he grew up may find his vowels broadening within a day or so.

When Americans from different backgrounds speak to each other, they hear accents in the speech patterns of the people they are addressing. They recognize that their differing accents represent different experiences and values and that they must overcome their differences in order to communicate. They recognize that the *voice* is a code. It means more than just the dictionary definitions of the words and the obvious meanings of the sentences.

They may instinctively respond by catching the code—it's really called **code switching**—to make communication easier and to show respect for the language customs of their new environment. The new code fills in some of the gaps between the people by giving them a shared language. When you have finished reading this section, you should begin to visualize and practice some of the unspoken assumptions that underlie the code called academic discourse.

Building a Code between Writer and Reader

The word **code** can mean either (1) a language which requires that you know how to interpret symbols in order to get to the meaning or (2) a system of beliefs, as in a code of ethics. We mean the term in both ways.

People's language and beliefs constitute a code: a set of assumptions shared by people who communicate with each other.

The old cowboy movies used to talk about the "code of the West," a way of life which was long on action and short on speech, as befitted the frontier environment of danger and hardship. People on the frontier valued physical courage and resourcefulness, and they built up a code of ethics around a rough sense of justice and hospitality. The code of the taciturn, independent westerner still means a lot to many Americans, as do the codes of the aristocratic southerner, the clever Yankee, and the cultivated Boston Brahmin. Texas has its code of expansiveness and display and California its code of trendiness and nonchalance.

Bumper stickers often send coded messages: "Proud to be an American." "Buy Union." "My daughter and my money go to Illinois State University." "Support your local police." You send a coded message by the way you dress, the friends and profession you choose, the college you go to, the clubs you belong to, and the person you choose to marry (or the choice not to marry).

You may switch codes in response to your natural desire to build a relationship with the person you are talking to. If you like the people you are with, you may try to sound like them. You may pick up their accents, you may talk about their subjects; you may use the words they would use.

But you know as you are consciously or unconsciously imitating someone's accent that the accent doesn't mean the same thing coming from you. You don't have the underlying experiences and values the accent implies. For example, many Americans admire British accents. But if we try to just "put on" an accent, we usually make embarrassing mistakes. George Bernard Shaw's play *Pygmalion* (the Lerner and Loewe musical version was called *My Fair Lady*) details the lapses that occur when someone is incompletely socialized to an accent.

When we switch codes, we switch assumptions, and when we switch assumptions, we change identities. Your self-image becomes an issue in code switching. You may switch codes in order to feel comfortable or achieve success in new surroundings, but you may also refuse to switch codes if you feel that the change is somehow not you. If your family speaks Spanish, Black English, or some other language or dialect at home, you may feel disloyal when you switch codes, as if changing dialects signifies that you have repudiated the environment in which you were reared.

The language of your country, region, or family has many associations for you—people, stories, conversations, traditions. To switch out of your "home" language, even temporarily, is to make a significant statement about who you are.

Code and Personal Identity

The authors of this book were both reared in environments which necessitated code switching between home and school. As adults, we have become so accustomed to the academic code that it is more comfortable for us than the nonacademic values and accents we learned growing up.

When we were younger, the code of our families seemed an impediment to achieving our goals. We recognized that gaining power in the college environment required valuing and learning the processes of abstract reasoning in fields such as philosophy and linguistics. We learned to see how literature conveys ethical principles and we learned to express ourselves in the language found in intellectual books and magazines. Above all, we learned that you have to compete. Our own children now find the academic world quite familiar, since they have been reared with those assumptions.

By their nature, assumptions are hard to identify. When you write a paper for a college teacher, for example, you probably feel the need to switch codes, to change the way you write somehow. You probably think something like, "I need to write formally." That vague sense of the need to write "formally" may lead you to make some surface changes, like avoiding contractions and trying to think of bigger words, but those features of academic texts just hint at a whole intellectual world built on an ethic of scholarship, logic, and argument. Once you get inside the academic world, you discover that there are actually quite a number of different codes representing worlds within worlds.

Throughout your college career, you'll become more and more aware of academic codes. Colleges have plans—curricular requirements—for socializing you to the various codes. The courses you take for your major and minor are the most obvious and the most detailed explorations of an academic code. You learn a body of information, a set of analytical methods, a set of values, and a language appropriate to a member of your profession. By the time you've been graduated, you will have learned pretty well what to say and do in order to gain acceptance in a particular profession.

Code and Community

Colleges also have plans for socializing you to the larger intellectual community. These core courses—those required for graduation but not for your major or minor—may help you to choose a major if you're uncertain. But even if you've chosen a major and a career, core courses help keep you abreast of issues that concern you in the larger community.

One of the larger community issues, for example, concerns the limitations of the academic code itself, the way the academic code inhibits the exchange of ideas. This issue comes up in debates over language, ethics, facts, and even methods of reasoning.

Do colleges provide an environment in which minorities, women, homosexuals, religious groups, or other victims of oppression can express themselves openly? Some colleges have instituted *speech codes*, ethical systems defining what may and may not be said, to try to make certain that powerful people do not silence oppressed groups with vicious language. Other colleges regard speech codes as inherently opposed to academic freedom, the concept that free speech is the ultimate value in the academic world. Within colleges that have speech codes and colleges that oppose speech codes, you'll find significant groups who oppose the institution's policies.

As another example, consider *grades*. In school, students and teachers treat grades as facts. We record them on transcripts and use them in making practical decisions about lives and careers. But all students have disagreed with a grade at one time or another; they have all been certain that a particular grade was not a fact or did not reflect the facts. Suppose someone writes racist or sexist opinions in an English essay. Should such papers receive lower grades because they reflect wrong-headed thinking?

Plagiarism—stealing or inadequately documenting words or ideas borrowed from someone else—is another code issue. So is *jargon*—the kind of inside language that makes it difficult to understand the writing of a professional. Where do you draw the line between language appropriate to your reader's level of sophistication and using technical language to prevent challenges to your ideas?

Curriculum is a code issue. Which ideas, books, and writers are important enough to be considered basic facts of a field? In psychology there have been debates between behaviorists and cognitivists. In English there have been debates between literature people and writing people, and even between groups within those two groups.

Your experience of college will make it clear to you that academic writers focus, almost obsessively, on building codes, clarifying them, and questioning them in order to rebuild codes. A restless search for a better idea, a broader theory, a more useful fact, or a clearer way of stating a truth embodies the academic code.

EXPERIENCE

➡ WARM-UP

1. Recall an incident in which you had to learn a new code in order to communicate with some person or persons in your environment. Describe the differences in code, the underlying differences in values and experiences, what you did and didn't do to accommodate the differences, and what the experience taught you about your values.
2. Make up a code for writing in college.
    a. Write down what you must do and what you must avoid.
    b. If you can, identify the sources of the rules in your code. What teachers, courses, books, or assignments have taught you the code that you write by?
    c. Compare your code with those other writers in the class produce. Do any of your rules contrast with or even contradict other people's rules?

➡ FOR YOUR WRITING PROJECT

3. Using a draft of a project you are working on now, identify the particular part of the academic community which would be most interested in your project. Does your project take a scientific view of the subject matter? An artistic view? A humanistic view? A technical or professional view? If you aren't sure, ask your teacher's opinion.

a. Consult the list of intellectual journals in Chapter 5 (Planning a Draft) in the Experience under the heading Planning for Your Audience. Then go to the library, look up an issue of a journal that represents the part of the academic community relevant to your project, and photocopy an article that interests you.

b. Analyze the article to discover the main features of its code.

- **Information:** What kinds of facts and ideas are most important to the article (statistics, equations, case histories, descriptions of techniques, quotations from other sources, and so on)?

- **Analytical Methods:** How does the writer reason about the information (analyzing processes, presenting and attacking arguments, defining terms, explaining and illustrating abstract ideas, and so on)?

- **Value Judgments:** What assumptions does the writer seem to use to evaluate the ideas and actions being discussed (in choosing subjects to write about, establishing personal credibility, distinguishing truth from falsehood, and so on)?

- **Language:** What special rules of language distinguish writing in this community from writing for the newspaper-reading public (e.g., terminology, format, sentence length, grammar, and so on)?

4. Keeping in mind the particular features of the academic code you have discovered, reread your draft and revise it to bring it more into line with the code of your academic community.

THE ETHICS OF REVISION

Your relationships with people combine with your personal voice and your response to your context to create a **persona,** the face you show to the world in your writing. By the time you have revised and re-revised a piece of writing, you may begin to wonder who has really composed your project. Have the revisions obscured your original intentions? Does this project still belong to you? When you have finished reading this section, you should understand how a writer's community prompts the writer to change personal views and personal ways of writing in order to build a relationship with readers. As you change your writing to meet the needs of the people who are your readers, you take part in the process that produces ethical maturity in people.

The Actor's Mask

The term **persona** originated in ancient Greek theatre, where it designated masks actors wore to represent the parts they were playing. You've probably seen the masks of comedy and tragedy, smiling and frowning faces. The audience knew what character, a deity or a famous person, the mask represented. The masks were great heavy affairs that covered the whole head of the actor and contained speaking trumpets to amplify the voice of the actor.

Of course, as the trumpets amplified the voice, they also changed it, just as the outer portion of the mask changed the faces of the actors. When the actor changed to a different part, he would simply change to a different mask, and the mask did part of the work of projecting the personality that the actor was playing.

Modern actors learn techniques to accomplish the purposes the masks accomplished for ancient actors, but even modern actors rely on certain stock elements of characters. We know what to expect when a character is playing a Tough Cop. We know that the cop will not act like a Teen-aged Nerd, a Career Woman, or a Sensitive Artist, and the actor uses our knowledge, either playing to our expectations by acting exactly as the stereotypical tough cop would act, or playing against them by acting out character traits we would associate with the teenager, the career woman, or the artist.

Different Masks for Different Parts

Writers create their personae from their own individual sense of who and where they are and who and where their readers are. In a personal letter to someone who knows you well, for example, you present yourself through a persona that you and your reader have built up between you over time.

If you write a letter to a parent, you are wearing the persona of Child. That is, you write from the part of you that is a child to the part of your reader that is a parent. Writing as a child to a parent may mean that you have to work within the context of an elaborate set of rules that you and your parent built up between you while you were growing up. If your relationship is easy and casual, you may be able to write candidly, using the same voice you would use to write to a friend your own age. If you are comfortable in your relationship with the parent you may feel that the persona is "you."

If, on the other hand, you are tired of being someone's Child, you may find yourself playing against the child in you and frustrating the expectations of the parent. Certain subjects—sex, for example—may change the rules of the context and thereby change your persona. Sex is difficult for many parents and children to discuss with each other. You can think of your own taboo subjects.

Unethical Masks

Your reaction to the persona resembles an actor's response to a part: some parts are easy while others are a stretch. That stretched feeling may be telling you that playing this part is asking you to play against your **ethos**—your personal beliefs and standards of behavior. That feeling may or may not be a sign that you are behaving unethically.

Of course, not all behavior that "feels wrong" is unethical. We all compromise every day in order to live in the world. We keep silent when it's someone else's turn to talk. We speak politely when we want to shout rudely. We disapprove of something we did or failed to do. And we have to decide whether we are compromising with someone or compromising our beliefs, being reasonable or being cowardly.

Which of the following sound reasonable and which sound like unreasonable compromises with oneself?

- "I wish I could just skip class and write. I'm going to be mad Monday morning when this isn't done."
- "I'm going to tell him I don't want to go out with him any more. He won't like it, but I can't stand any more pretending."
- "I shouldn't buy from that grocery store. The management abuses its employees."
- "I'd rather die a slow, painful death than go to that dull party. But I'll go; I don't want to hurt their feelings."

At some point, compromising shades over into selling out for the sake of your image. You've probably heard or read about the image-makers who work for politicians. These advertising people put together a campaign that they think will appeal to the voters. The image-makers use television, print media, and personal appearances to create personae to make their clients seem to typify the society's highest values: honesty, diligence, thrift, fairness, and so on.

Of course after the image-makers have finished sculpting every feature of a candidate's image to attract potential voters, voters can see little difference among candidates to use in making their choices. Thus campaigns become mudslinging affairs in which the image-makers become image-breakers, attacking an opponent by using slanted language, out-of-context facts and statements, and so forth. Once in office, the winner usually fails to live up to the image he or she used to win the election. Eventually, many voters lose respect for the whole process.

Processes of Ethical Development

Why do so many people disapprove of politicians' behavior? The theories of Lawrence Kohlberg (1958), a psychologist who has studied ethical behavior, may suggest an answer. Kohlberg believes that ethical develop-ment begins in the very young child and continues over a person's lifetime.

Role-Playing

In the **preconventional** stages, Kohlberg suggests that children learn to behave ethically, at first to avoid punishment, and later to get what they want. By acting out the role of good child, they mature into the **conventional** stage. They begin to believe in the role and want the approval of others for its own sake, which creates the sense that right behavior consists of doing what others expect. Eventually, people come to a law and order mentality, a belief in the value of law as an impersonal good, something that transcends individual rights.

Some people continue along the developmental path Kohlberg charts toward a **postconventional** belief in a simple social contract that tran-scends individual laws and requires that all people give up a portion of individual liberty in exchange for security. The final stage of Kohlberg's hierarchy—reached only by a few of the wisest people such as Jesus, Buddha, Joan of Arc, and Mother Teresa—involves a whole-mind and whole-body commitment to some universal ethical principle in the full knowledge that all principles are relative to time and place.

When we use the word *holy* to describe such people, we are often unaware that the word is related historically to the words *whole* and *healthy*. To commit oneself wholly to a principle is to experience wholeness, the sense that one's mind and body serve a single purpose. These people have chosen and embraced their roles fully, and history records the enor-mous energy and influence such people generate.

The process of ethical development begins when the person learns to play roles, because in playing roles we take another person's point of view. Most parents instinctively realize the importance of role-playing to moral development. "Now why did you take his toy away? How would you feel if someone took your toy away?" We have to experience another point of view to develop a mature understanding of ethical issues, which always present a conflict between two goods or two evils. One good—the pleasure of having the toy—conflicts with another good—the pleasure of receiving approval from others.

Role-Playing versus Playing the Role

We would hope political leaders would be people who had progressed a good distance toward a mature moral sense. It distresses us to see politi-cians "playing the role" like preconventional children who pretend to be "good" to avoid punishment or to seek tangible rewards. The image they project seems a childish pretense.

Kohlberg's hierarchy seems neat and persuasive, but like any system it has its problems. For one thing, we find it difficult to distinguish between behavior that is completely self-indulgent in a childish—even a criminal—way and behavior that is at the highest ethical level. Consider historical figures whom we suppose to exemplify the noblest aspirations of the human spirit.

Queen Elizabeth I, who won and retained power in a male-dominated world and whose reign produced many of the greatest works of literature in English, also ruthlessly executed people, such as Mary Queen of Scots, who disobeyed her. Mohandas Gandhi liberated India from British imperial rule by "peaceful" civil disobedience that involved his followers' standing passively while soldiers beat and killed them; Indian independence from England led to political squabbling and an eventual bloodbath between Moslems and Hindus, which still erupts from time to time.

While much good resulted from the lives of these people, we can see that they share with the Hitlers and Bloody Marys of history a willingness to sacrifice others' lives to their beliefs. On a less bloody and violent level, we can see the same paradoxes in contemporary political issues such as preserving the environment, providing equal educational opportunity to everyone, protecting freedom of speech, and promoting women's rights. Each of those worthy causes carries a price tag.

Ethical Masks

In short, we cannot do good without doing evil. As humans we carry that knowledge, but we nevertheless create images of ourselves as ethical people. Since we can't avoid doing harm and we can't be sure of our motivations, we owe it to ourselves and those around us to try to create a persona that shows who we are.

In ancient theatre, the **persona** revealed the character's **ethos**. The actor's mask showed the audience important features of the character the actor played. It was intended to make communication *more* clear, not less clear, to show the audience aspects of the character they might not have been able to see otherwise. The exterior told an important truth about the character's interior.

The particular truths we reveal in our actions as writers and speakers result from an internal conversation, a dialectic, between our ethos, our sense of self, and our persona, our sense of audience. "I really want to tell my mother to keep her nose out of my business. But I can't say it directly. I'll just avoid her. Well, I can't do that forever though. Maybe I can . . . ." The dialectic maintains the tension between the self and the society, the good and the evil we do. We don't keep secrets—not from the world, not from ourselves.

No piece of writing ever reveals completely who we are. As we near the end of a writing project, so many hands have touched the project and so many voices have joined our own that we may find the present version seems to obscure our original intention more than we like. If we feel uncomfortable with a piece of writing—feel that it has strayed from our original intention—we may experience reluctance to let go of it.

"I wanted to write about female language, but this is turning into a linguistics research paper. It sounds too male."

"I intended to write exactly what I thought about man-hating feminists. This reads like a wimpy endorsement of the National Organization of Women."

It's healthy for you as a writer to ask yourself whether you can live with the changes you have to make to present your work to an audience. If you can't live with the changes, you'll have to look for another audience or perhaps even accept the fact that you've written a journal entry, not a writing project. It's better to keep your ideas to yourself until you're ready for them to go out if the final draft is going to misrepresent you.

It's also healthy for you as a writer to try to accommodate other people's perspectives. Change never feels entirely comfortable because as a writer you always have your ego invested in what you think. Where your ego is involved, it's easy to convince yourself that you're acting out of the courage of your convictions when you're actually just being muleheaded. The final question to ask about a writing project is not, "Did it turn out exactly as I wanted it to?" but rather, "What have I learned from working on this project?"

As you think back over your interactions with others in your work on your project, you will be able to think of moments, large and small, when you found out something about your subject matter, about writing, about yourself, and about other people. It's worthwhile to take time to recall those moments.

EXPERIENCE

You'll need a draft of a writing project you have revised. If you have earlier drafts of the same paper, they will also be useful for this experience.

What have you learned about your subject matter, about writing, about yourself, or about others from working on this project?

1. Think back over the development of the project from the very beginnings, perhaps as far back as Part I of this book, or perhaps even further back to your original interest in the subject. Describe the most important changes your project has undergone. Have

those changes brought about changes in your beliefs or behavior as a writer?

2. Does the persona—the public self—you present in this project accurately reflect your ethos—your private self? Discuss any discrepancies that make you feel uncomfortable. Try to explain why these passages or qualities don't present the image you want to present.

Part V
Producing
the Final Draft

Remember the friend you outgrew when you were in grammar school? You played with him or her while you were small, but then one of you moved away, a new person your age moved into the neighborhood, or perhaps you just gradually saw less of each other.

Writing projects work the same way. Your life goes on, so at some point you have to say, "This is all I can do for now. I might pick this up again some time, but today I have to go on." When that moment comes, you start to disconnect psychologically from the project. At this moment, you've decided you're going to begin the final draft.

It's especially important for you to stay connected long enough to tie up all the loose ends properly. You'll feel more satisfied with yourself and the project if you pay intense attention to it one more time before you let it go, sort of like a going-away party. You should take one last look at the whole draft and then pay attention to the little details of grammar, punctuation, spelling, typography, and format that give the manuscript a final polish so that it looks its best.

Chapter 11, Editing Your Style, explains the process of reading to identify those final spots to polish, improving logical flow and sentence clarity, and managing tone and readability.

Chapter 12, Final Details, presents information on two styles of citing references and composing Works Cited lists. It closes with suggestions for effective, painless proofreading.

Chapter 11
Editing
Your Style

_____

_____

_____

THE FINAL DRAFT

Before you plunge into the thick of producing the final draft, you need to spend a moment evaluating the draft you have in hand to be sure you really are working on a final draft. You are ready for the final draft when you can turn your full attention to the process of editing. Like revising, editing happens continually as you write, and like revising, editing is a process of change. We use the two terms to distinguish the major, substantive changes of revision from the minor, formal changes of editing. No one quite knows where revising ends and editing begins. Different people draw the line between revising and editing at different places.

Some important research on revision (Faigley and Witte, 1981) suggests a distinction between rewriting that changes meaning and rewriting that preserves meaning. Our simple rule of thumb is that you begin the final draft when you think that you have all the major ideas in the paper in order, when preserving meaning becomes your primary focus. Once you've used the processes of addition, deletion, and rearrangement to put the major ideas into a shape that you, your peer readers, and your teacher all endorse, you begin to focus on rewriting that preserves those major ideas.

You have to give the project a thorough reading before you can decide whether you're ready to produce the final draft.

Reading to Edit

Think of something you've polished. It could have been a car, furniture, a coin, a jewel, or lenses in your eyeglasses. How do you know when something is polished? One way is to feel its smoothness when you run your hand or a cloth over the surface. If you've missed a spot, the cloth seems to drag a bit. You rub the spot with the cloth until you're satisfied that it's as smooth to the touch as the rest of the surface. Each time you look, you see another spot you could polish a little more.

Editing works like running a cloth over a surface: you find that your attention moves smoothly over some passages and speeds or lingers over others. When you read through a piece of writing and experience an *impulse* to change your speed, when you feel your interest drawn to a certain segment of the paper, you may be taking the first step in the editing process.

Unfortunately, unless you stop and think about the impulse or ask yourself what the feeling of interest means, you've no way of being sure what is happening. You don't get red lights and sirens to tell you that you have wandered off the subject. You don't get discreet little beeps to tell you a comma is missing. Your mind uses the same signal—*adjust your reading speed*—for every reading phenomenon. You may have discovered a misspelled word or a misplaced comma. A word might not seem quite right, or a sentence may seem too long or too short.

Understanding Your Impulses

How do you learn to interpret impulses during your reading process? You rely on experience—your own and other people's. You interpret the impulse as best you can, act on your interpretation, and then evaluate the change.

As a writer, you polish your work until it feels right, until your eye moves at a fairly even pace over the page. You interpret your impulses in the context of a writer's purpose: you want your readers to read at a steady pace unless, for the sake of clarity or emphasis, you cause them to slow down.

If you're reading your own text, you may interpret an impulse to slow down as a signal you should try to find something simple to change—spelling, punctuation or grammar. If none of those makes you able to read smoothly over the text, you may consider revising the meaning—adding, rearranging, or deleting information; reconsidering what a reader might need or expect; renewing your own sense of purpose in writing. Once you've made the change that satisfies you, your eye moves smoothly over the page. As you continue to read, you notice the seams and patches in the text where you've written something in or taken something out.

If you're reading another student writer's text, you may be more inclined to focus on easy-to-find problems like a misspelled word or a misplaced comma. It's a bit frightening to begin to change someone else's word choice or sentence structure since you might change the tone the person intended. But those are just the details a good final-copy editor should look for, because the writer may have missed the surface while getting the ideas in order.

If you're reading a published piece of writing, you may interpret impulses to slow down as a sign that the writer has said something profound or as a sign that you haven't understood and should reread. You're not so likely to criticize the piece of writing, since we all put a lot of faith in the printed word. Instead of changing the text, you may try to change your own understanding of the text.

That's the way you don't want to read when you are editing a text. The more authority you give the text, that is, the more you trust the writer to be an expert, the less you are likely to see details that need to be changed. Research studies (for example, Hake and Williams, 1981) have shown that readers will read right over errors and other inappropriate usage points if they think that the work is "finished" and if it appears in a respectable publication. Editing is what happens before the text appears in print, so the editor has to read in just the opposite way, withholding authority and looking for flaws in the surface.

Understanding and Acting on an Impulse during the Reading Process

Above all, you should know that *you must not ignore a nagging impulse about a piece of writing.* If you don't know what the impulse means, you should ask someone else to read it for you.

We'll give you a concrete example of the process we're talking about. The section you're now reading originally stopped in the paragraph which begins, "How do you learn to interpret impulses during the reading process?" above. The person who wrote it read over it, slowing each time at the end of the paragraph. He kept encountering a vague sense that the section was too short or needed its language changed. But he just couldn't find a change that satisfied him.

The other author read over it, and she was able to suggest a cause for the feeling. "The polishing metaphor sounds too much like you're saying editing is just looking for spelling errors. That's exactly the impression we don't want to leave. They need to know that the reading process sometimes leads to making major changes—rethinking the whole paper, responding to audience, and so forth. The thing they don't know how to do is to step back and look at themselves as readers."

The first author didn't see how her suggestion was going to help, but he tried rewriting to add her ideas. He wrote three new paragraphs. Then, over two months later, he looked at the section again and realized that he was trying to place editing in the context of reading in general and then to distinguish editing from other kinds of reading.

He wanted to be sure to convey the idea that reading to edit was a pretty fuzzy experience. That "polishing" feeling occurred in all sorts of reading. He sat down and wrote several more paragraphs on the spot to create the basic structure of the piece of writing you're now reading. Since he had consulted another writer whose authority he trusted, he felt more confident of his own authority. The changes brought out the implicit points he had somehow known remained to be discovered. As soon as the basic form and content worked properly, he was able to concentrate on adding final touches.

EXPERIENCE

1. Make at least two copies of a nearly completed writing project. Read the draft and record your thought processes in writing as you read.

    a. Read over the pages with pencil in hand and note where you slow or stop. Jot down the reason: "got this idea from Dad," "read this in the paper Sunday," "wonder if I need to say more here," "Is this clear?" "possible spelling error," "neat turn of phrase."

    If you feel the impulse to stop and revise something, go ahead. Otherwise, work all the way through the pages, making notations about places where you slow or stop, including where you pause to admire something.

    Once you've read the whole paper, take a second look at the notations you've made. These are the rough spots you're able to feel on the surface of your paper.

    b. Categorize the spots you've found as either *notations for revision* (major additions, deletions or rearrangements of content), *responses to other texts* (memories of conversations you've had or of something you've read), or *proof changes* (spelling, punctuation, and mechanical changes).

    Subcategorize the changes if there are enough of any kind to make subcategories possible. If you have responses to other texts or notations for revision, have another look at your paper to see if you've missed something.

2. Trade clean copies of your draft with someone and repeat the process described in 1 above, explaining your suggestions as well as you can.

3. Complete any revisions (additions, deletions, or rearrangements that make major changes in meaning) you find necessary before continuing through the rest of Part V.

IMPROVING LOGICAL FLOW

[Note: the opening paragraphs of this section are numbered for reference in an Experience which will follow.]

1. Imagine you're watching a detective mystery on television. Two people are arguing violently in the foreground. The camera focus

blurs and then a fireplace poker swims into focus from the background. What's probably going to happen next?

2. Suppose you are writing a poem. "O my luve's like a red, red rose, / That's newly sprung in June; / O my luve's like the melodie / That's sweetly played in _____." Is the right word for the blank *July* or *tune*?

3. Consider the following sequence of sentences (called a syllogism). "All men are mortal. Socrates is a man. Therefore Socrates is _____." What fills out the blank?

4. Of course the answers are, respectively, that (1) the poker is probably going to be used as a weapon soon since the director has taken the trouble to focus your attention on it, (2) the right word is *tune* since it rhymes with *June*, and (3) Socrates is "mortal" since he is a man and men are mortal.

5. What do these sequences have in common? The plot in the television program, the rhyme scheme in the poem, and the logic in the syllogism all lead you clearly from one point to the next. They lead you to expect what you're going to find. Arousing and fulfilling expectations creates what some people think of as **flow** (or **coherence**) in a paragraph.

6. **Flow** means different things at different points in the writing process. When you're writing, you may experience a sense that the words, sentences, and paragraphs are flowing easily onto the page. Reading your own work, you may often feel that it flows coherently.

7. When someone else reads your writing, flow becomes an altogether different matter. Sad to say, your personal sense that a piece of your writing flows as you write it or read it does not ensure that another reader will also find that it flows. Your thoughts, feelings, and experiences flow through your words for you personally in a way that other readers cannot share. We can illustrate this point with a return to the analogy of the detective mystery.

8. Suppose that the next thing that happened in the detective mystery was not that someone assaulted someone with a poker. Suppose that instead an airplane crashed into the house and killed both the people. You'd probably react with disappointment, thinking that the plot of the story had led you astray.

9. Planes do crash, and in real life one of them might crash into people who are having an argument in a room with a poker. This ending would cohere, make sense, to someone who witnessed the occurrence, but we expect stories to operate more logically than real life. Similarly, as you write, your thoughts occur in an order that reflects the flow of your life experience but that may not

seem to flow to other readers. As a courtesy to readers, then, you need to try to establish an order that fulfills their expectations to give them the experience of flow.

10. As water flows naturally downhill, paragraphs flow naturally from general to specific. A paragraph reads easily when you follow the natural direction of flow by giving a general idea and then a specific example. "Some people believe that evil is simply the absence of good. For example, a child may say cruel things to another child simply from a lack of understanding of other people's feelings." In these two sentences the general idea, that evil is the absence of good, becomes clearer in the context of the example.

11. Some principles of paragraph order tend to create the general-to-specific flow: question and answer, topic and comment, and cause and effect among others. You can illustrate this for yourself by rephrasing the two quoted sentences in the preceding paragraph as question and answer. Presenting ideas in familiar patterns like those can help to make a paragraph flow in an expected order for a reader. Such patterns help some writers to think in general-to-specific order. Outlines often help writers to deal with information in general-to-specific sequences too.

12. But when you read a paragraph, the basic unit you encounter is the sentence. Each sentence should flow into another sentence. So what makes sentences flow? Flow mostly develops from sticking to one subject. Like the director who focuses first on the people and then on the poker, you maintain flow primarily by bringing up a subject, and clarifying it for your reader, and then bringing up another subject that is related to the first one and clarifying the new subject for your reader.

13. Writers also use connective words and phrases, called **cohesive ties**, to create **cohesion** between the sentences. Two very common techniques are **transitional terms** and **topicalization**. Transitional terms are words and phrases like *for example, moreover, in addition, on the other hand,* and so forth.

14. These words and phrases underline the coherence, the logical relationships, between sentences, as *therefore* did in the syllogism about Socrates. They help to give a reader the flow feeling, but if you use too many of them, they begin to become noticeable and to detract from flow. You can prevent that from happening by using other techniques such as topicalization. Topicalization simply involves using some key words that recur in several sentences. They operate like the rhymes in a poem to give the reader the sense that everything fits together tightly. In paragraphs 11 and 12 above, the words *paragraph* and *subject* create topicalization. Note

that we allow ourselves to repeat the same word a few times in the interest of clarity rather than using synonyms to prove that we have a vast vocabulary.

Analyzing Flow in a Text

You can play an informative game with logical flow by trying to change the order of the elements in a piece of writing. In the discussion of flow that you've just read, for example, how could you rearrange the paragraphs to enhance flow or to create a different but still readable pattern of flow?

The version you have just read begins inductively, by asking you to consider some examples of flow before you know the term. Inductive order moves from the specific to the general, which is a little like asking water to flow uphill. You can make it happen, but it costs the reader a little more energy. Sometimes requiring readers to expend a bit of energy works like priming a pump or starting a siphon. Once you get the flow going it continues of its own volition. But sometimes nothing happens.

Suppose you wanted to revise this discussion to let the information flow downhill. If you were going to revise it to make it more deductive, more general to specific, *without leaving out any of the information,* would you begin with paragraph 6? Paragraph 11? Paragraph 12? Paragraph 13? Some other paragraph? How would the paragraphs follow in order?

Each of those paragraphs might begin the discussion of flow. Of course, whichever you chose, you'd have to do some rewriting to get the paragraphs to hang together. What parts of the paragraphs would you have to rewrite?

After you've arrived at an alternate order for the paragraphs, try underlining the parts of the paragraphs you'd have to rewrite. For example, if you decided to begin with paragraph 12, you'd have to do something about the first sentence, which begins "But when." A reader would think, "but what?" You might want other, more substantive changes, perhaps some additions. The changes you made would reveal your sense of the flow of the information.

Reordering the sentences in a paragraph gives you an even more focused look at the issue of flow. For example, how might you reorder the sentences in paragraph 5? If you began with the third sentence, "They lead you . . . .", you'd have to do something about "They." It works as a cohesive tie in the original, but it would confuse readers as the first word in the paragraph.

While we don't recommend this extensive tinkering with every paper you write, an occasional reconsideration of the order of information often tells you a good deal about how well your writing flows. The ideally coherent paragraph or writing project should fit snugly together like the pieces of a jigsaw puzzle. You won't ever create ideal coherence, but trying this technique will help you to see your writing from the standpoint of someone who does not know what is supposed to come next. You'll see how much more tightly your writing can fit together.

This experience and those that follow in Part V comprise two stages. In the first stage, you'll focus in a particularly disciplined way on a portion of a draft by doing analysis and revision. In the second stage, you'll apply that disciplined focus to the larger piece of writing to try to edit the whole draft.

EXPERIENCE

➡WARM-UP

1. Complete the exercise which begins at Analyzing Flow in a Text.

➡FOR YOUR WRITING PROJECT

For this experience you need a nearly completed draft of a paper you are working on.

2. Have readers help you analyze the flow of your paragraphs.
    a. Choose a passage of six to eight paragraphs from your draft and photocopy it. Cut and paste the paragraphs to put them in a scrambled order, retaining a record of their original order for your own information. Number the scrambled paragraphs as we have done above. Make several copies of the scrambled paragraphs.
    b. In class, trade your scrambled paragraphs for someone else's scrambled paragraphs. Read through your classmate's list and write down the numbers of the paragraphs in the order you think they should go.
    c. Repeat the procedure once or twice. Have another classmate rearrange your paragraphs while you rearrange his or hers.
        • If you find that your readers guessed right, congratulate yourself and write a short paragraph explaining how you think you created flow for them.
        • If they didn't guess right, look at the paragraphs to see what sorts of changes you could make to fill in logical gaps or underline logical relationships.
3. Have readers help you analyze the flow of your sentences.
    a. Choose one or two paragraphs from a nearly completed draft that seem to you to have problems with flow, and one or two that seem to you to flow well. Working one paragraph at a time, retype the sentences in some scrambled order. Arrange

them on the page as a numbered list of sentences and make several photocopies of your list.

b. In class, trade your scrambled list of sentences for someone else's scrambled list. Keep a copy of your sentences in their original order. Read through your classmate's list and write down the numbers of the sentences in the order you think they should go.

c. Then give another of your paragraphs to a different classmate, and so on until you have finished all the paragraphs.

• If you find that your classmates guessed right about the order of your sentences, congratulate yourself and then write a paragraph explaining how you think you created flow for them.

• If your classmates did not guess right, take a look at the sentences to see whether you can use a technique like topicalization or transitional terms to make the paragraphs flow more smoothly.

4. Reread your entire draft with a focus on logical flow. Mark passages that may need further editing and rewrite them.

CLARIFYING SENTENCES

"Your sons and your daughters shall prophesy, your old men shall dream dreams, your young men shall see visions."

The Old Testament writer Joel prophesies that in troubled times to come, people will see clearly what they have not been able to see before. In thousands of parallel statements like these, the King James Bible presents subtle stories and complex ideas in language both clear and elegant. While its seventeenth century word choice occasionally sounds archaic, the Bible remains a monumentally influential work for writers in English

You can understand the value of the Bible's clear, active style by reading the same ideas dressed in shabby, pompous, impersonal, academic language.

"Children—both male and female—will be engaged in the practice of creating prophetic statements. Furthermore, dreams will be had by people of advanced age, while visions will, on the other hand, be the province of those of lesser years."

How dreadfully this restatement diminishes the graceful thought and language of the Old Testament.

You can find such disagreeable writing everywhere, in legal documents such as consumer contracts, in the speeches of public officials, in the sets of instructions that tell you how to assemble your new stereo, in the textbooks you read in school. Most unclear writing results from two basic mistakes writers commit—either failing to think through what they're writing about or trying to sound impressive.

Sometimes writers compound the two errors. Have you ever thought, as you were reading a book, that the writer seemed to use language and logic that assumed you already understood the material? Does your heart sink when you see the words "Some assembly required" on a box because you have struggled with instructions that make sense only after you have completed the assembly? Can you explain (have you even read) the language in your credit card agreement, the lease on your apartment, or the loan on your car?

Dramatic Structure in Sentences

You can understand a basic fact about clarity if you think of how public performances work.

When you buy tickets for a concert, a movie, or a play, you try to get the best seats you can afford. Why? You want a clear view of the stage. It doesn't matter how good the show is if you can't see it. Writers operate with the same constraints. No one will know whether their ideas are good if their language obscures their meaning. Writers must give everyone a clear view of their messages.

In a movie or play, the director sets up (or "blocks") the scenes to focus the audience's attention on the story line. For each scene, the director decides which *actors* and *actions* make the most important contribution to the overall effect of the production. The director then moves the action around on the stage, bringing first one actor forward and then another; using lighting, costumes and props to focus the audience's attention; and keeping one goal constantly in mind: the audience must concentrate on the most important actors and their actions.

Actors as Subjects, Actions as Verbs

A researcher who has done important work on the problem of clarity in language (Williams, 1990) suggests a simple technique to help writers improve the clarity of their sentences. The subject of the sentence should name the primary actor, and the verb should name the primary action.

These lines from the poet William Butler Yeats ("He Wishes for the Cloths of Heaven") keep the important actors in the foreground.

"I have spread my dreams under your feet;
Tread softly because you tread on my dreams."

The actors are "I" in the first line and an understood "you" in the second line. *I* and *you* also serve as the subjects of their sentences. The words *spread* and *tread* express the actions and serve as the verbs of their sentences.

Suppose we were to rephrase those lines to read:

"My dreams are spread under your feet.
It is treading that must be done softly because my dreams will be
    trodden on."

Notice that the revision of the first sentence leaves out the actor, the person who is speaking. *Dreams* now serves as the subject of the sentence. Who did the spreading? You can't tell. Neither can you tell who must tread softly in the second sentence. The revision leaves out the person addressed, substituting *It* as the subject and *is*, which expresses no action whatsoever, as the verb. *More* words convey *fewer* ideas.

If you have read a good deal of intellectual writing, you may prefer the "sound" of the revision. We hope not. If you do, we hope to change your taste. We would like you to think of the revision as dark, overgrown, sprawling, and ugly—a sort of Frankenstein's monster. We wouldn't mind if you drove such sentences out as the villagers in the movie *Frankenstein* drove out the monster.

Finding the Important Actors and Actions

Like a movie or play, each piece you write works with a cast of major and minor actors, some props, and a background context or scene in which the actors operate. Your sentences will give your audience the clearest view of the story line if you keep the important actors and their actions out front in your sentences, the minor actors and props a bit further back, and the background—well, in the background.

Consider this example.

"He [the writer] has a dream. It anguishes him so much he must get rid of it. He has no peace until then. Everything goes by the board: honor, pride, decency, security, happiness, all, to get the book written."

In this passage from an interview, novelist William Faulkner (qtd. in Plimpton 32) talks of the *writer*, the writer's *dream*, and *everything* as major actors. *Having*, *anguishing*, and *going* are the major actions, and the book lies in the background.

Since Faulkner was speaking instead of writing, we might presume to change his language a little to put more significant actors and actions in the foreground.

We might rewrite the third sentence to read "Honor, pride, decency, security, and happiness all go by the board to get the book written." We might also note that Faulkner uses *has* in two different senses—to mean *possesses* in "He has a dream" and to mean *experiences* in "He has no peace until then."

We might improve "He has a dream" if we rewrote it to read:

"He dreams a dream."

We might rewrite "He has no peace until then" to read:

"He finds no peace until then."

That's the sort of revision you produce when you find actors and link them to actions. You find and bring out little dramatic actions which collectively produce the story.

Actor-Action Revision to Preserve Meaning

Let's look closely at another example. Suppose you were working with a sentence that said:

"There are times during sleep in which the movement of the eyes of the sleeper becomes rapid and shifts erratically up and down and from side to side."

The sentence is grammatically correct but stylistically awkward, full of wasted words and contradictory signals about verb number.

Notice how the plural noun *eyes* makes you stop and ask yourself whether the verbs *becomes* and *shifts* should be plural too. Notice that *There are, in which, of the eyes,* and *of the sleeper* extend the length of the sentence without improving its clarity or grace.

We can pull a better sentence out of this one. To begin with, we must ask ourselves which action matters most to the meaning. This sentence contains several actions, but the noun *movement* expresses the action most important to our purposes. The sentence seems to focus on eye movement.

We next ask ourselves, "What actor is performing the most important action?" In this case, the *eyes* are doing the moving.

In order to rewrite this sentence more clearly, we simply begin with the *eyes* as the sentence subject and *move* as the sentence verb. We then attach the rest of the information.

Our first attempt at the rewrite would be

"The sleeper's eyes move rapidly and shift erratically up and down and from side to side at times during sleep."

We have shortened the sentence significantly, from twenty-eight to twenty words. That's almost a third fewer words without deleting any of the meaning. In the process of shortening the sentence, we have given it more punch by moving the actor and action to the beginning of the sentence.

We can now see the sentence more clearly. Perhaps we can improve it a bit more.

We note that the verbs *move* and *shift* express similar ideas. It appears that *shift* simply specifies the sort of movement the eyes are performing. What if we got rid of *move*?

"The sleeper's eyes shift rapidly and erratically up and down and from side to side at times during sleep."

That version is a bit better still, and we have preserved the meaning of the original.

We've run out of changes that preserve the meaning, though. From this point, we can't take anything else away without changing the meaning of the sentence.

We may not like the way "at times during sleep" strings the sentence out. We could reorder the sentence to place "at times during sleep" at the beginning, but that change would diminish the punch of the sentence ever so slightly.

We could delete "at times during sleep" on the supposition that the context would provide that meaning to the reader, but we have to remain wary of such suppositions, for they lead away from clarity. We might compromise. We could reason that "during sleep" needlessly emphasizes a meaning implicit in the word *sleeper's*.

We would probably decide to move the phrase and go on to another sentence, leaving this sentence to read:

"At times, the sleeper's eyes shift rapidly and erratically up and down and from side to side."

The authors of this book routinely change sentences according to the actor-action formula, and, as a result we find that actor-action structures often appear spontaneously in our writing. However, we do not force ourselves to concentrate on actor-action revision until we have completed almost every other phase of a project, and even at that point we allow ourselves to leave some sentences as they stand.

EXPERIENCE

You'll need a piece of writing that you feel is close to being finished. Choose a brief section, one that sticks to one subject and that you can read in five minutes or so.

1. Identify actors and actions in this passage. At the top of a sheet of paper, enter two headings, Actors and Actions.

    a. Under the Actor heading, list the *people* who are involved in the section. For example, if you were writing about the analysis of dreams, you might accumulate a list of actors that included the dreamer, members of the dreamer's family, the dark man, the bird, the angel, the wise woman, and so forth. The passage might mention or imply all those people.

    b. Besides people, *things* may behave as Actors in your writing. So you might find that the dreamer's bed, notebook, eyes, or voice acted in the passage. You might also list the dreamer's father's house or the traffic outside the dreamer's bedroom. Absolutely anything mentioned or implied may act in the passage, though you will probably find that a few people and things do most of the acting.

    c. Under the Action heading, list actions: dreaming, talking, driving, tossing and turning, crying, laughing, hearing, and so forth—as many as you can find.

2. Now begin examining your sentences one at a time to find those that could benefit from actor-action revision.

- Try looking for verbs like *is, are, was, were,* and the various forms of *get, have, make,* and *come.* These vague verbs can carry several different meanings, so they often allow a writer to put the action somewhere else in the sentence.
- The phrases *it is, there is,* and *there are* also usually signal potential actor-action changes.
- Verbs you use frequently often disguise actor-action problems too. If you often find yourself writing a phrase like, "I would argue . . ." or "We may suggest . . . ," you might ask yourself whether you're really arguing or suggesting all those points. Perhaps you need a stronger or weaker action.

3. Identify the action in the sentence.

- What word in that sentence names the most important action?
- What actor is performing the most important action?

4. Rewrite the sentence so that it begins with the actor and the action in the subject and verb position. (Don't let the grammatical terms *subject* and *verb* frighten you; your instincts will carry you most of the way through this sort of editing.)

    After you have identified all the sentences that you could revise, you may decide that you want some of them left as they stand. That's all right so long as you can think of a reason better than "It sounds more formal."

5. Trade papers with someone and repeat steps 1–4. After you've finished, discuss the changes.

- Did you find it easier or more difficult to work with someone else's paper?
- Do you like the results as well as those you produced with your own paper?

6. Reread your entire draft with a focus on sentence clarity. Mark passages that may need further editing and rewrite them.

ANALYZING WORD CHOICE

According to scientific estimates, stars have a history that goes back about four billion years. Using a radio telescope, astrophysicists can tell us about the stars' chemical makeup, size, and distance from earth. In fascinating books like *A Brief History of Time,* a cosmological theorist such as Stephen Hawking can reason from the evidence of observation to offer explanations of the origin of the universe, and we can debate those explanations. Astronomers can read the stars as if they were words and sentences, gleaning theoretical and practical information from both individual stars and the groups they form.

Like words, stars also have a more personal dimension of meaning. Think of the clearest summer evening you can remember, and imagine the poet's view of the stars. Looking upward, you see innumerable points of light laid out against the background of the sky. The nearer, brighter lights are planets, bearing the names of figures from classical mythology: the gods of love and war. You may envision a woman on a sea shell and a man bearing a sword and shield. The more distant lights, the stars, form constellations if you can imagine lines from one star to another. The stars connect like words to make a story about a bear, twins, or a woman in a chair.

Look long enough at a page on which words are written, and you will undergo the varieties of experience of a stargazer. The words will vary from the familiar to the strange, from plain to fancy. Their meanings will swim clearly into view and blur into nonsense, state a fact or express an opinion, combine smoothly to form coherent groups or disperse into an assortment of black smudges on a white field.

The Denotative and Connotative Dimensions of Words

Of course the words don't change. They're just marks on a page. Readers' perceptions change.

You can look at a word with a scientifically dispassionate, analytical, objective eye in order to understand its **denotation**—its direct, explicit reference to an idea, or a person, or a thing. You can also take the poet's view by reading with an emotional, experiential, subjective intent to understand a word's **connotation**—the indirect and implicit associations a word calls up in your mind.

You build up your total understanding of a piece of writing out of denotative and connotative perceptions of how the words function in the context of the sentences, paragraphs, and larger units that contain them. Denotative and connotative meanings can cooperate or compete with each other, as we shall see.

Cloze Tests and Denotation

The denotations of words help you to understand the **gist**—the main idea—of a piece of writing. The more readily you can absorb the gist, the more readable you may consider the text.

To explain the relationship between word choice and gist more fully, we have provided a test based on a passage from an earlier point in this book. In order to create this **cloze test,** we've deliberately replaced every sixth word with a number. This test estimates how readily our readers can predict the words that will occur next in our writing. Studies of the reading process show that readers continually make intelligent guesses about what's coming next in a piece of writing

In the passage below, entitled "Feeling Defensive during Writing Classes," we have deleted every sixth word and replaced it with a number. Try to supply the words we've deleted. Make a list of the words you predict will be the correct replacements for the numbers.

- Before you attempt your predictions, **Skim** over the whole passage, keeping the title in mind.
- Then ask yourself the **Question,** "What would I expect to find in a passage about defensive feelings about writing?" Then answer your question. (Don't just say, "I don't know.")
- Then **Read** the passage and write your list.
- After you've listed your predictions, **Recite** your list to a classmate for the sake of comparison with his or her list.
- Then **Review** the list to see if you want to change anything before you compare your answers to our list.

Feeling Defensive during Writing Classes

If you're like us, you'll –1– be entirely happy at the –2– of criticism and the necessity –3– changing your words or your –4–. Your ego will always try –5– persuade you that you did –6– right the first time. After –7–, I worked so hard on –8–. If people would just read –9– carefully . . . .

Perhaps during class drafting or –10– sessions, you are annoyed or –11–. You have trouble concentrating or –12– grow bored. You find yourself –13– class or skimping on your –14– in doing assignments.

Suddenly you –15– seem to have as much –16– as you did, and you –17– to cut back on the –18– you expend for your writing –19–.

This condition is called "feeling –20–." You feel that way when –21– have a sense that your –22– is being invaded. If you –23–, you'll often find anger under –24– feelings, but you may even –25– defensive about acknowledging that you're –26. "Who, me? Angry? I *never* –27– angry!" (Growl, snap.)

You have –28– for good reasons, so it's –29– to be upset about letting –30– defenses down. It may help –31– verbalize your feelings if you –32–. If you say, "I'm embarrassed –33– this," or "I hate showing –34– work before it's finished," you –35– find you are able to –36– on to do the lesson.

A cloze test can be used to test a person's reading ability or, as in this case, to estimate whether a piece of writing fits its intended reader. The number you predict correctly gives you a sense of how well the paragraphs we have selected match your knowledge and reading ability.

Check your predictions against the following list of words.

You don't have to predict the exact word: synonyms will do.

1. never	13. skipping	25. feel
2. prospect	14. effort	26. defensive
3. of	15. don't	27. get
4. ways	16. time	28. defenses
5. to	17. have	29. natural
6. it	18. work	30. your
7. all	19. class	31. to
8. it	20. defensive	32. can
9. more	21. you	33. by
10. revising	22. territory	34. my
11. embarrassed	23. look	35. may
12. you	24. defensive	36. go

If you and the paragraphs suit each other well, you should have predicted at least 90 percent of the words correctly. In this case, 90 percent would be 32 right out of 36. If you guessed almost 100 percent right, you would probably find this passage boringly predictable; if you only guess right 60 percent (22 words) of the time, you would find the passage stressful to read because you would often have no idea what was coming next. If you try this technique with some of your other textbooks, you'll begin to see in clear, quantitative terms why you gallop through some subjects and limp through others.

In the passage we have just analyzed, many readers find that the first sentence presents them with the most difficulties in predicting word choice. Readers are accustomed to finding the main idea near the beginning of a paragraph, so the lack of information at that point is especially disconcerting.

The term *cloze test* suggests the source of the difficulty in predicting the word that replaces the number in the test. When we remove words from a sentence, we are testing your ability to close out—to complete—the meaning of the sentence. In the first sentence, you don't have much information—only the title—to use to achieve closure.

In order to help you to compensate for that difficulty, we instructed you to use a set of reading strategies called **SQ3R**. Before you began predicting, you were to Survey (skim) the whole passage, and Question yourself about the passage. Then you were to Read the passage to make your list. Then we instructed you to Recite the list to someone else to check your understanding, and finally to Review the list to determine whether you needed to adjust your interpretation.

The cloze test and SQ3R method demonstrate, in an oversimplified and schematic way, how you build up your understanding of the gist of a piece of writing. As a writer, you can use the cloze technique to estimate how well the words you have chosen convey the meanings you intend. Readers who use the SQ3R method should be able to understand your gist well enough to score 90 percent. If you find that readers' scores fall below that mark, you may be sure that occasionally your meaning is growing blurry before readers' eyes.

In order to remedy such difficulties, you must first ask yourself whether the problems reflect the need for some major revision of the passage. Once you have ruled that possibility out, you can turn to other small-scale changes to assist readers in getting the gist.

When a reader tells you what word he or she predicted would fill the blank, you may simply elect to use that word. You may discover that another word or a simple restructuring of a sentence will contribute clarity to the passage. Or you can use **boldface** or underlining to help readers pick the most important words out of a passage. If you emphasize a term, readers will usually expect you to define it immediately as well.

For larger sections and even more important terms, you can use subheadings such as the one that follows this sentence.

Lexical Sets and Connotation

Since people operate both logically and emotionally, words operate in complex ways as well. Take our cloze test passage as an example. We chose that passage because we were worried about its **tone,** the emotional coloration of the words. Words can have as many shades of tone as people have emotions: angry, happy, sad, afraid, bored, euphoric, weepy, sentimental, light, brooding, calm, lethargic, passionate, sexy, crabby, enthusiastic, and a thesaurus-full of others.

As you may have noticed by this time, we like to maintain a very positive tone in our discussions of writing. We think people learn more when they focus on rewards rather than punishments, and we know that we enjoy classes more when everyone feels upbeat. So we have misgivings about even bringing up negative attitudes. But we know that ethereal sweetness and sublime light do not always permeate every moment of the writing process. And we know that people do have to deal with problems. So we wrote the section you just read and then debated with ourselves whether to leave it in. If we were curious (which we were) about how much negativity we had conveyed in the passage, we could use the list of answers to the cloze test to analyze the tone by creating something called a lexical set—a group of words that bear similar meanings (Cummings and Simmons, 1983). Then we can focus on the connotative dimensions of the meanings of the words.

To begin with, we look at the list and rule out words that serve merely connective functions—words that do not contribute materially to the tone. Trying to rule out as few words as possible, we nevertheless have italicized the following for deletion from our list.

1. never	13. skipping	25. feel
2. prospect	14. effort	26. defensive
3. *of*	15. don't	27. get
4. ways	16. time	28. defenses
5. *to*	17. *have*	29. natural
6. *it*	18. work	30. your
7. all	19. class	31. *to*
8. *it*	20. defensive	32. can
9. more	21. you	33. *by*
10. revising	22. territory	34. my
11. embarrassed	23. look	35. may
12. you	24. defensive	36. go

Having ruled out some words, we can now focus on sorting the rest of the words into categories. We read through the list looking for words that might bear negative connotations. In this instance we are focusing on the words in isolation from the context. We would like to think about the connotations those words may carry with them from previous contexts in which we have seen them.

In reading the list, we perceive several clearly negative words. We also see a number of ambivalent words that can go either way depending on their context. We can't find any clearly positive words.

Negative Words	Ambivalent Words	
never	work	prospect
embarrassed	revising	all
defensive (3)	effort	more
don't	feel	you (3)
skipping	ways	time

The analysis has convinced us that the passage sounds too mopey to leave as it is. Since we are dissatisfied with the tone, we might try to find synonyms for *embarrassed* and *defensive*. But if we replaced them with *awkward* and *uncomfortable*, we would take the risks a writer always takes when trying to invent a **euphemism** (a pleasant word for an unpleasant concept). Some readers might think we were being evasive. Others might simply miss the point altogether. A longer sample from that same section might give us different results. But a glance at the rest of the section convinced us that the results would not differ. Logically then, we should revise the section or cut it. We decided to cut it.

As a writer, you can use this sort of analysis to discover the tone that underlies your approach to your subject matter. You can quantify the degree to which your tone is angry, happy, sad, afraid, bored, euphoric, weepy, sentimental, light, brooding, calm, lethargic, passionate, sexy, crabby, enthusiastic or anything else. Often, the tone will not surprise you. But you may be surprised to learn that you have not expressed feelings with as much consistency as you imagine.

Using the same list, you can ask yourself questions about the level of word choice you have used. English vocabulary usually can furnish at least two and frequently three levels of formality. Often people perceive more formal words to sound more learned, and they try to use learned words when they write for college audiences.

The list of words we've produced contains few terms we could identify as formal or learned. Perhaps *defensive* might qualify as formal since we have borrowed the term from psychology. Instead of *prospect*, we might have used a less formal term such as *idea*. But we might have created a much more formal tone had we talked about "absenting oneself" from class rather than "skipping." Our consistent use of the second person pronoun (you) also creates a strongly informal influence on tone.

All in all, we try to keep our tone at the level of intelligent conversation, the sort of talk in which literate people comfortably mix informal personal reactions with the language of intellectual debate and analysis. We find that this tone comfortably represents our relationship with writers. The tone is appropriate to a situation in which we have to be able to work closely together on a manuscript without losing track of the formal academic world in which college writers have to function.

The cloze test and lexical sets can help you to understand how word choice influences the meaning your readers carry away. These analytical tools can also suggest some changes in the manuscript.

EXPERIENCE

You'll need a nearly completed manuscript of a writing project you're working on. Choose a passage of no more than 300 words. The passage should seem to you to need some work on word choice.

1. Create a cloze test of the passage.
    a. Type or write out a new version of the passage, deleting every sixth word. Leave numbered blanks where the missing words go. Make several copies of your new version.
    b. Type or write out a list of the missing words.
    c. Trade copies of the passage with several members of your class.
2. Try to supply the words your classmate has deleted. Make a list of the words you predict will be the correct replacements for the numbers.
    *   Before you attempt your predictions, **Skim** over the whole passage, keeping the title in mind.
    *   Then ask yourself the **Question,** "What would I expect to find in a passage about [the subject of the passage]?" Then answer your question. (Don't just say, "I don't know.")
    *   Then **Read** the passage and write your list.
    *   After you've listed your predictions, **Recite** your list to a classmate other that the writer for the sake of comparison with his or her list.
    *   Then **Review** the list to see if you want to change anything before you compare your answers to our list.
    a. Use your list of the missing words to score your classmates' tests. Give them credit for synonyms of the missing words.
    b. Use a fresh copy of the test to collate their answers. In each blank, enter a check mark for an incorrect answer.
    c. Now examine the words your classmates had the most difficulty predicting correctly. Consider making one or more of the following changes:
        *   Replace the word with the word your classmates supplied.
        *   Rephrase the sentence to make the meaning clearer.

- Boldface or underline important words in the passage to help readers understand the gist.
- Insert subheadings in the passage to help readers understand the gist.

3. Describe the emotional response you want your writing to evoke. Then read through the list of words (the "answers" to the cloze test) you compiled for Step 1.

   a. Eliminate "empty" words unless you have a good reason to believe that you need to work on them. We define empty words as prepositions (such as *to, at, under, with*), pronouns (such as *he, she him, her*), conjunctions (such as *and, or, for, nor, yet, so*), and articles (*a, an, the*).

   b. Sort the remaining words into groups which seem to have meanings in common.

   c. Give the lists descriptive labels.
   - What attitude, tone, or level of style do the lists suggest?
   - Are you satisfied with that attitude, tone, or level?

   d. Trade your original list with a classmate and repeat steps a through c above. Discuss your results.

   e. Reread your entire draft with a focus on tone. Mark passages that may need further editing and rewrite them.

Chapter 12
Final
Details

DOCUMENTING SOURCES

Paying debts has its own satisfactions. Sometime during the first week of each month, the authors of this book sit down to sort out our bills and pay them. Utilities, mortgage, credit cards, charitable contributions—anyone who looked at the bills we pay could get a pretty clear view of what we value. It feels good to have done it. We know we're on good terms with all the people who have done things for us or given us things. If we've kept good records, we can look back months or years later and remember the experiences associated with the debts.

Writers pay their intellectual debts by simply acknowledging the source. Basically, they just say, "Thank you." Before you can say you have finished a writing project, you must compile a tidy list of those from whom you have borrowed words and ideas. The list may bear the title "Works Cited," "Bibliography," or "Works Consulted." Within the body of the writing project, you identify the particular points at which your sources' ideas have helped you, using footnotes, endnotes, or parenthetical citation.

Your list of Works Cited tells your reader about your interests and the patterns of your thought. We all develop our ideas by adding to, deleting from, and rearranging the ideas of other people. We list our sources not to prove that we read a great deal but to emphasize those articles and books that have most influenced our thinking in a particular project.

In order to arrange sources in a predictable pattern, each academic discipline requires a certain system of documentation. Two of the most prevalent are the systems of the Modern Language Association (MLA) and the American Psychological Association (APA). We have provided here two brief check lists based on the documentation styles of those two organizations. If you can't answer questions about documentation from our lists, you'll need to consult the manuals that detail the styles. Most libraries have copies of the *MLA Handbook for Writers of Research Papers* and the *Publication Manual of the American Psychological Association*. As we write this, both those manuals are in their third edition. You should consult the most recent edition.

MLA

Here is a simplified version of the Modern Language Association style.

1. Always mention your source within the text of your paper like this:

   Careful fieldnotes will not guarantee a good ethnographic study, but the absence of such notes can destroy credibility (Spradley 1980).

2. Your readers can identify this source by consulting your Works Cited list at the end of your paper. The entry for the information above would appear like this:

   Spradley, James P. *Participant Observation.* New York: Holt, 1980.

3. To quote directly or to stress the authority of the source being paraphrased, mention the name of the source in the sentence. Then include just the page number (or numbers) at the end in parentheses, like this:

   In *Grammar and Good Taste,* Dennis Barron complains that ordinary English teachers are "forced to arbitrate the language disputes of everyday life" (227).

4. Indicate an indirect quotation—something quoted from another source not available to you— by a parenthetical reference with "qtd. in":

   Joseph Conrad said of his fiction that his task was "before all, to make you *see*" (qtd. in Hersey 54).

5. The final section of a paper is the Works Cited list of all sources mentioned in the paper, using **hanging indention**: after the first line of each entry, subsequent lines are indented five spaces.

6. Use note numbers for **informational notes** only (notes containing material pertinent to your discussion but not precisely to the point). Include these content notes at the end of your paper just before your Works Cited list and entitle them "Notes." Before deciding to include them, ask yourself whether you ought to either include the information in the text or delete it altogether.

7. To refer to more than one work by the same author, include a shortened title in the text:

   (Barron, *Good Taste* 23).

8. To use a source written or edited by more than three people, use only the name of the first person listed, followed by the Latin phrase "et al." or "et"—and—"alia"—others.

> Aimes et al. discuss the need to review theoretical language constructs (9).

9. Generally avoid lengthy quotations. Quote directly only if the exact wording of the quotation is important to the point.
   To quote more than four typed lines, indent the quotation ten spaces and omit the quotation marks. Cite the page number in parentheses two spaces after the period:
   Thoreau describes his peculiar way of starting a conversation with nature in "The Ponds" section of *Walden*.

> When, as was commonly the case, I had none to commune with, I used to raise the echoes by striking with a paddle on the side of my boat, filling the surrounding woods with circling and dilating sound, stirring them up as the keeper of a menagerie his wild beasts, until I elicited a growl from every wooded vale and hill-side. (120)

10. Omit any mention of page or lines. Do not even include abbreviations for these terms. Use numbers alone.
11. Use abbreviations for *vol., no., chap.,* and *trans.* (meaning volume, number, chapter, and translated by).
12. Use regular (not roman) numerals throughout except in cases where custom requires the roman numeral (such as James I, Elizabeth II). Use small roman numerals for citing page numbers from a preface, introduction, or table of contents. You may use roman numerals to indicate act and scene in plays:

> In *The Importance of Being Earnest*, I, i, we meet both John and Algernon . . . .

13. In the Works Cited list, do not repeat any author's name; use three hyphens, followed by a period, followed by the usual information.

> ———. *Grammar and Good Taste*. New Haven: Yale UP, 1982.

Sample Entries for a List of Works Cited

Alphabetize and use hanging indention.

1. Book with one author:

> LeFevre, Karen Burke. *Invention as a Social Act*. Carbondale: Southern Illinois UP, 1987.

2. Reprint of an earlier edition:

Whitman, Walt. *Leaves of Grass*. 1855. Rpt. New York: Viking, 1959.

3. Revised edition:

Foss, Sonja K., Karen A. Foss, and Robert Trapp. *Contemporary Perspectives on Rhetoric*. 2nd ed. Prospect Hts, IL: Waveland, 1991.

4. Book with two authors:

Knoblauch, C. H., and Lil Brannon. *Rhetorical Traditions and the Teaching of Writing*. Upper Montclair, NJ: Boynton, 1984.

5. Book with more than three authors or editors:

Young, Richard E., et al. *Rhetoric: Discovery and Change*. New York: Harcourt, 1970.

6. Work in several volumes:

Blom, Eric, ed. *Grove's Dictionary of Music and Musicians*. 5th ed. 10 vols. New York: St. Martin's, 1961.

7. Essay in a collection, casebook, or critical edition:

Finlay, Linda Shaw, and Valerie Faith. "Illiteracy and Alienation in American Colleges: Is Paulo Freire's Pedagogy Relevant?" *Freire for the Classroom: A Sourcebook for Liberatory Teaching*. Ed. Ira Shor. Portsmouth, NH: Heinemann, 1987. 63–86.

8. Work in an anthology:

Jennings, Elizabeth. "Poem in Winter." *The Norton Anthology of Poetry*. Ed. Alexander W. Allison, et al. New York: Norton, 1975. 1234.

9. Work in translation:

Machiavelli, Niccolo. *The Prince*. Trans. Christian E. Detmold. New York: Simon, 1963.

10. Anonymous book:

Beowulf. Trans. Kevin Crossley-Holland. New York: Farrar, 1968.

11. Newspaper articles:

(signed)
Greene, Bob. "What's Bad for General Motors . . . ." *Chicago Tribune* 24 Dec. 1991: 2.1.
[section 2, page 1]

(unsigned)
"Are Interest-Rate Cuts Any Match for This Recession?" *New York Times* 23 Dec. 1991: 3.5.

12. Magazine articles with no volume number:

(signed)
Diamond, Jared. "The Ethnobiologist's Dilemma." *Natural History* June 1989: 26+.

(unsigned)
"Earthbound Telescopes Take on Hubble." *Scientific American* November 1991: 121.

13. Periodical articles:

(with continuous page numbering)
Harris, Muriel. "Composing Behaviors of One- and Multi-Draft Writers." *College English* 51 (1989): 174-91.

(with each issue paged separately)
Terkel, Studs. "The Good War: An Oral History of World War II." *The Atlantic* 254.1 (July 1984): 45–75.
[vol. 254, issue 1]

14. Article from *Dictionary of American Biography:*

W[hicher], G[eorge] F. "Emily Elizabeth Dickinson." *DAB* (1964).

15. Anonymous pamphlet:

Aaron Copland: A Catalogue of His Works. New York: Boosey & Hawks, n.d.

16. The Bible:

The Dartmouth Bible. Boston: Houghton Mifflin, 1961.

The Oxford Annotated Bible. Revised Standard Version. New York: Oxford UP, 1962.

[List any Bible version other than the King James. Cite chapter and verse in parentheses in the text of your paper this way: (Matt. 12.1–3). Underline only the titles of bibles other than the King James version.]

17. A letter in a published collection:

Millay, Edna St. Vincent. *Letters.* Ed. Allan Rose Macdougall. New York: Harper, 1952.

18. An unpublished or personal letter:

Lewis, C. S. Letter to an anonymous lady. 4 June 1941. Lewis Archives. Wheaton College, Wheaton, IL.

19. Personal or telephone interview:

LeGuin, Madeline. Personal interview. Iowa State University, Ames, Iowa, 14 June 1979.

Koertge, James. Telephone interview. 14 January 1990.

20. Review:

(signed)
Hoffman, Daniel. "Life Was One Long Midnight." Rev. of *Edgar A. Poe* by Kenneth Silverman. *The New York Times Book Review* 22 December 1991: 1+.

(unsigned)
Rev. of *JFK. Chicago Tribune* 26 December 1991: 1.10.

21. Film:

Schatzberg, Jerry, dir. *Honeysuckle Rose.* With Willie Nelson and Dyan Cannon. Warner Brothers, 1982.

22. Lecture:

Olbert, Scott. "Myers-Briggs Type Indicator." Illinois State University Modern Theories of Rhetoric class presentation. Normal, 24 October 1989.

NOTE: For all sources such as movies, TV shows, recordings, or works of art, include enough information to permit an interested reader to locate the original source. Be sure to arrange this information in a logical fashion, duplicating as far as possible the order and punctuation of the entries above. Consult your teacher or a librarian for suggestions about documenting unusual material.

APA

The American Psychological Association documentation style is used in social science and education. Like the MLA style, the APA requires in-text citation instead of footnotes.

Differences:

1. APA does not spell out the author's first name.
2. APA lists the date just after the author's name.

3. APA does not cite page numbers except when a direct quotation is used; then the APA style includes the page number in the in-text citation.
4. APA treats titles as if they were ordinary sentences, capitalizing the first word of a title, the first word following a colon within a title, and proper names.
5. MLA uses no punctuation when designating a page number, while APA uses a comma to separate the information.
6. Although both APA and MLA use hanging indention for citations, MLA titles the section "Works Cited" whereas APA titles the section "References."

In general, the following guidelines apply to the APA style.

1. Always mention your source within the text of your paper in parentheses, like this:

   Musicians sometimes buy as many as one hundred and fifty reeds in order to find one or two that will work for their instruments (Schmidt, 1991).

2. Your readers can identify this source by consulting your References list at the end of your paper. The entry for the information above would appear like this:

   Schmidt, Karen F. (1991). "Good vibrations, musician-scientists probe the woodwind reed." *Science News, 140,* 392–393.

   [Note that capitalization is like an ordinary sentence.]

3. To quote directly or to stress the authority of the source being paraphrased, mention the name of the source in your sentence. Then include just the page number (or numbers) at the end in parentheses, like this:

   In "Good Vibrations" Karen Schmidt (1991) explains how "fretting over reeds affects virtually every musician who plays oboe, bassoon, or clarinet" (p. 392).

4. To quote indirectly from another source not available to you, use "cited in" in your parenthetical reference. The following example cites an essay written by Stephen Jay Gould:

   Gould explains the name Conway Morris gave the *Hallucinogenia* in Morris's words, saying it was named for "the bizarre and dream-like appearance of the animal" (cited in Gould, p. 16).

5. In a source written or edited by more than two people and fewer than six, cite all authors the first time you refer to the source in the

text. For all the following references in the text, cite only the surname of the first person listed, followed by "et al."

Ryan et al. (1985) discuss the effects of self-regulation on student learning.

In the References list at the end of your paper, list all authors of the source.

Ryan, Richard M., Connell, James P., & Deci, Edward L. (1985). A motivational analysis of self-determination and self-regulation in education. In Ames, Carole & Ames, Russell (Eds.), Research on motivation in education (volume 2): The classroom milieu (pp. 13–51). Orlando, Florida: Academic Press Inc.

When there are only two authors, join their names with the word *and* in running text:

Knoblauch and Brannon (1985) discuss the need to allow writers to control their own texts.

6. In parenthetical text and the References list, join authors' names with an ampersand (&). If the author's name is not given, use a shortened title instead. In your abbreviation, be sure to use at least the first word of the full title to send the reader to the proper alphabetized entry in your "References" section.

7. If you are quoting more than 40 words, begin the quotation on a new line and indent five spaces, but run each line to the usual right margin. Omit the quotation marks. Do not single space the quotation. Give the necessary citation in parentheses two spaces after the final period:

In *The New Complete Afghan Hound,* Constance Miller and Edward Gilbert (1988) discuss the exotic history of this amazing hound:

> Tales, reeking with the incense and romantic mystery of the Baghdadian Mid East [sic], tell that the Afghan Hound jealously guarded harems of beautiful concubines and was the pampered pet of Kings' daughters. The Afghan peoples, in rare reference to the breed in native writings, referred to the hound as having been a zealous herder of flocks of sheep, a courier, guard and mascot for war-lords of the tenth century A.D., and as an animal that primarily made a reputation as a hunting dog extraordinaire in the company of tribal chieftains and kings. (p. 17)

8. The References list must be alphabetized, beginning on a new page, listing all sources mentioned in the paper.

To cite two or more works by the same author or authors, sequence the works chronologically, earliest work first. For more than one work published in the same year, sequence alphabetically according to the name of the book or article and identify with an a, b, c, and so on following the date:

Jung, C. G. (1921). *Psychological types.* (R. F. C. Hull, Trans.). Princeton: Princeton University Press.

Jung, C. G. (1956a) *Symbols of transformation: An analysis of the prelude of a case of schizophrenia* (2nd ed.). (R. F. C. Hull, Trans.). Princeton: Princeton University Press.

Jung, C. G. (1956b) *Two essays on analytical psychology.* (R.F.C. Hull, Trans.). Princeton: Princeton University Press.

Use abbreviations for *Vol., No., chap., trans., ed., Ed., rev. ed., 2nd ed., p.,* and *pp.* (meaning Volume, Number, chapter, Translated by, edition, editor, revised edition, second edition, page, and pages). Use official U.S. Postal Service abbreviations for states, such as IL for Illinois.

Sample Entries for APA Reference Page

Alphabetize and use hanging indention.

1. Book with one author:

   LeFevre, K. B. (1987). *Invention as a social act.* Carbondale: Southern Illinois University Press.

2. Reprint of an earlier edition:

   Whitman, Walt. *Leaves of grass.* (1959). New York: Viking Press. (Original work published 1855)

3. Revised edition:

   Foss, S. K., Foss K. A., & Trapp, R. (1991). *Contemporary perspectives on rhetoric* (2nd ed.). Prospect Hts, IL: Waveland Press.

4. Book with two authors:

   Knoblauch, C. H., & Brannon, L. (1984). *Rhetorical traditions and the teaching of writing.* Upper Montclair, NJ: Boynton.

5. Book with more than two authors or editors:

Young, R. E., Becker, A., & Pike, K. (1970). *Rhetoric: Discovery and change.* New York: Harcourt, Brace, and World.

6. Work in several volumes:

Blom, E. (Ed.). (1961). *Grove's dictionary of music and musicians* (5th ed.) (Vols. 1–10). New York: St. Martin's.

7. Essay in a collection, casebook, or critical edition:

Finlay, L. S., & Faith, V. (1987). Illiteracy and alienation in American colleges: Is Paulo Freire's pedagogy relevant? In I. Shor (Ed.), *Freire for the classroom, a sourcebook for liberatory teaching* (pp. 63–86). Portsmouth, NH: Heinemann.

8. Work in an anthology:

Jennings, E. (1975) Poem in winter. In Allison, A. W. (Ed.) *The Norton anthology of poetry* (p. 1234). New York: Norton.

9. Work in translation:

Machiavelli, N. (1963) *The prince.* (M. E. Detmold, Trans.). New York: Simon & Schuster.

10. Anonymous book:

Beowulf. (1968). (Kevin Crossley-Holland, Trans.). New York: Farrar, Straus, & Giroux.

11. Newspaper articles:

(signed)
Greene, B. (1991, December 24). What's bad for General Motors . . . . *Chicago Tribune,* p. 1.

(unsigned)
Are interest-rate cuts any match for this recession? (1991, December 23). *New York Times,* p. 5.

12. Magazine articles with no volume number:

(signed)
Diamond, J. (1989, June). The ethnobiologist's dilemma. *Natural History,* pp. 26, 28, 30.

(unsigned)
Earthbound telescopes take on Hubble. (1991, November). *Scientific American,* p. 121.

13. Periodical articles:

(with continuous page numbering)
Harris, M. (1989). Composing behaviors of one- and multi-draft writers. *College English, 51,* 174–91.

(with each issue paged separately)
Terkel, S. (1984). The good war: An oral history of World War II. *The Atlantic, 254*(1), 45–75.

14. Unpublished dissertation listed in abstracts:

Brozick, J. R. (1977). An investigation into the composing process of four twelfth grade students: Case studies based on Jung's personality types, Freudian psychoanalytic ego psychology and cognitive functioning. *Dissertation Abstracts International, 38,* 31A–32A.

15. ERIC citation:

Fagan, W. T., Jensen, J. M., & Cooper, C. R. (1985). *Measures for research and evaluation in the English language arts, volume 2.* Urbana: ERIC Clearinghouse on Reading and Communication Skills.

NONSEXIST LANGUAGE

Your school no doubt has a regulation about nonsexist language in all official documents, but we want to stress a need to double-check your final draft for any slips. The guideline most schools use is the 1974 formal policy statement of the National Council of Teachers of English. Copies of the statement are free upon request from NCTE, 1111 Kenyon Road, Urbana, IL 61801. Ask for "Guidelines for Nonsexist Use of Language." Some of the suggestions in this pamphlet are to

1. Use *people* or *humanity* to refer to human adults, not *man* or *mankind.*
2. Use plurals rather than *he* or *his.* If you must refer to an individual, use an example so that you can refer by gender. Rather than saying "One should read his history assignment," say, "Tom should read his history assignment before band practice," or "Sally should read her history assignment today because she has a test tomorrow." Almost all *his/her* questions can be avoided by being specific, and your writing will be improved at the same time.

3. Use titles for jobs that are not gender related: *chair* or *chairperson* rather than *chairman* or *chairwoman, police officer* rather than *policeman* or *policewoman.*
4. Use the same words to describe women and men who do the same activity. Write *doctor,* not *lady doctor.* Write *Twain, Hemingway,* and *Welty* (not *Twain, Hemingway,* and *Eudora Welty*).
5. Write about people respectfully: not *my girl* but rather *the secretary.*

A good rule when rereading for nonsexist language often may be to decide whether you would want to be referred to by the term you are using. Then double-check the rules, too.

PROOFREADING THE FINAL DRAFT

If you have any perfectionist tendencies, proofreading is the time to give them free rein. Whether you're a perfectionist or a slob, you need a friend, a teacher, or editor to tie you to your keyboard until the manuscript is perfect. That's right—*perfect.*

Readers expect your final draft to be absolutely without error. You'll realize the truth of that statement if you think about your own experience of reading. When was the last time you read a magazine article that was handwritten? Have you read many newspapers that allowed the writer to draw a line through misspelled words and write the correct spelling above them? Do you expect books to have typographical errors on every page?

Many people groan when the subject of proofreading comes up and groan quite loudly when they hear the word perfect. Years of exposure to spelling tests, grammar exercises, punctuation rules, bibliography and footnote formats, and the like may bring on shudders when you think of dealing with the host of details that stand between you and the absolute end of a project.

It may interest you to know that professional writers rely on editors to help them proofread copy because proofreading is too much to face alone. Even with the best of intentions and a lot of time spent on the task, most people simply can't see all the changes that need to be made. So it makes sense to share the labor with other writers. As you work through manuscripts together, you can share information, consult with your teacher about problems, learn more about the language, and give your manuscript a proper sendoff.

In fact, when the authors of this book do proofreading sessions, we try to create a slightly festive atmosphere. Some music, drinks, and snacks can help counteract the nasty experiences everyone suffered with grammar and spelling drills in earlier years. A sign-up sheet works nicely to spread the responsibility for the party.

As we sit at a table or on the floor with pieces of manuscript scattered around, we're glad to have the help of others as copy editors. We find that when copy editors point out an error, they are usually right. We also find that writers know how to correct most of their own errors without further explanation when editors point them out. Some few errors require explanation from the editor or, as a last resort, from the writer's teacher.

We also find that people sometimes believe whatever they have already done is right and are willing to kill and be killed over the placement of a comma or the spelling of a word. So we bring a supply of reference books to proofreading sessions, and we refer to them to resolve disputes. For questions of punctuation, we use *The Chicago Manual of Style*, published by the University of Chicago Press. For questions of usage (such as the difference between who and whom, whether we're allowed to use contact as a verb), we like *The Harper Dictionary of Contemporary Usage*, edited by William and Mary Morris and published by Harper. We bring along the style manuals of the Modern Language Association and the American Psychological Association. And of course we bring along a college dictionary.

We set up one rule for the proofreading session. Proofreaders should search only for problems of spelling, punctuation, grammar, format, and typography (such as extra spaces or uneven margins). The writer has decided that he or she has done as much with the content as needs to be done for the moment, so comments from a proofreader suggesting new ideas or tinkering with the logic or development will be neither appropriate nor appreciated.

Proofreading Procedures

Proofreading can either be written or oral. In the written version, you simply hand off a copy of your paper to someone in class, who reads it and hands it off to someone else for another reading. When several people have read it, you use their corrections to create a final draft.

Oral proofreading involves one person reading the manuscript aloud while the others follow along on their copies, making notations where they believe they have found an error. One session with a manuscript read aloud works as well as two or three individual silent readings. They both take about the same amount of time in class.

The proofreader makes two marks, one on the error and another in the margin, to make it easy for the author to find the notations. If you want to use the official proofreader's marks, you can find them in your college dictionary. Otherwise you can write brief notes explaining any notations you think aren't clear.

If you are reading aloud, you should read slowly and distinctly so that people have enough time to pay attention and make their notations. If you are following along, you should make two marks wherever you think an error may have occurred—a check mark above the error and another check mark in the margin beside the line containing the possible error, so that the author can find the marks readily after you've finished. Once you've read through the manuscript together, you can return the marked-up copy to the author, who will collate the marks onto a master copy of the manuscript. If you or your teacher notices patterns of errors in your writing, you may want to do some focused work on error analysis. We have outlined this work in step 5 of the Experience that follows this section.

Preparing a Portfolio for Submission

Near the end of your writing course, your teacher may ask you to assemble several final drafts into a portfolio you submit to demonstrate the depth and breadth of your work. You should choose the writing that best represents what you can do and what you are interested in. Once you have chosen the projects, you may find that you want to do some revision before you submit the final copy; often you can see a manuscript more objectively after some time has elapsed. Be sure that your two best pieces of writing are the first and last projects in the portfolio.

In addition to your projects, you will need to prepare a letter introducing the portfolio to your reader. In your letter, you should describe each project in turn and, since you are submitting the portfolio for your writing course, you should describe the processes by which the projects were written and revised. Be sure to acknowledge by name those who gave you advice and assistance. Your teacher may be especially interested in your explanations of how you used reader comments to revise your work.

The final copy of the portfolio should be typed double-spaced on good quality $8\frac{1}{2} \times 11$ inch white paper with margins of at least an inch all round. The pages should be numbered consecutively beginning with the second page. Leave space for a table of contents page, which you prepare after all the other pages are finished. Begin a new page when you begin a new project. Leave no typographical errors or hand-corrections. Your teacher will tell you whether he or she wants the portfolio paper-clipped, stapled, or bound together.

You'll find that teachers lavish praise and other rewards on carefully prepared portfolios, and you'll find, during your last year in college, that having several attractive writing samples will make you more competitive in the process of searching for a job.

EXPERIENCE

You'll need copies of a manuscript that you have decided is finished, as many copies as there are people in your proofreading group (groups of two to four people work best).

1. Have a proofreading session in class.
    a. As a group, decide whether you want to do a written or an oral proofreading.
    b. Hand out your copies and conduct the proofreading.
    c. When you get back your marked-up copies, transfer all the notations to one copy and make any changes you know how to make.
    d. Consult with your editors about marks you don't understand. Try to resolve questions and disagreements with reference books.
    e. Consult with your teacher about any remarks that still mystify you after you consult with your editors.
2. Compare the responses your editors have made.
    Note where the editor(s) agreed with one another's responses. Make any changes most or all editors considered necessary. Double-check with reference books any changes you aren't sure of.
3. Look at the changes an editor suggested but which you don't plan to make. Divide them into two categories:
    •   changes you wouldn't make because you're not sure how to make them, and
    •   changes you wouldn't make because you don't think they'll help you accomplish your purpose.
4. Consult with your teacher about changes you're not sure how to make. Then explain in writing why you prefer not to make the rest of the changes.
5. Learn to analyze your errors to control the damage that persistent errors cause in the effect of your writing. Sometimes persistent errors recur from project to project. Certain persistent errors may send a signal to the teacher (and, of course, to other readers) that the writer has not fully mastered Standard English. A teacher may suggest some additional work to focus a writer on ways of controlling errors that damage a writer's credibility.
    a. You'll need drafts of several writing projects. They may be projects for this or any other course.

b. Read through the projects, noting with a check mark any point at which you believe you've found an error. After you've checked over a whole manuscript, use reference books to resolve as many of the problems as you can.

c. Make an appointment with your teacher or a tutor in your college's writing center to discuss your remaining check marks. Your teacher or tutor will be able to help you determine whether your check marks indicate errors.

d. In consultation with your teacher or tutor, sort the errors into categories. You could start with the categories of Spelling, Grammar, Punctuation, Usage, and Manuscript Format.

e. In consultation with your teacher or tutor, find, list, and categorize any remaining errors. You have now created an error analysis document, your personal reference work that focuses on errors you commit.

f. When you proofread a manuscript, refer to your error analysis document to try to anticipate and correct persistent errors. You won't find every one of them, but then none of us is perfect. You will substantially increase your correctness, and you will be better able to focus on the errors you actually commit.

Appendix
Writing for
Evaluation

_____

_____

_____

Throughout the book we have focused on slowly developed and much-revised writing. In Writing for Evaluation, we take up a kind of writing we have not discussed so far. College will often call on you to write one-draft essays quickly for the purpose of evaluation—for entrance, placement, and competency examinations of various kinds; for essay examinations in courses; for scholarship competitions; and for professional credentials. This sort of writing persists through college and if you attend graduate or professional schools, you will continue to write for evaluation.

We know that in your career as a student you've experienced evaluation over and over again. In the final chapter of the book, we therefore give you the opportunity to experience evaluation from the teacher's side, as a person who reads essays and makes decisions about them. We think you'll find it interesting and informative to experience the powerful position of evaluator, and once you understand the process of evaluation in more detail, you'll be able to respond with improved effectiveness to the inevitable announcement: "Put away all notebooks and books. Open your test booklets. Begin."

SUBJECTIVE VERSUS OBJECTIVE EVALUATION

You write for evaluation when you take the tests that school requires. The writing might be an essay test for history, political science, philosophy, or literature. It might be a contest essay you write to win a scholarship. It might be a placement essay you take to enter a college writing program or a competency essay you take in order to graduate. It might be an autobiographical statement you write to get into medical school or a hypothetical case you analyze to get into law school. It might be a comprehensive exam for a master's degree or a doctorate. Later on in a career you might deal with stringent time constraints and strict criteria of form as you write proposals that compete with other proposals for funds, or articles or stories that compete for the limited number of spaces editors allow in a magazine or a book.

When you write for evaluation, you are putting yourself in the position of the musician giving a recital, the athlete competing at a sport, or the actor playing a part: you are giving a performance. You know that you need to study and practice before a performance. You probably know that it's important to treat tests of all kinds as performances. You need to give yourself practice tests and time constraints to try to anticipate the problems that are certain to occur.

The Process of Evaluation

You may think you already know how evaluation works. After all, it's happened to your writing over and over again. You think of red pens poised like hawks over helpless manuscripts. "Awk!" they scream as they strike, and when they leave, the writer's ideas and feelings have been reduced to a lifeless grade.

You probably accept the marks on your mechanical errors because those seem objective. You can use a handbook to look up commas and semicolons, parallel and periodic sentences, connotation and denotation, and all the other paraphernalia of print. But where does the grade come from? Does the teacher add up the number of red marks or is evaluation just subjective?

Indeed evaluation is **subjective:** that is, an evaluator uses his or her personal understanding and values to arrive at a judgment about the quality of a piece of writing. You shouldn't think of it as "just" subjective, though, because a teacher's judgment is based on a great deal of deeply considered experience with writing and reading. When a teacher puts a grade on a paper, he or she is saying in a shorthand way that this paper belongs to a certain *category* of papers. As a result of writing, reading, studying, and teaching for years, a teacher sees enough papers to begin noticing similarities in them.

Suppose for example that you were writing a letter to a high school principal who had decided to ban junk food from the school cafeteria. Would you talk about the students' rights to freedom of choice in their food? Would you discuss the healthful effects of eliminating junk food from the diet? Would you deal with both those issues? Would you take some other line of approach?

Stop for a moment to think about how you would approach the subject, supposing you could either support or condemn the principal's decision.

The authors of this book have administered that topic to many, many students from grade school through college age and found that virtually all writers will discuss freedom of choice. Few writers will emphasize the health issue. An important group of writers will deal with both issues.

The Primary Traits of Successful Essays

In fact, if we divide all the essays on the junk food topic into two piles, one containing the more successful essays and another containing the less successful essays, in the stack of more successful essays we tend to find a balanced discussion of *both* freedom of choice and health. In the stack of less successful essays, we usually find that the majority of essays focus on the freedom of choice issue.

Other qualities distinguish more successful from less successful essays, but a comprehensive approach to the topic is a very reliable and important one. So now, when we see an essay that is written on this topic, we immediately begin to form a conclusion about whether it is more or less successful based on whether it deals with the whole question, not just one side.

Can we make a rule, then, that you have to always present both sides of every issue in order to write well? Not necessarily. You certainly have to consider both sides of a controversial issue to write well, but under different circumstances you might elect to write differently. In this case, since you are addressing your essay to the principal, a person more powerful than you, you have to demonstrate that you understand both viewpoints if you are to gain the principal's attention. If you were writing to the students to organize a strike, you would probably try to whip up an emotional commitment to just one side.

Each writing problem has a unique solution. As you gain writing experience, you encounter writing problems that resemble problems you have already solved, but you never find the ultimate solution or the rule that applies to every writing situation.

But wait a minute. Aren't there universal constants like organization, grammar, sentence structure, and spelling? Don't people really evaluate writing according to whether it's clear and correct? Yes and no. Naturally a reader evaluates a piece of writing according to whether its organization makes it easy to follow and whether the writing is mechanically good enough to make the writer seem literate. But you can write nonsense or inappropriate commentary that is perfectly spelled and organized.

A reader mixes spelling, content, organization, and a host of other considerations into a judgment of a piece of writing. It usually works out that the papers that take a successful line of argument on the junk food topic also manage to seem to be literate. It may be that writers who take an appropriate line of argument are also careful about proofreading and organizing. Or it may be that choosing the right line of argument makes everything else fall into place easily. Or it may be that readers are less likely to notice minor flaws if the writer is making a good argument.

Traits and Categories

At any rate, experience teaches a reader that papers will tend to fall into categories. As we read papers on the junk food topic, we can't help noticing that one category of papers takes only one line of argument and another category takes two. Some papers are two pages long and some are longer. Some have lots of examples and some don't have so many. Some mention outside information the writer has found in reading and some don't. Some are neatly written and some aren't. Some follow proper manuscript form and some don't.

After a while all those categories begin to come together, and an evaluator looks at a paper and sees a whole sequence of categories it falls into— two lines of argument, four pages long, lots of examples, neatly written, supported by references to other texts, presented in the proper format, and so forth. Such papers inevitably become the ones readers like best. Occasionally you'll see a miserably researched paper that has splendid organization and content, but such anomalies are rare. You might suppose that it's "just subjective" to like such papers best, except that the authors of this book always find, when we ask the opinion of a number of people, that certain papers receive almost unanimous approval. If a great many people arrive at a similar judgment, we can say that the judgment has objective value, even though people arrived at the judgment subjectively.

Experienced evaluators have memories stocked with dozens of papers on many subjects. Each new paper an evaluator reads is compared against papers the evaluator has seen previously. The judgment begins forming instantly, as soon as the evaluator picks up the paper. The process resembles sorting items into stacks. Comparing the paper against other papers, the evaluator uses all the categories that experience has provided and arrives at a decision about whether the paper seems to belong in the "best" stack or the "second-best" stack.

The first decision, about the relative success of the paper, gives the evaluator the possible range of scores. Once the evaluator has made the first decision, he or she refines the decision to determine how successful the paper is.

If the evaluator is working with a 9-point scale, papers that fall into the above-average level of success may earn a score of 9, 8, 7, or 6. Papers that fall into the average-and-below level of success will earn a 5, 4, 3, 2, or 1.

Of course a writer may work like fury on a paper, learn from the experience, and still not produce a paper that is as successful as other similar

Of course a writer may work like fury on a paper, learn from the experience, and still not produce a paper that is as successful as other similar papers, just as a writer may dash off a paper to which many people give high marks. We all tend to personalize the evaluations people put on our writing, to take them subjectively as compliments or criticism. We can also learn to view these evaluations objectively as information—nothing more, nothing less. The following exercise will help you to view evaluation as an informative process.

EXPERIENCE

This experience uses a competitive exercise to let you in on the process of evaluating writing. You'll develop a common assignment (for instance, to write a narrative, a book review, an essay on a topic like addiction, or a letter to an audience of high school students), and write an essay on it. The whole group will read and score the essays without knowing who wrote them. This experience causes some anxious moments for most writers, but every writer we've worked with agrees that the information gained is worth the anxiety.

1. To begin with, list some topics you wouldn't mind writing a brief essay about.

   These might be issues in the news right now. Is the government enacting some legislation about taxes, the environment, or civil rights that you like or don't like? This might be a chance to debate it. Is something happening on campus in student government, the Greek system, or the dorms that you think bears some investigation? This might be the occasion to go find out some facts. Would you like to write something silly about UFO abductions, Elvis sightings, or the importance of the number three? In class, contribute your topics to a list your teacher puts on the board. Then vote for the assignment that seems most interesting to you, but be prepared to accept the majority's choice.

2. Next, determine what potential published context this assignment might fit. Would you like to write an article for a magazine, an editorial for a newspaper, or a letter to a public official? If some other context occurs to you, suggest it. Once again vote for the context you prefer.

3. Finally, set any rules you would like about details such as length, format, levels of formality, and so forth, so that everyone has a common understanding of the assignment. Once again, vote for the rules you prefer.

4. Once you're comfortable with your understanding of the assignment, complete it and make enough copies for everyone in your

5. In class, hand out the copies of your paper to everyone in your class. You in turn will get a copy from everyone else. Then, using all the papers except yours, begin sorting the papers into two stacks, an upper group and a lower group, based on your understanding of the assignment. It's easiest to just throw papers into two stacks first without worrying whether the stacks come out exactly even.

6. Once you've made two stacks, count them and move essays around if necessary to get stacks that have roughly the same number of papers.

7. Once you've got two stacks, repeat the process and divide the upper and lower stacks into two stacks each for a total of four. Next to the social security number on the paper, write the number of the stack into which you put the paper: 4 for the stack of papers you liked best, 3 for the stack you liked next best, 2 for the next, and 1 for the stack you liked least. Then sort the papers into numerical order by social security number.

8. Look over the stack numbered 4 and describe the qualities those essays had in common. What was it you liked about them? Try to be specific, noting both your general impressions and the particular spots in the papers that gave you those impressions.

EVALUATING WRITING COLLABORATIVELY

The next stage in evaluation is comparing your own responses to other people's responses. Although evaluators work from the subjective standpoint of personality and experience, they also belong to a society of readers and writers from whom they draw many of their values. When we compare our responses to those of other evaluators, it's easy to see what we share and what we don't share. If we share an opinion with a number of other people, we can conclude that the opinion is objective at least in part, even though we feel as if we have arrived at the opinion subjectively.

We have all learned to value clarity, correctness, elegance, factuality, imaginativeness, originality and a host of other qualities in writing. When you sorted the papers, you used your understanding of those concepts to make the judgment that one paper belonged in the upper half and another belonged in the lower half. The question is, how much do you agree with others on which of the papers exemplify the traits everyone likes? In order to compare responses, work through the following experience.

EXPERIENCE

1. In class, combine your rankings with those of your classmates to arrive at a group definition of the categories. Your teacher may

EXPERIENCE

1. In class, combine your rankings with those of your classmates to arrive at a group definition of the categories. Your teacher may make a chart on the board or the overhead and ask you to raise your hand to vote for which category each paper belongs in.
2. Note where you agree and where you disagree with the categories of the class as a whole.

   You'll probably find that you pretty much agree with the way the class has put papers into the upper and the lower half. You may agree a little less with the way your class has assigned papers to the various quarters, but you'll be able to see what qualities cause a paper to be placed in those quarters. Your teacher may share his or her rankings with you, explain how the rankings relate to grades, and discuss any discrepancies between his or her rankings and those of your class.
3. You can give a paper four points for every person who categorized the paper in the top quarter, three points for the next quarter, two points for the next, and one point for the last quarter. Adding the scores will give you a rank for all the papers.

DEVELOPING EVALUATION CRITERIA

You've just experienced in a concrete way a *process* like the process by which experienced readers—teachers, editors, employers, and, yes, writers—evaluate writing.

It's a sorting process, more or less. It's subjective because you use your own judgment and people disagree on the details. But there must be something objective about evaluation, too, since people can agree on their perceptions of how papers should be categorized.

As you gain greater experience with papers, you'll become comfortable with sorting them into stacks and pretty confident of your judgment. You'll agree with most people on most papers, but you'll also become aware of personal likes and dislikes that cause you to evaluate a paper higher or lower. You'll come to regard some of your personal preferences as right for you, and you'll hang onto them even though other people don't share them. You'll decide that some of your feelings about writing are too weird to hang onto; that's good, too. Finally you won't need to sort papers into stacks because you'll have the categories in your mind.

A good way to accelerate the process of learning the categories is to try to write down the criteria you use in assigning papers to the four stacks. You'll notice that the papers in each of the stacks have common qualities that you can look for in assigning new papers to those stacks.

EXPERIENCE

1. Skim all the papers to get a sense of the difference between upper- and lower-half papers.

   Try to focus on qualities upper-half papers have in common with each other, and do the same for lower-half papers. Take notes as you read. You'll feel a strong desire to assign papers to upper and lower half based on how well they're spelled and punctuated. That's okay. Mechanical accuracy is important. But look past mechanics. You'll probably find fancy language impressive too. You'll want to assign papers to categories based on how big the words are and how elegantly the sentences are arranged. That's okay too. But try to look past language.

2. Reread the assignment.
   • How have the more successful papers followed the assignment?
   • What about organization? Do upper-half papers offer a clearly logical pattern? Do lower-half papers read a little like a list?
   • Do upper-half papers sound more personal? Do lower-half papers sound like someone writing an English assignment?
   • Do upper-half papers offer lots of examples, or one very well chosen example? Do lower-half papers offer fewer examples or obvious examples?
   Note any patterns and write them down.

3. In class, compare your descriptions of the categories with those your classmates have developed. Get your teacher's reaction to the categories. As a group, develop a description of the papers in each of the four categories.

4. Reexamine the papers and rank them again using your written criteria. You may find that you'll agree even more with the rankings everyone has given the papers, though some disagreements will remain. Be sure to keep your copies of the papers for later reference.

   By this time, you'll find that much of the mystery has been removed from evaluation. Your teacher may choose to repeat this paper-sorting experience with other assignments for your course. You may use the methods yourself in an evaluation group you organize outside of class.

Bibliography

Aristotle. *The Rhetoric of Aristotle.* Trans. Lane Cooper. Englewood Cliffs, NJ: Prentice-Hall, 1932.

Atkinson, J. W., and G. H. Litwin. "Achievement Motive and Test Anxiety Conceived as a Motive to Approach Success and Motive to Avoid Failure." *Journal of Abnormal and Social Psychology* 60 (1960): 52–63.

Austin, J. L. *How to Do Things with Words.* Cambridge, MA: Harvard UP, 1962.

Bakhtin, Mikhail. "The Problem of Speech Genres." *Speech Genres and Other Late Essays.* Trans. Vern W. McGee. Austin: U of Texas P, 1986.

Baron, Dennis E. *Grammar and Good Taste.* New Haven: Yale UP, 1982.

Bernstein, Basil. *Class, Codes, and Control.* New York: Shocken, 1975.

Berthoff, Ann E. *The Making of Meaning.* Upper Montclair, NJ: Boynton/Cook, 1981.

Brandt, Deborah. "Toward an Understanding of Context in Composition." *Written Communication* 3 (1986): 139-157.

Brannon, Lil, and C. H. Knoblauch. "On Students' Rights to Their Own Texts: A Model of Teacher Response." *College Composition and Communication* 33 (1982): 157–166.

Bruffee, Kenneth. "Collaborative Learning and the 'Conversation of Mankind.'" *College English* 46 (1984): 635–52.

_____. "Social Construction, Language, and the Authority of Knowledge: A Bibliographical Essay." *College English* 48 (1986): 773–90.

Burke, Kenneth. *A Grammar of Motives.* New York: Prentice-Hall, 1945.

Csikszentmihalyi, Mihaly. *Flow: The Psychology of Optimal Experience.* New York: Harper, 1990.

Cummings, Michael, and Robert Simmons. *The Language of Literature: A Stylistic Introduction to the Study of Literature.* Oxford: Pergamon, 1983.

Daly, J. A., and M. D. Miller. "The Empirical Development of an Instrument to Measure Writing Apprehension." *Research in the Teaching of English* 9 (1975): 242-249.

Elbow, Peter. "Reflections on Academic Discourse: How It Relates to Freshmen amd Colleagues." *College English* 53 (February 1991): 135–155.

Emig, Janet. *The Composing Processes of Twelfth Graders.* NCTE Research Report No. 13. Urbana, IL: NCTE, 1971.

Erikson, Erik H. *Adulthood.* New York: Norton, 1978.

Eysenck, H. J. *The Inequality of Man.* San Diego: Edits, 1975.

Faigley, Lester, and Stephen Witte. "Analyzing Revision." *College Composition and Communication* 32 (1981): 400–414.

Fennick, Ruth. "The Creative Processes of Prose-Fiction Writers: What They Suggest for Teaching Composition." Diss. Illinois State, 1991.

Fisher, Walter. *Human Communication as Narration: Toward a Philosophy of Reason, Value, and Action.* Columbia: U of South Carolina P, 1987.

Flower, Linda. "A Cognitive Process Theory of Writing." *College Composition and Communication* 32 (1981): 365–387.

_____. "Writer-Based Prose: A Cognitive Basis for Problems in Writing." *College English* 41 (September 1979): 19–37.

_____, et al. *Reading to Write: Exploring a Cognitive and Social Process.* New York: Oxford, 1990.

_____, and John R. Hayes. "The Cognition of Discovery: Defining a Rhetorical Problem." *College Composition and Communication* 31 (1980): 21–32.

Foss, S. K., Karen A. Foss, and Robert Trapp. *Contemporary Perspectives on Rhetoric.* Prospect Heights, IL : Waveland, 1985.

Foucault, Michel. *The Order of Things: An Archaelogy of the Human Sciences.* New York: Vintage-Random, 1966.

Franz, Marie Louise von, and J. Hillman. *Jung's Typology.* Dallas: Spring, 1985.

Gere, Anne Ruggles. *Writing Groups: History, Theory, and Implications.* Southern Illinois UP, 1980.

Hairston, Maxine C. "Not All Errors Are Created Equal: Nonacademic Readers in the Professions Respond to Lapses in Usage." *College English* 43 (1981): 794-906.

Hake, Rosemary L., and Joseph M. Williams. "Style and Its Consequences: Do as I Do, Not as I Say." *College English* 43 (1981): 433-51.

Hillocks, George Jr. *Research on Written Composition.* Urbana, IL: NCTE, 1986.

Hymes, Dell. "Competence and Performance in Linguistic Theory." *Language Acquisition: Models and Methods.* Eds. R. Huxley and E. Ingram. New York: Academic, 1971.

Jensen, George H. *Personality and the Teaching of Composition.* Norwood, NJ: Ablex, 1989.

_____, and John K. DiTiberio. "Personality and Individual Writing Processes." *College Composition and Communication* 35 (1984): 285–289.

Jung, Carl G. *Man and His Symbols.* Trans. W. S. Dell and C. F. Baynes. New York: Harcourt, 1933.

_____. *Psychological Types.* Trans. R. F. C. Hull. Bollingen Series 20. Princeton: Princeton UP, 1921.

Kohlberg, Lawrence. "The Development of Modes of Moral Thinking and Choice in the Years Ten to Sixteen." Diss. U of Chicago, 1958.

LeFevre, Karen Burke. *Invention as a Social Act.* Carbondale: Southern Illinois UP, 1987.

Lepper, M. R., D. Greene, and R. E. Nisbett. "Undermining Children's Intrinsic Interest with Extrinsic Rewards." *Journal of Personality and Social Psychology* 28 (1973): 129–137.

Lunsford, Andrea, and Lisa Ede. *Singular Texts/Plural Authors.* Carbondale: Southern Illinois UP, 1990.

Macrorie, Ken. *Telling Writing.* 3rd ed. Rochelle Park, NJ: Hayden, 1980.

Maslow, A. H. *The Farther Reaches of Human Nature.* New York: Viking, 1971.

Moffett, James. *Teaching the Universe of Discourse.* Boston: Houghton Mifflin, 1968.

Myers, Isabel Briggs. *Gifts Differing.* Palo Alto: Consulting Psychologists, 1980.

_____, and Mary H. McCaulley. *Manual: A Guide to the Development and Use of the Meyers-Briggs Type Indicator.* Palo Alto, CA: Consulting Psychologists, 1985.

Ong, Walter J. "The Writer's Audience Is Always a Fiction." *PMLA* 90 (January 1975): 9–21.

Perelman, Chaim, and Lucie Olbrechts-Tyteca. *The New Rhetoric: A Treatise on Argumentation.* Trans. J. Wilkinson and P. Weaver. Notre Dame: U of Notre Dame P, 1969.

Perl, Sondra. "Understanding Composing." *College Composition and Communication* 31 (December 1980): 363–369.

Plimpton, George. *The Writer's Chapbook.* New York: Viking, 1989.

Porter, James. *Audience and Rhetoric.* Englewood Cliffs, NJ: Prentice-Hall, 1992.

Rose, Mike. *Writer's Block: The Cognitive Dimension.* Carbondale: Southern Illinois UP, 1984.

_____. "Rigid Rules, Inflexible Plans, and the Stifling of Language: A Cognitivist Analysis of Writer's Block." *College Composition and Communication* 31 (December 1980): 389–401.

Shor, Ira, ed. *Freire for the Classroom.* Portsmouth, NH: Heinemann, 1987.

Tannen, Deborah, ed. *Spoken and Written Language.* Norwood, NJ: Ablex, 1982.

Toulmin, Stephen. *The Uses of Argument.* Cambridge, England: Cambridge UP, 1958.

Vygotsky, Lev. *Thought and Language.* Cambridge, MA: MIT UP, 1938.

White, Edward M. *Teaching and Assessing Writing.* San Francisco: Jossey-Bass, 1985.

Williams, Joseph. *Style: Ten Lessons in Clarity and Grace.* Chicago: U Chicago P, 1990.

Young, Richard E., A. L. Becker, and Kenneth L. Pike. *Rhetoric: Discovery and Change.* New York: Harcourt, 1970.

Index